WHAT'S COOKING
IN THE KREMLIN

◇◇◇◇◇◇

From Rasputin to Putin,
How Russia Built an Empire
with a Knife and Fork

WITOLD SZABŁOWSKI

Translated from the Polish by Antonia Lloyd-Jones

PENGUIN BOOKS

PENGUIN BOOKS
An imprint of Penguin Random House LLC
penguinrandomhouse.com

First published in Poland as *Rosja od kuchni: Jak zbudować imperium nożem, chochlą i widelcem* by Grupa Wydawnicza Foksal, Warsaw

Map by Cyprian Zadrożny

LIBRARY OF CONGRESS CATALOGING-IN-PUBLICATION DATA
Names: Szabłowski, Witold, 1980– author. | Lloyd-Jones, Antonia, translator.
Title: What's cooking in the Kremlin : from Rasputin to Putin, how Russia built an empire with a knife and fork / Witold Szablowski ; translated by Antonia Lloyd-Jones.
Other titles: Rosja od kuchni. English
Description: New York : Penguin Books, 2023. | "First published in Poland as Rosja od kuchni: Jak zbudować imperium nożem, chochlą i widelcem by Grupa Wydawnicza Foksal, Warsaw"—Copyright page. | Includes bibliographical references.
Identifiers: LCCN 2023010788 (print) | LCCN 2023010789 (ebook) | ISBN 9780143137184 (paperback) | ISBN 9780593511176 (ebook) |
Subjects: LCSH: Cooks—Russia (Federation)—Interviews. | Cooking—Political aspects—Russia (Federation) | Food habits—Russia (Federation) | Russia—History. | Soviet Union—History. | Russia (Federation)—History. | Cooking, Slavic. | LCGFT: Cookbooks.
Classification: LCC TX649.A1 .S9413 2023 (print) | LCC TX649.A1 (ebook) | DDC 641.509247—dc23/eng/20230317
LC record available at https://lccn.loc.gov/2023010788
LC ebook record available at https://lccn.loc.gov/2023010789

Printed in the United States of America

1st Printing

Set in Arno Pro

Designed by Jessica Shatan Heslin/Studio Shatan, Inc.

Acclaim for *What's Cooking in the Kremlin*

"If you want to understand the making of modern Russia, read this book."
—Daniel Stone, bestselling author of *The Food Explorer*

"A riveting account of a uniquely sumptuous cuisine prepared in often grotesque and dangerous settings."
—Paul Freedman, author of *Ten Restaurants That Changed America*

"As a chef and the daughter of Soviet Jewish refugees, I have experienced a lifelong fascination with, mingled with repulsion toward, the food on my ancestral table. *What's Cooking in the Kremlin* gracefully captures this perpetual tension—it is what inevitably arises when an extraordinary cuisine becomes a weapon deployed against the very people who've made it."
—Bonnie Frumkin Morales, author of *Kachka: A Return to Russian Cooking*

"[This book] is more important now than ever with the Ukraine conflict. The chapter about the famine in Ukraine was especially touching for me, as my grandparents and great-grandparents lived through it. You won't be able to put it down!"
—Tatyana Nesteruk, author of *Beyond Borscht*

"By turns poignant and playful ... [with] engaging stories and oral histories given by cooks who survived the vagaries of the Kremlin's whims and who toiled through the great afflictions of collectivization, the Siege of Leningrad, the Chernobyl disaster, and more."
—Darra Goldstein, author of *A Taste of Russia*

"This book will make your mouth water. Witold Szabłowski's delicious dive into Russian imperial history comes complete with recipes for Stalin's favorite Georgian walnut jam, the blockade bread that people ate during the World War II Siege of Leningrad, and the turkey in quince and orange juice served to Winston Churchill and Franklin D. Roosevelt in Yalta in 1945. . . . [It] explores how the way to the famed Russian soul has always been through the collective stomach."
—Kristen R. Ghodsee, author of *Everyday Utopia*

ABOUT THE AUTHOR AND TRANSLATOR

Witold Szabłowski is an award-winning Polish journalist and the author of *How to Feed a Dictator* and *Dancing Bears*. When he was twenty-four he had a stint as a chef in Copenhagen, and at age twenty-five he became the youngest reporter at one of Poland's largest daily newspapers, where he covered international stories in countries including Cuba, South Africa, and Iceland. His features on the issue of migrants flocking to the EU won the European Parliament Journalism Prize; his reportage on the 1943 massacre of Poles in Ukraine won the Polish Press Agency's Ryszard Kapuściński Award; and his book about Turkey, *The Assassin from Apricot City*, won the Beata Pawlak Award and an English PEN award and was nominated for the Nike Award, Poland's most prestigious literary prize. Szabłowski lives in Warsaw.

Antonia Lloyd-Jones has translated modern fiction, reportage, poetry, and children's books by several of Poland's leading authors. In 2019 her translation of *Drive Your Plow Over the Bones of the Dead* by Olga Tokarczuk, winner of the Nobel Prize in Literature, was shortlisted for the Man Booker International Prize. She is a former cochair of the UK Translators Association.

In memory of Leokadia Szabłowska

CONTENTS

CULINARY MAP OF RUSSIA AND THE FORMER SOVIET UNION, POLAND, AND AFGHANISTAN

RUSSIA

5

Tallinn

ESTONIA

4

9

12

Riga

LATVIA

8

LITHUANIA

Vilnius

11

Minsk

10

Moscow

Warsaw

BELARUS

3

Astana

POLAND

14

Kyiv

KAZAKHSTAN

13

UKRAINE

15

MOLDOVA

6

Chișinău

1

2

Bishkek

GEORGIA

Tbilisi

UZBEKISTAN

KYRGYZSTA

ARMENIA

Baku

Tashkent

TURKMENISTAN

TAJIKISTAN

Yerevan

AZERBAIJAN

Dushanbe

7

AFGHANISTAN

1. New Athos, Abkhazia

Here stands one of Stalin's favorite summer dachas. One of its kitchens prompted the idea of writing this book.

2. Gori, Georgia

This is where Joseph Stalin was from, as was his half-brother—later his food taster and personal chef—Alexander Egnatashvili. During World War II, Egnatashvili fought an uneven battle against Lavrentiy Beria, the chief of Stalin's secret police, for his beloved wife's life.

3. Fairy-Tale Forest pioneer camp, Chernobyl

A team of cooks from the Rivne Nuclear Power Plant cooked at this camp for the first clean-up crews working at Chernobyl following the disaster. Most of them are no longer alive.

4. Moscow

Here at the Kremlin, master chef Viktor Belyaev cooked for many years and was then in charge of the kitchens.

5. Leningrad

The siege of this city cost the lives of around 1.5 million people. Those who died there included Vladimir Putin's brother and uncles. We learn about the blockade from Tamara, who was a baker there.

6. Baikonur

It was from here that Yuri Gagarin, the first man in space, took off on his historic journey. Maria Kritinina cooked for him. On page 160 you can find her personal recipe for borscht.

7. Bagram

Here at a Soviet airbase in Afghanistan, Mama Nina cooked for the pilots. In civilian life she was a shoemaker and head of the Party cell at a shoe factory in the Soviet town of Kubinka.

8. Yekaterinburg

This is where tsar Nicholas II, his family, and his most faithful servants spent the final months of their lives. They included the chef Ivan Kharitonov, who was executed along with the tsar.

9. Kuntsevo

Stalin's secret dacha was situated on the outskirts of Moscow. There was a farm and fish ponds here so that Stalin could have food from trusted sources.

10. Gorki Leninskiye

This is where Vladimir Ilyich Lenin spent the final years of his life. His top secret chef, Shura Vorobyova, cooked for him here, giving him buckwheat against his doctors' orders.

11. Ilinskoye

This is the site of the sanatorium for Communist Party members where Spiridon Putin, grandfather of the Russian president, cooked. He is also buried here.

12. Star City near Moscow

This is where Faina Kazetskaya cooked for the future astronauts. Here too she gave Yuri Gagarin raw milk just before the ill-fated flight in which the first man to go into space was killed.

13. Velyka Rostivka

Half the residents of this village were murdered by Stalin during the Great Famine in the 1930s. Two cooks' daughters survived, some of the last living witnesses to those events.

14. Viskuli

Here the leaders of Russia, Belarus, and Ukraine brought down the Soviet Union. Polina Ivanovna, who cooked for the Belarusian Chairman of the Council of Ministers, prepared wild boar goulash for this occasion.

15. Yalta

This was the site of the conference at which the Allies divided Europe. From a culinary point of view it was a tour de force, prepared by Alexander Egnatashvili. In 1944 hundreds of thousands of Crimean Tatars were deported.

PREFACE

As I write these words, it has been several months since Russia unleashed its cruel war against Ukraine. Unfortunately, for that very reason this book has become extremely topical. To research it, I traveled the length and breadth of Russia, Ukraine, Belarus, and several other former Soviet republics. I spoke to some unusual cooks, including Viktor Belyaev, the head of all the Kremlin kitchens, who had a major heart attack soon after Vladimir Putin's accession to power and had to retire; the cooks responsible for feeding the frontline troops during various conflicts instigated by Russia; the cooks who worked at Chernobyl after the nuclear disaster; and people who survived the Great Famine, cold-bloodedly planned and executed by Stalin.

Today I couldn't have done the research for this book, because I wouldn't be allowed to enter Russia or Belarus. And if I were, I'd soon be arrested for writing the sorts of things you'll read here. In fact, in the course of my research I had to explain myself several times to the police, and I was once interrogated by the Russian special services. I managed to complete the work only because it never occurred to any of Putin's state

agencies that it's possible to show the mechanisms of power—
Putin's and his predecessors'—through the kitchen.

I have no doubt that it is possible. Just as I'm quite sure that
in the present conflict too, the cooks on both sides are stretch-
ing their skills to the limits to fill the stomachs entrusted to
their care. These are people like thirty-five-year-old Natalya
Babeush from Mariupol, Ukraine, who has a warm and gentle
smile. Before the war she worked as a high-pressure-boiler
engineer at the Azovstal steelworks, where her husband also
worked. When the war began and the Russians were approaching the city center, she and her husband moved into the
steelworks, which has hundreds of underground passages and
shelters. It was easier to hide out there than at home during the
Russian attack and subsequent siege of the city. Natalya and her
husband ended up in a bunker where more than forty people
were sheltering, including eight children. The youngest was
only two.

While there, Natalya quickly became a cook, making meals
for everyone on a primitive stove, using a scorched saucepan,
the only one she had. Soon she was doing something that seems
to come naturally to most cooks—the ones featured in this
book, and the world over: she raised morale. She joked, she
roped people in to help, and when she found some paper and
crayons, she organized drawing contests for the children. She
helped others to endure the hell of the siege. The smallest children couldn't say her name properly, so she told them to call her
Auntie Soup. And that's how she's remembered: Auntie Soup
from the Azovstal works.

Natalya and her husband were successfully evacuated a couple of weeks before the defenders of Azovstal surrendered on

the orders of President Zelensky and the Ukrainian chief of staff. They had spent more than two months underground. In that time many of their friends had died. Natalya still weeps whenever she talks to journalists. But she's surprised to be asked for a recipe—what was on the menu in the Azovstal bunker? One or at most two cans of Spam, immersed in 30 liters (8 gallons) of water. (Natalya was able to get water from the plant's industrial tanks.) That's all they had to eat at the besieged steelworks, so everyone was permanently hungry. Every day, every second could have been their last.

The people who got out of there alive had various culinary requests. Some of them wanted pizza, while others longed for sushi or a juicy steak. The first thing Natalya ate was a slice of bread and butter—just like the women who survived the Great Famine, who still think of a plain piece of bread as the greatest treat they can imagine.

So people's tastes don't change when they've been to hell and back. Nor does politics change in Russia, the country that has built its power with a knife and fork—and famine. As I write this, Putin is trying to pressure other countries into giving him a free hand in the war against Ukraine by threatening to prevent ships carrying Ukrainian grain from leaving their ports. If the ships don't sail, many countries in Africa and the Middle East will risk experiencing famine. Russia is deliberately blackmailing the world: either you meet us halfway, or more people will die of hunger, not just in Ukraine but also the world over. This book explains why it's in Russia of all places that a regime could come up with such a diabolical idea.

But there is a glimmer of hope. Following each of Russia's "interventions"—Putin never refers to the war in Ukraine as a war but insists on calling it "brotherly intervention"—the blinders imposed by propaganda have fallen from the eyes of the Russians. That's what happened to Mama Nina, the cook you'll meet in the chapter about the war against Afghanistan. Only there did she realize she'd been conned by the politicians, and millions of Soviet citizens came to have the same realization.

I am certain the same thing will happen this time too. By attacking Ukraine, Putin has made a major error, one that might cost him his power—or even his life. For many years it has not been the people in the streets who have overthrown Russia's dictators but palace coteries, including members of the staff: bodyguards, cooks, and chauffeurs. Perhaps there's already a cook at the Kremlin who's going to add a few drops of poison to Putin's soup, whether it's borscht, shchi, or ukha.

I hope one day I'll have the chance to ask them what kind of soup it was.

INTRODUCTION

All at once the smells of gasoline, fruit wine, and partly digested fried fish hit my nostrils. The gasoline was coming from a cutter that had headed out to sea around an hour ago, and the wine and fish must have been from the stomach of the drunken janitor who had thrown up under my window. There I lay in bed, still half-asleep, listening to the roar of the Black Sea and watching some policemen representing the Republic of Abkhazia—a self-proclaimed orphan of the Soviet Union recognized only by Russia—as they searched my room. In the doorway stood the flustered manager of the holiday resort where I was perching for the night, repeating, not exactly to me and not exactly to the policemen, "Not meant to be here. I don't know how he got here."

He was telling the truth. He didn't know.

So for the second or third time I explained that I'd arrived late at night, that the drunken janitor—the same man who would later sing bawdy songs in Russian, and later still vomit under my window—had let me in and said I should go to bed, that we'd settle up in the morning.

When the police found nothing suspicious on me, it started to dawn on the manager that he'd made a mistake and set the functionaries on an innocent man. Luckily the policemen let it drop. They made some jokes, took a few Russian rubles off me for a cup of tea, and were gone.

I was left with the manager, who was feeling pretty stupid. He made coffee in a small pot, first for me and then for himself, and we drank it in silence while he wondered whether to try to placate me. He decided to give it a try and offered me a glass of chacha—a very strong spirit made of grapes—to go with my coffee (I refused it, because it was seven in the morning). Then out of the blue he asked if I knew where we were.

"In New Athos, in Abkhazia," I replied, yawning.

But the manager violently shook his head, saying that it was true, but not entirely. And that I was to follow him. So we drank up our coffee, and off we went. First he unlocked a chain hanging on a gate, then he led me through a secret tunnel that ran under the street and a few dozen yards beyond. All of a sudden, we were in a garden of paradise. I'm not exaggerating. Around us grew both pine trees and palms; the milk from coconuts that had fallen and cracked against the asphalt was flowing down the path. Two beautiful black horses were licking it up, and two more, bays, were grazing a short way off. As we walked along the path, brightly colored birds chased one another between the bushes.

Beyond all this, the path began to lead uphill.

On the way we passed a sign that read PROPERTY OF THE PRESIDENT OF ABKHAZIA—NO ENTRY. Beside it stood two agents who were there to guard the grounds, but the manager waved to them and they let us through. Green-and-brown lizards raced underfoot, and bird after bird screeched overhead. Finally the asphalt ended, and we were standing outside a small green house on a hillside. The view was stunning: palm trees, forest, and the turquoise sea looming below.

"This place is top secret. It used to be Stalin's summer dacha," said the manager. "He came here on vacation every year toward the end of his life. The house where you slept was built later on, but it's also part of his estate."

Suddenly it all made sense. For decades this place had been accessible to only a small number of people. Stalin had died, the Soviet Union had collapsed, but no one had rescinded the order to keep it as hidden as possible from the eyes of outsiders. The cottages were probably rented to tourists illegally—maybe even Stalin's villa was rented out. Who knows—in a nonexistent country, anything's possible. But tourists from Russia, a common sight here, are one thing, while someone from Poland is quite another. That's why the manager panicked and called the police.

I started wondering how I could see inside the dacha. And the manager seemed to read my mind.

"I don't have the key." He spread his hands. "But my colleague has it. If you'd like, I'll ask him to let us in this evening."

So I spent the day touring the sights of New Athos, and then went back. The manager was already waiting with several other men. One of them was named Aslan; tall and graying, he was the one who had the key, and in the days of the Soviet Union he'd recorded conversations with the people who'd worked at Stalin's dacha. He let us in and told us step by step how it had been built, when exactly Stalin had arrived here, in which room and on which bed he'd slept.

Meanwhile, the other men made a bonfire and started to cook lamb shashliks. They put raw onion on some plates as well as *adjika*, a sauce for the meat made of hot red peppers, garlic, herbs, and walnuts. They also poured chacha—now was the right time to drink it. They all worked here on the dacha grounds: one was the gardener, another the watchman, and a third looked after the horses. They were old enough to remember the bloody war that had erupted in 1992, following the collapse of the USSR, when—with Russia's help—Abkhazia had broken away from Georgia. We raised a toast to our meeting, we drank, and I wondered how to ask them what they thought about the war and what it had brought to their quasi-mini-country. Luckily the manager read my mind again.

"Russia, Georgia, what a pair of fuckers," he said, chasing the chacha with watermelon. "Both of them are only after our beaches and our money. We shed blood, and that just makes things worse."

The others nodded in agreement.

After the war Abkhazia separated from Georgia, but though once rich—it was known as the Soviet Côte d'Azur—the country came to a complete standstill. The only things they live on here are mandarin farming and Russian tourists. Because no one except Russia has recognized their statehood, hardly anyone but Russians ever comes here; within the mountain landscape, the richly decorated buildings are now buried in the undergrowth.

"Life hasn't been good since Stalin's day," the manager went on, as his pals poured us each another glass of chacha. "He understood this land. He ate our bread, he ate our fish, he ate our salt."

The others nodded again.

"Stalin was like us. He ate the same things as the ordinary people," said the man who cared for the horses. "Over there, behind the dacha, is his kitchen. My grandfather worked there as a servant, he told me."

We drank up again, and the chacha started singing in my head. As the shashliks roasted on the open fire, I went to take a leak. I chose a spot just behind Stalin's kitchen, and on my way back I peeked inside through the window. As in the dacha, everything there was original—the burners, the floor, the table, even the pots and stools. I began to wonder who the cook had been who'd worked here. What had he made for Stalin? Had he wanted to run away from this place, or had he stood beside the Sun of Nations and bathed in his warmth?

It was just then, feeling slightly tipsy, that I first had the thought that I'd like to know if Stalin really did eat like "the ordinary people." If so, then why? And if not, then why did they think he had?

So that was how, on a warm evening around ten years ago, the idea for this book was born.

It spent a few years marinating inside me, and once I finally got down to some serious work on it, I traveled throughout several of the former Soviet republics. I talked to the chefs of Communist Party general secretaries, cosmonauts, and frontline soldiers, and to cooks from Chernobyl* and from the war in Afghanistan. I soon discovered that Stalin hadn't eaten like the

---

*In this book, the name "Chernobyl" is used historically to designate the site of the nuclear power plant where in April 1986 one of the reactors exploded, causing a major disaster. In the days of the Soviet Union, the name of the city was spelled in its Russian form, "Chernobyl," though now, as a city in Ukraine, its name is spelled in Ukrainian, "Chornobyl." As the story of the cooks that is told in chapter XIII is about the immediate aftermath of the 1986 disaster, the Soviet-era name is used here.

average Abkhaz at all, nor like the average Soviet citizen. And along the way I discovered several other culinary secrets—both his and his successors'.

In this book you will learn how, when, and why Stalin's cook taught Gorbachev's cook to sing to his dough. How Nina, a cook during the war in Afghanistan, forced herself to think about something pleasant in the hope of imparting her good mood to the soldiers. How in Chernobyl, a few weeks after the catastrophe, a competition was held for the best canteen, and who won it.

You'll read about Stalin's food tester, who fought an unequal fight against the tyrant and his cronies in an effort to save his wife's life. You'll also find a recipe for the first soup to have flown into outer space. And for pasta with turtle doves, eaten by the last tsar, Nicholas II. You'll find out why Brezhnev hated caviar.

And you'll read about people who had nothing to eat at all: in Ukraine, when Stalin tried to break its back by starving its citizens, and during the siege of Leningrad.

But above all you'll see how food can be a tool for propaganda. In a country like the Soviet Union, every pork chop fried and dished up in every canteen and restaurant from Kaliningrad to the Arctic Circle, from Kishinev to Vladivostok, was of service to propaganda. What the general secretary of the Communist Party ate and what the ordinary citizen ate were political. Just as the USSR did for decades, Russia still feeds its people on propaganda.

It's no accident that Vladimir Putin, grandson of the cook Spiridon Putin, is in charge there. You'll read about both of them in this book.

I'm told that these days you can visit Stalin's dacha in New Athos legally—you just have to buy a ticket for around fifteen rubles. But as I learned from friends who went there a few years after I did, there's still no entry to the kitchen and the door is locked.

This book aims to unlock it.

WHAT'S COOKING
IN THE KREMLIN

I

The Last Tsar's Chef

She's in a neatly pressed suit and her hair is dyed blond. She has invited me to her apartment because her legs ache and she prefers not to go out, but for the past two hours she's been keeping me at a distance. We're sitting in the living room, having tea served from a samovar and some extremely stale cookies.

All her life, Alexandra Igorevna Zalivskaya has worked at an institute of higher education, and has developed a suspicion of others that's typical of Russian state organizations; to let anyone come close, she must first form an opinion of them. And that takes time. So she spends two hours telling me about her great-grandfather Fyodor Zalivsky, who worked in the kitchen of the last tsar, Nicholas II; she doesn't remember him, but he left the family a souvenir cup and a photograph of the tsar and his wife. And every time, as if reading from a book, she says, "His Highness Nicholas II," never just "the tsar," and if she's talking about Nicholas, his wife, and their five children it's "the holy imperial family." She watches to see how I'll react.

Because to a Russian, a Pole is always a bit of an enigma: we're sort of similar, but we give things quite different names and don't understand them in the same way. She knows I want to ask her about a friend of her great-grandfather's, the tsar's last chef, Ivan Kharitonov. She also knows that Kharitonov's descendants have refused to give me an interview. Mrs. Zalivskaya has to sort it all out in her head.

Ivan Mikhailovich
Kharitonov

Eventually something falls into place: some algorithm in her mind decides that although I'm a Pole I'm not too bad, and she can trust me. And something happens that I will experience over and over again in Russia. Mrs. Zalivskaya takes two shot glasses and a bottle of Moskovskaya vodka from the minibar and says that's enough chatting here, let's go to the kitchen. And in the kitchen, by applying some special magic of her own, in under fifteen minutes she has covered the table in zakuski, or hors d'oeuvres: pickled mushrooms, pâté, a macédoine (if you don't know what this is, please read on patiently), the pickled gherkins and sauerkraut that are standard fare on every Russian table, Olivier salad (also known as stolichny salad or simply "Russian salad"), and plenty of other little dishes that she must have had ready long before my arrival. But first she had to form an opinion of me before she could invite me from the living room into the soft underbelly of every Russian home, where favorite guests are received and where a person is as open as they can possibly be.

"Do start with the pâté, Witold Miroslavovich," she says.

"It's one of my great-grandfather's original recipes, straight from the tsar's kitchen. In my family it's always made like that for Easter."

So I help myself to pâté, a finger-thick slice, first because I like it, and second to please my host. I pile some gherkins on top. We raise a toast—to our meeting, to friendship—and moments later my taste buds are enjoying a soft meaty substance just like the kind enjoyed by tsar Nicholas II and his family, until the Bolsheviks put them up against a wall and shot them.

1.

The best place to start the story of the tsar's most loyal chef is at the end, on the last night of Kharitonov's life. So let's begin like this:

He made them supper, they crossed themselves, they ate.

It wasn't the first time that Ivan Mikhailovich Kharitonov, a portly forty-eight-year-old with slicked-back hair, had had his hands full. Ever since the Bolsheviks had imprisoned the former tsar and his family in 1917, he had been the only chef to stay with them. Of the hundreds of people who had worked at the court before then, the five most loyal had remained, including Lyonka Sednev, the kitchen boy. Many times the Bolsheviks told them they should abandon the tsar and save their own lives, but they always refused. As the head of the group that guarded and subsequently shot the workers recalled years later: "They declared that they wanted to share the fate of the monarch. We had no right to forbid them."

But that last evening the Bolsheviks sent the underage

Lyonka to the city. They told him he'd be met by his uncle, who had also worked for the tsar.

Though Lyonka had no way of knowing, by then his uncle had been dead for several weeks.

Kharitonov had known the tsar since early childhood; it was customary at court for the Romanov children to play with the servants' children, and Nicholas and Ivan, whose father had served Alexander III, were almost the same age. Famous for his unemotional child-rearing, Alexander wanted his children to be familiar with the so-called simple life.

But the time for games had soon ended. At the age of only twelve, Ivan Kharitonov had become a kitchen boy. Through hard work, persistence, and talent, his father had risen from an orphan raised in a children's home to a senior position at court, and he had been appointed to the nobility by the emperor. It was he who had advised his son to build a culinary career. He had arranged for him to go to France, where the young Kharitonov became a master chef, learning from the world's best.

But under arrest in Yekaterinburg, where the Bolsheviks had imprisoned the former tsar, it was all meaningless. Since the tsar's abdication, the quality of his food had steadily been lowered, and not even the best chef could do anything about it. He could only make sure it happened as gently as possible. And since a master chef can cope in any circumstances, Kharitonov achieved mastery in this too.

That evening they had supper at eight, after which the former tsar and tsarina played bezique, their favorite card game and their way of killing time in prison. Meanwhile, in the commandant's office their guards prepared six pistols and eight revolvers. The tsarina went to bed at half past ten. She still managed to devote a sentence in her diary to Lyonka, the kitchen boy: "We're wondering if we'll ever see him again," she wrote with concern, because just as Kharitonov had grown up with Nicholas, Lyonka was the favorite companion of their only son, the tsarevich Alexei.

She was right: they never saw the boy again. The entry about the kitchen boy was the final one in her diary.

2.

"The tsar's entourage consisted of nothing but remarkable people," Mrs. Zalivskaya tells me between a pickled mushroom and another shot of vodka. "And just as the Romanovs were a dynasty, so there were whole dynasties of cooks, pastry chefs, and waiters too. It seemed that however poorly people lived in Russia the tsar would never know hunger, so the fathers trained their sons and daughters, to be sure they'd always have work. My great-grandfather Fyodor worked there because his father had trained him; I don't know his first name, but I know poverty drove him to Saint Petersburg from near the city of Suzdal. But there were others who had worked there since the days of Catherine the Great. My great-grandfather was friendly with the pastry cook Potupchikov, for instance, whose family had apparently been with the tsar for two hundred years. Potupchikov taught him to serve frozen strawberries flavored with lemon juice, almonds, and violet petals."

There were more than twenty pastry chefs, responsible for the cakes and also for the fruit, the nonalcoholic drinks, and the rolls that were a favorite of Alexandra Fyodorovna, wife and great love of the last tsar of Russia. The man in charge of them was the baker, Yermolaev, whose arms were shaved to the elbows and who moonlighted as an actor at one of the Saint Petersburg theaters.

"My great-grandfather didn't like the tsarina," says Mrs. Zalivskaya. "She was a German, she spoke Russian badly and treated the servants badly too. She put ideas into the tsar's head and introduced Grigori Rasputin to the court, and that was the start of all the trouble that finally led to them shooting the Romanovs. As you know, there were lots of scandals involving Rasputin, and he was even accused of an affair with the tsarina. But my great-grandfather never had a bad word to say about the tsar. He always said he was a good man. Too good to rule Russia. What does 'too good' mean? He was very sensitive, he took everything personally. The way things were in those days, Russia needed somebody much tougher."

The alcohol department, with a staff of fourteen, was responsible for stronger drinks, including brewing kvass. In his youth the tsar liked to drink a lot—his diary from those years is full of juvenile games with alcohol playing a leading role. After ascending the throne he settled down, but even as an adult he would drink a few glasses of port with dinner, and on his travels, a glass of strong Polish plum vodka that his viceroy sent from Warsaw.

Around 150 people were employed in the typical kitchen that prepared meals for the imperial tables, ten of whom cooked for no one but the tsar, his family, and their private guests. Four cooks specialized in roast meat, and four more—including Ivan Kharitonov—in soups. Apart from the specialists there was a whole host of apprentices, transferred on a daily basis from sponge cakes to sourdough, from sourdough to aspic, and from aspic to the team that decorated the dishes. In those days it was one of the world's two or maybe three best kitchens.

Let's take a look at a standard breakfast menu. On October 10, 1906, the imperial family was served cream of asparagus soup, lobster, leg of wild goat, celery salad, peaches, and coffee. On September 10, 1907, they were served pearl barley soup (with pickled gherkins, carrots, and peas), potato pancakes, salmon pâté, roast beef, chicken breast, pears in sherry, and a cranberry tart with sugar.

The lunches were just as lavish. A typical meal on May 28, 1915, a year after the start of World War I, was like this: fish soup, zander, roast meat, salad, vanilla cream. On June 26, 1915: pâté, trout, dumplings, roast duck, salad, ice cream. December 30, 1915: fish soup, dumplings, cold ham, roast chicken, salad, ice cream.

Then there was afternoon tea, with cookies and cakes in the leading role, and supper. The tsar took his meals quite late: breakfast was usually at one p.m. At five p.m. the entire family assembled for tea—a habit introduced by the tsar's wife, Alexandra Fyodorovna, who as a granddaughter of Queen Victoria had been brought up at the British court. Dinner was at around eight in the evening, and supper often well past midnight.

But despite this richly laden table, sometimes the tsar ate nothing but an egg or two, and his wife would eat only some vegetables. Both of them watched their figures, and Nicholas weighed himself several times a day.

"They threw away a great deal of food," says Mrs. Zalivskaya, spreading her hands. "But he was the tsar. He couldn't just be served two eggs for breakfast. The appropriate ceremony had to be observed."

If Nicholas did allow himself to eat a little, his favorite dish was pasta with turtle doves.

In Nicholas II's day the maître d'hôtel—the man in charge of the imperial kitchen and dining staff, responsible both for what was served and for the cooks and the waiters—was Jean Pierre Cubat. Ivan Kharitonov had met him earlier in France. For Kharitonov he was a mentor, but also a friend with whom he corresponded and shared memories of vacations in Crimea.

Mrs. Zalivskaya forces me to drink another toast—to Polish-Russian friendship—and to have another slice of pâté. Then I force her to drink in memory of her late great-grandfather, may he rest in peace.

"My great-grandfather never imagined he'd become a first-class chef," she tells me, wiping her mouth after the toast. "He was the son of a second-class cook, and repeating his father's journey was quite enough for him. Cubat the Frenchman gave up working for the tsar in 1914, when World War I began. At a time of unrest he preferred to go home to his family in France. But his place was immediately filled by another Frenchman, Olivier."

(This Olivier is sometimes mistakenly credited with creating the famous Russian vegetable salad. In fact, it was invented by another Frenchman of the same name, but half a century earlier.)

The Frenchmen raised the imperial cuisine to such a high standard that it looked as if no Russian cook would ever be maître d'hôtel at court.

"Kharitonov aspired to it," says Mrs. Zalivskaya. "Everyone at the court knew that, including my great-grandfather. But they were all sure that any new head of the imperial kitchen would be a Frenchman. The court cuisine was greatly influenced by French cooking, and it was quite natural that it had to be the responsibility of someone from France. So no one expected Kharitonov to become the maître d'hôtel, or that it would happen in the most dramatic circumstances imaginable."

3.

Historians are pretty much in agreement that Nicholas II was a good man but a lousy tsar. And considering he had to deal with the greatest crisis in the entire history of the Romanovs, it's no wonder he couldn't cope with it. According to the old Russian calendar, he was born on May 6, the day when the Orthodox Church commemorates Job—the old man on whom God inflicted all the misfortunes in the world—and from his early years the tsar often said it was no accident. (Nor was it by chance that Leo Tolstoy called him "a pathetic, weak, and stupid ruler.")

His coronation was a disaster. On May 26, 1896, half a million Russians gathered at a parade ground in Khodynka because they had been promised free food and commemorative cups. When the stalls were opened in the morning, the crowd rushed forward, trampling over two thousand people, of whom more than a thousand died. That same evening, as if nothing had happened, the tsar danced at a ball given in his honor by the French ambassador.

The Russians never forgave him. The rift between the tsar and his subjects began on that very day, and from year to year it continued to widen.

Matters were made worse by the imperial couple's prolonged lack of a male heir; Alexandra gave birth to four girls in a row: Olga, Tatiana, Maria, and Anastasia. But the birth of their long-awaited son not only failed to solve the couple's problems; it also brought new ones. From early childhood the little tsarevich, Alexei, suffered from hemophilia. The tsar and tsarina sought help first from conventional doctors, then from all sorts of charlatans, faith healers, and pseudo-physicians. That was how the village preacher Grigori Rasputin appeared at their court, a man who through his sexual excesses added scandal after scandal to the already damaged reputation of the imperial family.

So the clouds had been gathering over the Romanovs for a long time when the toughest moment came, with the outbreak of World War I. Russia joined the conflict in July 1914 and took a beating right from the start. On August 20, the day of the Battle of Gumbinnen, for lunch the tsar was served patés, pork goulash, crab pilaf, and poularde stuffed with snipe and peaches.

Disaster was ever nearer.

4.

Power was slipping from Nicholas's hands by the day. The people were tired of the ineptly conducted war. The soldiers mutinied. When in March 1917 even the State Duma turned against the tsar, Nicholas decided to abdicate.

The Provisional Government sent him to his palace at Tsarskoye Selo, where at first the Romanovs' living standards did not change much—they were still surrounded by chefs, waiters, and stewards. The most significant change was that after the tsar abdicated, the French maître d'hôtel, Olivier, took off.

Suddenly there wasn't a single Frenchman at court to be his successor.

"Ivan Kharitonov received the title," says Mrs. Zalivskaya. "It was the crowning achievement of his career, but a sad one: he became head of the kitchen staff of a tsar who was no longer tsar. My great-grandfather went on working at court. Kharitonov invited everyone for a glass of cognac. But it really was just one small glass: the staff working for the former tsar was to behave with dignity."

In the first few weeks the court continued to operate in much the same way. A few days after the abdication, Kharitonov filled in the kitchen order form as follows: three apples, eight pears, six apricots, and half a pound of jam, plus a carafe of the dessert wine cherry kagor. But soon after, the government began its repressions. First the Romanovs were no longer allowed fruit, and the flowers were removed from their rooms. The budget for their food was reduced too. Later on things went further: gearing up for the legal action that the people of Russia were to bring against the tsar, supposedly Prime Minister Alexander Kerensky forbade the tsar and tsarina to sleep in the same bed; they were to spend as little time together as possible, to prevent them from preparing a common line of defense. Fortunately for them, this did not last long.

So for breakfast Kharitonov served the imperial family a healthy diet of oatmeal, pearl barley with mushrooms (1.5 rubles per portion), or rice rissoles. For dinner in this difficult period there were Pozharsky rissoles (made with minced chicken or veal) at a cost of 4.5 rubles each. For those watching their weight he made pasta rissoles, at a cost of 1.5 rubles each. And when the end of the accounting period was near—the tsar's budget for food was calculated every ten days—to save money he served potatoes roasted in the embers, which the imperial family loved.

In late July 1917 Kharitonov began to serve the tsar macédoine, a cheap and impressive dish of finely diced vegetables or fruit, often with the consistency of aspic, which he must have learned to make in France. He made the vegetable version with carrots and turnips, then added beans and peas and seasoned it with butter. A sweet macédoine was made of diced fruit: bananas, grapefruit, oranges, strawberries, and apples, with a splash of rum or jelly, just as fruit salad is made today. By then Kharitonov was having to rack his brains to feed Nicholas and his family.

After the Romanovs had been at the Tsarskoye Selo a few months, the government decided that they should be transferred to Tobolsk in Siberia—they would have to move from a palace into the governor's former residence. The new maître d'hôtel stopped receiving money from the state purse to feed Nicholas; from now on Citizen Romanov would have to feed himself, his family, and his retinue at his own expense.

The Romanovs were still eating fairly normally, or at least they were not going hungry. One day Kharitonov would make them borscht, pasta, potatoes, and rice rissoles for dinner; another day solyanka (sour soup), potatoes, turnip-and-ice purée; and yet another day shchi (cabbage soup) and roast piglet with rice. But from then on they would only fare worse, especially after October 1917, when the revolution erupted in Petrograd (as Saint Petersburg was renamed in 1914) and the Bolsheviks, led by the charismatic Vladimir Ilyich Lenin, took total power.

The October Revolution—the event that ultimately led to the death of the entire Romanov family—did not particularly trouble Nicholas. Many years later Vasily Pankratov, who guarded the tsar in Tobolsk, wrote in his memoirs that Nicholas became agitated only when he heard that the crowd had forced its way into the Winter Palace in Petrograd and cleaned out . . . the wine cellars. The alcohol in there had been worth more than the equivalent of five million dollars. The Bolsheviks ordered that it be poured into the Neva, and although not everyone obeyed and plenty of people managed to get drunk, much of the wine flowed off to the Baltic Sea.

The gulf between what happened in Petrograd and Nicholas II's understanding of it shows how divorced from reality he was by then.

Meanwhile, Kharitonov had increasing difficulties buying basic produce. Nicholas was cut off from his money, and most of his property had been requisitioned by the state. So the chef had to tour the houses of the wealthy, asking them to support the imperial kitchen with donations. He often came away with nothing: many people, even those who were well off, did not support the tsarist system, especially "Nicholas the Bloody," as the Russians called him. Others were afraid of the Bolsheviks.

"My great-grandfather followed the tsar to Tobolsk too," says Mrs. Zalivskaya. "But there, as I'm ashamed to admit, the Bolsheviks started to brainwash him. They said there was no tsar anymore, and no magnates, that everyone was equal. And that my great-grandfather didn't have to be a cook all his life, but could be a professor, for instance, a general, or a minister. That was typical of their nonsense, you see. We are all immune to it now, but poor Fyodor was hearing it for the first time in his life, and he believed it. He abandoned the tsar, went back to his family in Petrograd, and for a while became a militant communist. It is not for us to judge the deeds of our forebears, Witold, but I am a little ashamed of him. At any rate, the man whom I regard as a real hero is not my great-grandfather, but Ivan Kharitonov, who stayed with the tsar to the bitter end."

5.

Following the victory of the Bolshevik revolution, the tsar and his family were forced to move again, from Tobolsk to Yekaterinburg. Here they were no longer the imperial family, but prisoners. The nooses around their necks were tightening.

They made the journey in stages, first Nicholas and Alexandra, then the children, who stayed in Tobolsk a little longer because of the tsarevich Alexei's condition. On short notice, Kharitonov went with the second group. He wasn't given the chance to say goodbye to his wife, Yevgenia. Until now, she and their six children had bravely followed him, but this time she was only able to wave farewell through the window. Someone suggested he should give her his gold watch, which, apart from his cufflinks engraved with the imperial eagle, was the most valuable gift he had received for his loyal service. But he just waved, thinking he'd be back soon. And if not, why worry her now?

All he left at home was a copy of the Bible with a personal dedication from the tsarina.

In Yekaterinburg the cook set about his work with great energy. Nicholas II and his relatives had home-cooked dinners once again, rather than what the Bolsheviks brought them from the local canteen. The tsar, who kept an extremely boring diary in which he loved to write about food, mentions Kharitonov's return as follows: "June 5. Tuesday. Since yesterday Kharitonov has been preparing our meals. He's teaching my daughters how to cook, how to knead dough in the evening, and then bake bread in the morning! Wonderful!"

Alexandra, Nicholas's far more laconic wife, also noted Kharitonov's return in her diary: "Dinner. Kharitonov made a pasta cake."

So the chef tried to function just as before. But in Yekaterinburg nothing was the same anymore.

"The tsar was a prisoner, and at every step the Bolsheviks showed their disdain; even making a cup of tea involved asking the guards for permission," Mrs. Zalivskaya tells me. "They were only given modest, soldiers' rations to eat, and often not even those arrived."

Once again Kharitonov tried to make up for the lack of supplies by buying on credit from local families, and often by simply begging. But he usually met with refusal. Only the nuns from the local Novo-Tikhvinsky convent supplied the Romanovs with basics like milk, eggs, and cream.

The guards often kept the former tsar and his family company at dinner. Sometimes they would dip their spoons into the soup of one of the grand duchesses and remark, "They're still feeding you pretty well." Soon Yakov Yurovsky, the commander of the guard, forbade the nuns from bringing eggs and cream for the prisoners. "We have been brought meat for six days, but so little that it was only enough for soup," noted Alexandra in her diary.

6.

On July 15 something astonishing happened: Yurovsky not only allowed eggs from the convent to be served but also ordered the nuns to prepare another fifty for the next day. For whom were they intended? No one could guess.

The following day, fourteen-year-old Lyonka Sednev was sent to the city to meet with his uncle, who until recently had also worked for the Romanovs. The kitchen boy, on whom the Bolsheviks seem to have taken pity, was the only one of the prisoners at Yekaterinburg to get out alive.

The rest were woken in the middle of the night. They were told to pack and that White Army forces, the enemy of the Bolsheviks, were approaching the city. Indeed, shots had been heard all day from the Ipatiev House, where they were being detained.

"Well, we're moving out," said Nicholas. They crossed the courtyard, then went through a double-leaf door into the cellar. Nicholas went first, carrying Alexei, followed by Alexandra, the grand duchesses, and the servants. In the cellar the footman, Trupp, and the cook, Kharitonov, stood beside the grand duchesses.

To the end they thought they had been brought down there purely as a prelude to the move. Only moments before the execution did Yurovsky make a short speech betraying his real intentions, and then his men opened fire.

The first to die was the tsar, followed immediately by Kharitonov and Trupp. But the grand duchesses had precious gems sewn into their clothes, and the bullets bounced off them. The Bolsheviks had to finish them off with shots at close range.

The fifty eggs supplied by the nuns from the Novo-Tikhvinsky convent were provisions for the group of local peasants who were to dig graves for the Romanovs.

After the execution the assassins transported the bodies

beyond the city by truck. But the site they had chosen for the burial turned out to be swampy, and the corpses kept floating to the surface. On top of that, the peasants employed to dig the graves were more interested in robbing the corpses (and fingering their intimate parts) than in helping bury them.

Yurovsky, in charge of the operation, had the corpses stripped naked. Then he secured the many precious gems hidden inside their clothes (Alexandra had a gold bracelet weighing a pound sewn into her brassiere, and the grand duchesses had plenty of large diamonds), broke their bones, and poured acid over their faces. All so that no one would ever be able to recognize the remains.

The tsar's body was thrown on top of his cook's, with the tsar's ribs landing on Kharitonov's head.

Seven decades later, in 1991, archaeologists extracted more than nine hundred bones from a pit dug next to a marsh. It took them several months to establish that they belonged to nine people.

Several more months passed before they established who was who in the grave.

The easiest to identify were the tsarina and her maid Anna; they were the only middle-aged women, and beside Alexandra's skull was found a very modern denture that the maid couldn't have afforded.

The skeletons were then examined by comparing the skulls to photographs. It was laborious, not least because the skull that was finally identified as that of Kharitonov had only its upper part, including the edges of the eye sockets. Either he had been shot straight in the face, or the Bolsheviks had proceeded to smash his skull to pieces.

"Witold Miroslavovich," says Mrs. Zalivskaya, drinking only half a glass at a time by now because of her high cholesterol. She's saying that this is the last one, but after what she's about to say, we must have another drink. "There's one thing you have to know. I was very interested in Kharitonov, because he worked with my great-grandfather and they knew each other well. I have spoken to everyone who might know something. I have read everything I can find. I've been to meetings with investigators and anthropologists." At this point she pauses, because it's a very delicate matter. "And they all say, unofficially, that what is buried today in Saint Petersburg in the grave of Saint Nicholas II, the last tsar of Russia, is in fact a mixture of bones belonging to both the tsar and his cook."

"The cook is lying in the same coffin as the tsar?" I ask to make sure.

"So they say." She spreads her hands sadly. "Significant, isn't it?"

MENU
◇◇◇
Turtle Doves and Pasta

In 2020 the Russian newspaper *Komsomolskaya Pravda* asked the famous chef Igor Shurupov to re-create Nicholas II's favorite recipe, which was turtle doves and pasta. The trouble is, since the tsar's death these medium-sized birds have become virtually extinct and are now strictly protected. Shurupov advised using pigeon or quail as a substitute.

For the dish to taste similar to that enjoyed by the tsar, one must marinate several quail overnight in vinegar, then drain them, stuff them with thin pieces of ham, and fry them for an hour and a half in a frying pan.

To go with these birds, the tsar liked to have homemade pasta made of white flour and potatoes.

The turtle doves were not shot, to save the ill-fated Nicholas II from finding pellets in them. Instead, peasants employed by the court would scatter sunflower seeds to lure the birds into an open field, then throw large nets over them and strangle them by hand.

II

Lenin's Cook

> We are not utopians . . . We know that not every laborer,
> not every cook will be able to run the country from one
> day to the next. VLADIMIR ILYICH LENIN

1.

Welcome to Gorki Leninskiye, the place where Vladimir Ilyich
Lenin spent the final days of his life. I know you're particularly
interested in the topic of food, so let's go to the kitchen where
the cooking was done for him—I've been to fetch the keys already. I'll tell you all about Shura Vorobyova, Lenin's cook,
whom I've been looking for evidence of, and who for many
years remained in the shadows—for who would ever have seen
the leader of the world proletariat employing servants, right?

But first I'll tell you about this place. We're standing outside
the house where Lenin came to live after the assassination

attempt carried out by Fanny Kaplan. He was to recuperate here. Many of the famous photographs of him were taken here, in the park. Sorry? I didn't hear what you said. Including the one where he's goggle-eyed? Yes, sir, that picture of the ailing Vladimir Ilyich a few days before he died was taken in the garden of this house. But I would rather you spoke of him with greater respect, though of course I know you are a Pole; I was expecting to have a hard time with you. I know that in Poland you don't like him and that you tell plenty of lies about him. What's that? Syphilis?! Well, quite—you can see what I mean. No, I don't know the relationship between bulging eyes and venereal diseases. It was Lenin's enemies who spread rumors about his alleged shameful illnesses, but don't forget that they were supporters of the tsar. They hated Lenin to the marrow of his bones. They'd have done anything to discredit him: accuse him of living in luxury or of sexual excesses.

But nothing of the kind really happened. Throughout his life, sir, Lenin lived and ate extremely modestly. They say his one and only true love and passion was revolution, and that makes a lot of sense. Well, please don't say any more. Let's start at the beginning.

On the second floor we have the telephone room, with an old telephone, and the library. A narrow staircase leads to the third floor. At Lenin's request extra inside banisters were installed that allowed him to go up and down the stairs without disturbing the staff.

On the third floor we have Lenin's bedroom, the dining room, the study, and the bedroom of his wife, Nadezhda Krupskaya.

In the study there's a small desk standing in front of a wide window that overlooks the park. Some of the newspapers, books, and journals that Lenin read are spread out on the table, and there are also some envelopes and letterhead stamped with CHAIRMAN OF THE COUNCIL OF PEOPLE'S COMMISSARS. Here is the bed in which he died. Please take a few minutes for your thoughts. Ready? Let's go on.

Vladimir Ilyich came from a family that had climbed up the ladder of the tsarist administration. His father managed to join the Russian elite, becoming head of the education department for the Simbirsk region, but financially he was a long way from being wealthy. An expression of his aspirations was the fact that—like the elite in those days—the family ate white bread, rather than the black bread that was typical for the country-side and for the poorer peasant strata. William Pokhlebkin, a pioneer of Russian culinary literature, wrote in an article about Lenin's diet that the white bread had an impact on the rest of his life. Although the black bread might not have tasted as good, it contained lots of vitamins and minerals, which the white bread did not—but white bread was what the richer people ate, so Lenin's father wanted to eat it too. But of course the rich men provided themselves with minerals from other sources that the Ulyanov family couldn't afford. Lenin never made up for what he didn't get from his bread in childhood. That's why he was so very sick at the end of his life. This was one of the reasons he lacked the strength to pull himself to-gether after the assassination attempt, so he died prematurely.

As a little boy, Volodya did eat regularly enough—his mother was from a family of Volga-district Germans and took great care of domestic *Ordnung*, including mealtimes. To the end of his life Lenin showed up on time for every meal and was very annoyed if anyone else was just a minute late. His child-hood also gave him a dislike of sweets—his parents only of-fered them to his sisters; in those days sweets of any kind were regarded as unmanly.

But as soon as Vladimir Ilyich left home to study, he stopped eating regularly and immediately contracted a stomach dis-order that bothered him, with greater or lesser intensity, throughout his life. Paradoxically, he only ate better when the tsar cracked down on him. The first time he ended up in prison, where things may have been bad for him but where he was fed regularly, his problems abated. He left prison, went back to his student-revolutionary life, and instantly started to complain of stomach trouble again.

The same thing happened when the tsar sent Lenin into exile in Siberia, to the village of Shushenskoye on the Lena. For the eight rubles he had at his disposal, he received board and lodging with a local family. Nadezhda Konstantinovna Krupskaya, a friend from the Socialist Party, came to join him; she had been exiled to Siberia too and had begged the officials to send her to the same place as Lenin. It's hard to say what he thought about her arrival, but it definitely didn't please his family. His sister Maria couldn't bear Krupskaya. She thought her ugly and intrusive, with as much charm as a herring; she thought her brother deserved someone much better.

But Lenin didn't complain; he valued the great support he had in Krupskaya for revolutionary matters, though to the end of his days he often said that he had never met any woman capable of reading *Das Kapital*, understanding a railroad time-table, or playing chess well.

So thanks to the tsar, Lenin and Krupskaya had a three-year

"vacation" in Siberia. And for the first time since leaving prison he had regular meals, three times a day, and it was good, healthy, fatty Russian cooking: pelmeni, ukha (fish soup), shchi (cabbage soup), and rassolnik (cucumber soup), as well as baked fish, which he often caught himself, and the meat of game animals that he often hunted himself. Suffice it to say that when Krupskaya's mother came to visit them in exile, at the sight of them she exclaimed, "But you're in fine form!"

Krupskaya's mother would accompany them for many years. One of the first things she did upon arriving in Siberia was to establish a kitchen garden, where she and her daughter planted tomatoes, cucumbers, chives, dill, onions, and garlic. In winter they pickled the cucumbers. This added the ideal variety to their good Siberian peasant diet. Lenin never ate better in his life.

When their exile ended, neither Lenin nor Krupskaya had any intention of giving up their revolutionary activities. It would clearly be dangerous for them to stay in Russia, so they began a nomadic life in Europe—they lived in France, England, Switzerland, Poland, and many other places. But although they were revolutionaries, they had a very traditional approach to running a house: Krupskaya was meant to run it. But by her own admission she knew how to make only three dishes: scrambled eggs . . . using one, two, or three eggs. And the truth is that in exile, Lenin's diet consisted mainly of scrambled eggs. Eating nothing but eggs won't kill you, but your body won't be getting many of the elements it needs, including vitamins, and sooner or later the inadequacy of this diet will make itself known.

That is exactly what happened to poor Vladimir Ilyich.

What's more, Lenin had grown up with the habit of drinking raw milk. His sister died in Saint Petersburg of typhoid fever, and according to Pokhlebkin, the scholar I mentioned earlier, no one should die of that particular illness in peacetime in a city where there is access to running water. Pokhlebkin believed, and I agree with him, that Olga fell sick because she was in the habit of drinking milk that hadn't been boiled. But what's reasonable in the countryside, where you can drink the milk straight from the cow, is a completely different matter in the city, where the milk has had to make a journey, in the course of which it could be infected by bacteria.

In short, Lenin liked fresh milk too, and it can't have been good for his health either. So scrambled eggs washed down with fresh milk? I hate to think how many brain cells he killed with that diet.

There's an interesting story about Lenin's brain, perhaps you know it? Stalin wanted to prove that Vladimir Ilyich was a genius whose mind worked differently from that of an ordinary person. To prove it, they removed poor Lenin's brain—of course it was after he died, what are you saying?! Ah, I get it—I say something seriously, and you start making silly jokes again. I shall ignore that remark. So the brain was removed from Lenin's dead body, and then it was cut into thirty thousand slices. In those days they didn't know how to do the relevant research in Russia, so while most of it remained in Moscow, several of those slices were taken to Germany, where the German scientists were to work on them. Except that Stalin was expecting some incredible result, but they told him that Lenin's brain was a brain like any other. There was nothing extraordinary about it. And Stalin never had those results published. What he did was pointless, because that was exactly where Lenin's strength lay—he was no stronger or wiser than anyone else, nor did he have a differently constructed brain. He was just like every Russian, not particularly tall, bald, of average looks. But he was far more hardworking and determined. He had read about communism and revolution, and he believed that he, a boy from a small village, could bring about a better life for people all over the world. And he did it! Isn't that a fine story?

On the other hand, it's sad to think that, because of Stalin, to this day Lenin's sliced-up brain is still stored at the Moscow Brain Research Institute, which was founded after his death. I'm sorry? They could have tested it for what? Syphilis? Well, exactly—here I am, telling a fine story, and you're showing a fixation on Lenin's sex life. No, Witold Miroslavovich, I must disappoint you; among the thirty thousand slices of Lenin's brain, no evidence of cerebral syphilis was found. In any case, tests for syphilis were performed while he was still alive, because toward the end his eyesight weakened, and the doctors tried to establish what was ailing him. That possibility was excluded. Really, the next time I hear that there's someone from Poland, I shall refuse to lead the tour. How many times can one listen to such nonsense?

Let's return to the kitchen, then maybe you'll focus for a while. I'll tell you a curious fact. Lenin was never interested in food—whatever they served him, he ate. He wasn't a man of taste—he was more like a man with no taste buds. I've been telling that joke to the tourists all year. You see? I like to make jokes too, though I speak to the point, like Lenin. Vladimir Ilyich didn't know how to say what he thought about food: asked if he liked the taste of something, he simply shrugged; he couldn't understand that sort of question at all. One time, while in exile in Stuttgart, he and Krupskaya got terrible food poisoning. As soon as they came home from the restaurant, Krupskaya decided they must summon a doctor. As luck would have it, at the time Lenin had fake documents in the name of a Finnish . . . cook. But when the doctor started questioning him, asking exactly what he and Krupskaya had eaten, Vladimir Ilyich couldn't name a single thing.

The doctor soon realized there was something strange about this case. Apart from the usual fee for his visit, they also had to pay him a small fortune for not reporting their illegal presence to the authorities.

For most of their time abroad, Lenin and Krupskaya ate once a day. Shockingly, Lenin still preferred to eat eggs washed down with milk. Theirs was a different generation, so they knew nothing about the effects of food on the human organism. But plainly, everything in Vladimir Ilyich's life was subordinate to one single aim: revolution.

Another incident having to do with food occurred in Paris. When Lenin and Krupskaya were leaving an apartment that was too expensive for them, the man moving in to replace them was a Pole, who wanted to question his compatriots—at the time Poland was part of the Russian empire—about the price of beef, goose, and other meats at the local market. Upon hearing these questions, Lenin made such an awful face that his family joked about it for years, encouraging various people at every opportunity to go and ask Volodya about the price of goose.

In exile, Lenin wrote a lot and worked on organizing the

Socialist Party. He was constantly going to assemblies and meetings or on trips away. Of course he was fully aware that many people in Russia were suffering from starvation, but most of his concerns were on a higher plane than organizing food. The only thing I can remember about food from his writings is an interesting demand that Russia should stop wasting potatoes on vodka production, as it could be made from peat. Lenin was a great enemy of vodka; the only alcohol he tolerated, perhaps because of his mother's German heritage, was beer. But once he came to power, he fought against alcohol and the way the tsar had intoxicated and stupefied the Russian people. Making moonshine was punishable by execution. "Better to die than to trade in vodka," he used to say.

While Lenin and Krupskaya were in Stockholm, Lenin's mother began sending them packets of smoked fish and Russian candy. In her letters, Krupskaya, who loved sweets, was very grateful to her for these packets but feared that they made her gain weight. She tried to encourage Lenin to eat chocolates and candy, but he remembered from his childhood that sweets are for women, or possibly for the sick, but not for a healthy man in his prime, as he regarded himself. Other friends sent them cherry jam, halvah, and raisins, but Lenin didn't eat those either.

Their years in exile were largely idyllic, especially compared to what happened to them later.

2.

When World War I broke out, Lenin was living in Poronin, Poland. I know you used to have a fine museum dedicated to him there, but it was closed down after the change of government. They wanted to close us down too, and then they wanted to put up a sign about Lenin's harmful role in history. Eventually they brought us all the furnishings from Lenin's study and apartment in the Kremlin, which in the communist era had been a museum, including the kitchen. There's even a leaky pot used by both Lenin's sister Maria Ulyanova and Nadezhda Krupskaya, and which the Polish chauffeur Gil helped them patch. If a leaky pot won't convince you that they lived modestly, then I really don't know what else will.

Anyway, when the revolution broke out, Lenin came to Petrograd to lead it. You can read the rest of that story in any history textbook. Though nowadays you'll be told that upon coming to power he carried out repressions, and that people starved because of him. But in reality, when Lenin came to power, Russia was steeped in anarchy. Nothing was working properly, and the tsar's former men put stumbling blocks in the way of the Bolsheviks, who were having to fight on five fronts simultaneously. The Bolsheviks believed they could win as long as they were ruthless and determined. They shot people dead? Yes, they did. Did they have an alternative? No, they had no alternative. And I don't want to discuss it with you. Please simply accept that this is how I see it, just as I accept that you see it differently.

Vladimir Ilyich started coming to Gorki—which today we call Gorki Leninskiye—not long after the victory of the revolution. At first he wasn't keen on these expeditions; he thought his place was at the heart of events, in the new capital, Moscow. But in 1918 when he was shot, his health declined badly, and Gorki was the ideal place to recuperate. Here's a curious fact: Lenin was shot just as he was talking to one of the women about how hard it was to buy bread. We know this thanks to Stefan Gil, the Pole who was Vladimir Ilyich's driver and who saved his life that day, because when the leader was shot, he sped him to the Kremlin. In fact, Stefan Gil's life story is unusual too, because earlier he was tsar Alexander's chauffeur and worked for the imperial family for many years. To me that's proof that if someone connected with the old regime was ready to work for the revolution, Vladimir Ilyich had no objection.

So it took a long time to find a suitable place for Lenin: on the one hand it had to provide all the essential comforts, but on the other it couldn't look like a palace, because he would have found that unacceptable.

Gorki had previously belonged to Zinaida Grigoryevna Morozova, an extremely wealthy woman whose third husband had been the imperial viceroy of Moscow. And it was ideal for Lenin: the luxury wasn't ostentatious but there was a telephone, thanks to which Vladimir Ilyich could make important decisions whenever necessary, and there was also hot water, which in those days was not common at all. But the furniture was elegant enough for Ilyich to ask the staff to put plastic covers on it. He was embarrassed to live in such luxury.

I'm sorry? What do you mean, he stole it? From Morozova? Witold Miroslavovich, that's no way to talk. It was a sanatorium! He merely borrowed it to restore his health!

The sanatorium was first established at Gorki for members of the Party. A full staff was employed, including cleaners and cooks. One of them was probably Spiridon Putin, grandfather of the president of our country, Vladimir Putin. So the president has said in interviews.

And here at last appears the cook you've been waiting for. Her name was Shura Vorobyova, she was just over thirty years old, and she worked first in the kitchen at the sanatorium, then later exclusively for Lenin, Krupskaya, and their guests. Let's go down to the kitchen; just a moment, I'll open the door. We've been wanting to open it up to tourists for a long time, but so far very few people have had the chance to see it. The pots, the plates, the knife sharpener, the stove, and the stove lids are all original, from Lenin's time. From Morozova's day there's still an underground tunnel that was used to carry food from the out-building, where we are, into the main house. In the cellars the food was divided into portions and put on the plates, and from there it was taken straight into the dining room on the ground floor.

We don't know much about Shura. She came from Gorki village, and she wasn't perfect, because one of the few memories of her comes from Lenin's bodyguards and involves a theft. Apparently she stole a rug. Vladimir Ilyich forgave her, which was very typical of him, and she was eternally grateful to him. And fed him to the best of her ability.

In the Soviet Union one wasn't allowed to say that Lenin had a cook or personal servants. It was always stressed that he and Krupskaya lived like ordinary Russians, and that at home either Krupskaya, Lenin's sister Maria, or Krupskaya's mother cooked. And there was plenty of truth in that, because for years on end that's exactly how they lived. But the fact that they had a professional cook at Gorki, for the first time in Lenin's life, was passed over. And I suspect that some of the records having to do with Shura were thrown away, though the shopping lists she wrote out herself have survived. How did she know how to write? I don't know. In those days it wasn't common among peasant children, but she wrote quite proficiently. Perhaps she had worked for Morozova, the previous owner?

Morozova had brought Latvians to work at her property, because in those days Latvia was the place where agriculture was the most advanced, and her estate included an orchard, a garden, an apiary, and an orangery. Most of the cut flowers sold in Moscow in those days came from her nurseries.

So the state took over not just the residential buildings but also a well-run farm and its staff. One of the first sovkhozy—state farms—in Russia was created there. Almost all the Latvians who were already working there stayed on, though they were less productive than in Morozova's day. This showed in the statistics, and Lenin couldn't understand why it was happening. Maybe for the first time in his life he saw that the beautiful theories he had in his head couldn't always be put into practice, or at least not easily. He used to go and question the workers at the sovkhoz about why they had worked more productively for the capitalists, but now that the farm belonged to the state—in other words, to all of them, as he saw it—they weren't doing as well.

So there were cows mooing right next door to Lenin's house, hens running up to it, and bees making honey. Most of the resulting produce went to Vladimir Ilyich's table, but not all of it, because some went to the sanatorium, some to a nearby school, some to an orphanage, and some to other places, just like the food from any other sovkhoz. To this day our bees are the descendants of the ones that made honey for Lenin. Several walnut trees have survived too. Even our apple trees are descended from the ones in that orchard.

Lenin scrupulously accounted for everything that was brought to him; he would not accept anything for free. One time two fishermen from the Volga brought him a sturgeon as a sign of their appreciation. Shura Vorobyova set about preparing the fish; she scaled and gutted it and began chopping it into pieces. Everyone in the house, including the bodyguards, was looking forward to trying it.

Until Lenin arrived, and asked what sort of fish it was and where it had come from. And when he learned that it had been given to him, he grew terribly angry, said it was inadmissible in a country where so many children were going hungry, and then had the fish taken straight to the nearest orphanage.

3.

I know what you're going to say, Witold. That it all sounds like the fairy tales about Lenin printed in the communist era and has nothing to do with the truth. Well, since the change of government our museum has done a lot to make sure our visitors can get to know Vladimir Ilyich as he really was—to move away from Leninism toward Lenin, the man, who lived, loved, and had emotions. And also ate. I've been working here for more than twenty years, and his personality never ceases to amaze me.

Unfortunately, even here at Gorki, his favorite foods were still eggs and milk. There's an interesting story about that. A year after the assassination attempt, Lenin had another lucky escape. He was traveling through Moscow in his limousine when a gang of bandits blocked the road. They threatened him with a gun and told Stefan Gil to get out of the driver's seat, and then they robbed the most important person in the country of his car. There was nothing particularly odd about it. Felix Dzerzhinsky, another Pole who was close to Lenin, was only just developing plans for the leader's security; in the same era, some reckless thieves had stolen his previous car from right outside the Kremlin. But the curious thing is that during this attack Lenin let the robbers have the car, and only asked them to let him take a bottle of milk with him.

Lenin's life in Moscow was very intense. When he took power, he had everyone against him: World War I was going on and Russia was taking a beating; the civil war was going on, and the Whites, who supported the tsar, were trying to overthrow communism; the peasants were organizing themselves against the Bolsheviks too, as were the imperialist countries, furious that somewhere in the world the ideals of communism were being put into practice. And on top of all this he was still introducing reforms and trying to build a new country on the smoldering ruins left by the tsar. No wonder he was exhausted. In a short period of time he had several strokes, one of which left him in a wheelchair—and he never got out of it again.

Toward the end of his life he was very feeble and sickly. Stalin must have brought in all the doctors he could find, including the world-famous specialist Otfrid Foerster, who came from the then German city of Breslau.

Lenin found these doctors terribly annoying. Each one gave different advice; each one thought up a new dietary restriction. Foerster told him to drink broth to give him strength and categorically forbade him to eat buckwheat, which, as befitted a Russian, Lenin loved—he even used a buckwheat metaphor in one of his letters: "We are not children, to be fed political buckwheat." Shura Vorobyova, who fed him as a mother feeds her child, cooked and served him buckwheat behind the backs of the German doctors. Memoirs have survived in which Lenin's visitors say that whenever Shura served him buckwheat, although he couldn't speak by then, Lenin smiled. I know, Witold, that in the West they give buckwheat to the dogs; maybe you do that in Poland too? But here it's the staple of many people's diet. Perhaps if Lenin had eaten more of it in childhood, he'd have received all the essential micronutrients he never absorbed because he only ate white bread, and he'd have lived longer. We shall never know. But I am deeply grateful to Shura Vorobyova for disobeying the doctors and serving Vladimir Ilyich our own Russian antibiotic—buckwheat.

And now, to finish, I'll take you to a special place. Please sit down here, by this bed. This is where Vladimir Ilyich Lenin, the greatest revolutionary and the greatest visionary of his time, breathed his last breath. Think of him what you wish, that's your business. But if his dreams had come true, both you and I would be living in a far better world than we do today.

MENU
◇◇◇

Scrambled Eggs Using Three Eggs

Oil or lard, for frying
3 eggs
Salt and black pepper

Heat a frying pan, then add enough oil to coat the pan. Break the eggs into the pan. Be careful not to beat them, because what Lenin and his wife called "scrambled" eggs was actually fried eggs.

The eggs are ready when the yolks and the whites are both set. Season to taste with salt and pepper.

Lenin certainly didn't do this, but if you want to introduce variety to your eggs, add cherry tomatoes, ham, medium-firm or semi-hard cheese, or salmon. And eat them with avocado.

MENU
◇◇◇

Buckwheat with Vegetables

1 cup (170 g) buckwheat
Assorted frozen vegetables, such as peas, diced carrots, or
*   diced celery*

Toss the buckwheat into a pot. Add 2½ cups (600 ml) of water and bring to a boil. Add the vegetables and simmer until the buckwheat is soft.

It's not just Lenin and his cook; many other Russians believe in the magical and therapeutic properties of buckwheat. Some even call it "Russian Viagra." Indeed, buckwheat lowers cholesterol and triglycerides, increases vigor, and even rejuvenates (though dead and in his mausoleum, Lenin is still in fine form!).

But to keep healthy we recommend using unroasted buckwheat (rather than the roasted kind commonly consumed in Russia), as eaten by the father of the revolution.

OVERHEARD IN THE KITCHEN

Let's not swallow whole the stories told by the tour guide at Gorki Leninskiye, the place where the leader of the world proletariat breathed his last.

We cannot be sure either way on the question of syphilis, because apparently, although he never thought about anything except revolution his whole life, during his time in France Lenin used to frequent brothels. Rumors that he could have caught a revolting illness there that affected the rest of his life—and the fate of the world—were very common among his contemporaries, and to this day have many adherents among historians.

On the other hand, we do know for sure that Lenin inflicted repressions on the Russian people at a scale previously unknown in the history of the country. In the tsarist era, around a thousand people were shot dead each year for various crimes. That's a lot, but when the Bolsheviks came to power, the figure rose to fifty thousand.

People in the countryside began to starve, initially because of unsuccessful collectivization. But Lenin, who couldn't understand why the sovkhoz attached to his residence was more productive under the capitalists than the communists—this story sounds highly credible—was also incapable of understanding why there was no food. He blamed it all on the kulaks, the richer peasants, though their wealth was often limited to just one or two cows. The Bolsheviks started ruthlessly requisitioning food from the peasants, so that they had nothing to survive the winter. In Tambov province the peasants responded with armed resistance. The campaign against them, led by Mikhail Tukhachevsky (who was later one of the commanders during the Polish-Soviet War and later still a victim of Stalin's purges), cost the lives of more than a quarter million people.

The history of the sovkhoz at Gorki is also a little more complicated than the propaganda would have us believe. Lenin's dream was that the farm attached to the sanatorium where he was resting—he always stressed that Gorki was not his property but that of the working class, who had simply lent it to him—would be a model sovkhoz. The farm workers themselves asked for it to be named Lenin Farm, and it was meant to be a living advertisement for the revolution.

It certainly had the potential. Before the revolution it had cowsheds for 145 cows, a piggery, henhouses with modern incubators, a dairy, a smithy, a metalwork and carpentry shop, and an icehouse, all with access to running water, a sewage system, and electricity, which in those days was extremely rare. Before the war Morozova's farm was a front-runner at every agricultural competition; at a contest in Moscow just before World War I, it scooped all three first prizes. But the Bolsheviks were such poor administrators that under them, even this model farm fell into ruin; barely two years after they came to power, a commission that came to see how it was doing found an ailing small holding where the corn had not been ground and the people were emaciated. It took many years for the farm to get back on its feet, which did happen after Lenin's death, but it never recovered to its former standard.

Upon taking power after Lenin, Stalin played a fine practical joke on his dead predecessor by having Lenin's body embalmed and building a mausoleum for it on Red Square. Vladimir Ilyich would certainly not have wanted a quasi-religious cult to develop around his mummified body. His life companion, Nadezhda Krupskaya, tried to protest, but in vain. Stalin, a failed Orthodox priest, realized that people need gods and idols to give their lives meaning. The embalmed leader of the revolution was ideally suited for the role of a divinity, so he came to rest—and still rests today—in Moscow's central square.

Meanwhile, Stalin didn't forget that Krupskaya had opposed him. They had never liked each other anyway. Once, when visiting Lenin at Gorki, he had berated her for something, saying that if she didn't change her behavior, the Party would choose another life companion for Lenin. By doing so, he came extremely close to harming his own political career, because Lenin broke with him for some time after that.

Following Lenin's death, there was nobody to protect Krupskaya anymore. She went on living partly at Gorki and partly at their old apartment in the Kremlin. As one might expect of such a greedy person, she died in 1939 after being poisoned by a cake. It is highly probable that the cake was sent to her by Stalin. By then, a dozen years after the revolution, poison was becoming one of the Kremlin's favorite methods for getting rid of people.

The Lenin Museum at Gorki agreed to send me the one surviving picture of Shura Vorobyova. Indeed, the Bolsheviks knew that having servants would ruin Lenin's image, so for many years her presence at Gorki was a strictly guarded secret. In the picture, you can see Shura (short for Alexandra) standing in the snow, which is near a side door to the house at Gorki.

Her apron hasn't been ironed. She's smiling, but she looks cautious; perhaps she's just shy.

Lenin once said that not every laborer and not every cook "will be able to run the country from one day to the next." But Shura Vorobyova doesn't look as if she's been trained to run anything at all. She looks like a typical cook and housekeeper for the rich, and there were plenty of rich people in Russia before the revolution.

Shura Vorobyova

Despite the evil he did, Lenin, of all the men who ruled Russia and the Soviet Union, was the closest to the people and the most interested in them. So perhaps the moment he hired a cook was the first small but significant instance when the revolution started to part ways with the people it was meant to help. After that, things would only get worse.

Stalin inherited not just power from Lenin but also an efficient apparatus of terror. He made ruthless use of it. Political prisoners constructed most of the flagship buildings and projects undertaken during his rule: they laid tracks, built airports, and dug a canal between the White Sea and the Baltic. Millions died doing hard labor and in the Gulag, the system of political prisons.

Millions more, who rebelled against the people's power, were starved to death.

III

The Great Famine

"We ate whatever we could find. Mold. Tree bark. The flesh of dead animals. We dug up burdock. Or picked linden leaves; they're quite bitter but bearable. Especially if you have no alternative," says Hanna Basaraba, and the gentle smile never leaves her face. "Sometimes I'd go to the field and dig holes in the ground in search of rotten potatoes," she adds a little later. "But for that you had to have strength, and I rarely had any. I was six years old, and I can remember being hungry nonstop, absolutely all the time."

1.

Let's start the story like this.

Roman Kabachiy is a Ukrainian historian. He's handsome, with a rakish mustache and a thick head of hair. He's also an excellent singer—a passion he inherited from his father, who ran the school choir for many years and is now retired.

It's hard to believe that Roman, so full of life and optimism, might not have been born at all.

We're in a car, zooming from Kyiv toward the village of Velyka Rostivka, where Roman's mother is from and where he spent every vacation as a child. Roman knows that there are still several women in Rostivka who remember the Holodomor (the Great Famine)—an event that occurred almost ninety years ago, at the turn of 1932 and 1933. In those days Stalin starved more than six million Ukrainians to death. Every seven minutes someone in Ukraine died of starvation.

The Vinnytsia province where Rostivka is located is one of the areas where the suffering was greatest. The local historians estimate that in the region of Podolia alone, which includes the city of Vinnytsia as well as the villages of Velyka Rostivka ("Big Rostivka") and Mala Rostivka ("Small Rostivka"), between 1.5 million and 2.5 million people died.

And that was just the first of the plagues that were to affect not just Ukraine but also the whole of Europe in the years that followed. In that same winter of the famine, on January 30, 1933, Adolf Hitler took power in Germany.

So we're in the car, eating sunflower seeds, and Roman is telling me his family history.

"My grandmother Vera, my father's mother, was twenty-three and had lost her first husband during the famine; when they had nothing left to eat, he'd gone to the neighbor's to pick a few beets. They spotted him, beat him up, and stabbed him with a pitchfork. He died out there in the field. Today it seems unthinkable—to kill a man for a few beets. But the people he tried to steal from were fighting for their own lives too."

We stop at a roadside café. Roman shows me a map to explain the extent of the famine. Or, in fact, three famines.

"The first time was just after the Bolsheviks came to power, at the turn of 1920 and 1921," Roman says, circling southern Ukraine on the map, because this is where the famine was at its most acute. "On that occasion millions of people died in Russia too, mainly in the Volga region."

Then came the second famine, from 1932 to 1933.

"That one was aimed specifically at Ukraine. Stalin engineered it because Ukraine was rebelling against the Bolsheviks. There was the occasional peasant uprising here—many people opposed the collectivization of the countryside. So people died of hunger while the Ukrainian grain was carted off to Russia. That was when almost everyone died in Rostivka, my parents' village." And Roman points on the map at a strip of land running from the Polish border across central Ukraine, where we are, all the way to Kharkiv.

"And the third?" I ask.

"It happened right after the war, from 1946 to 1947. Stalin tried to finish us off again, as if two famines and two world wars in thirty years weren't enough. Not much is said about it, but one and a half million Ukrainians died that time too."

2.

We're driving into Velyka Rostivka from the direction of Mala Rostivka, its twin village, separated from its sister by just two small hills. There's an Orthodox church that dates back to 1776, an unusual wooden structure probably built by the Cossacks.

"The communists closed it down in the 1930s, like most of the Orthodox churches in Ukraine," says Roman.

After that it fell into disrepair, until a few years ago, when one of the local farmers had it renovated at his own expense.

We stop for a while between the two villages. From up here we can see the entire district: the villages stretch along little streams that flood the whole area in the spring.

"That's why people rarely had orchards here. Their trees got flooded," says Roman. "Places like this beside water were known as *berehy*—riverbanks. The ground here was extremely fertile." He leads me into the field we have parked alongside, then tells me to pick up some of the earth. It's as black as night and very rich. "That's *chornozem*—black earth," says Roman. "The best soil imaginable—everything grows in it. During World War II, the Germans exported it by train to the Third Reich. When you think about it, it's even harder to believe so many millions of people could have starved to death on this earth."

The history of the other half of Roman's family—his maternal grandmother's side—also involves the berehy along which Rostivka was built.

"My grandmother was from a family where there were three children before the famine." According to family legend, once upon a time, in the 1920s, people toured the villages exchanging traditional Ukrainian *rushnyki*—beautifully embroidered pieces of cloth that are laid at a young couple's feet before their wedding—for food. At the time the woman from next door was at my great-grandmother Lizaveta's house, and both of them wanted to buy the rushnyki from a visitor. But my great-grandmother said to the neighbor: 'Forgive me, but you are at my house, so I have priority.' The neighbor was deeply offended and left in a fury, and on her way out she uttered a curse: 'May you never be able to lay those rushnyki at anyone's feet.'

"Some of my family members believe to this day that the neighbor cast a spell on us, because first of all my great-grandmother's son died, then one of her daughters, and then my grandmother Marika fell seriously ill too. They were sure she was going to die, and they'd never lay the rushnyki at anyone's feet.

"Until one day Marika's father took her to the market in the nearby town. My great-grandfather left Marika in the wagon. When he came back he saw a Gypsy woman beside his daughter. He was about to chase her off when the woman said: 'Your daughter is wasting away. Why should she have to die? I know how to help her.' And she told him to keep bathing my grandmother in three streams, until the girl said she wanted some borscht.

"So they did it. They bathed her, until one day she actually said she wanted some borscht. She ate it and got better. She survived her illness, and the years of famine too. But her parents didn't: both my great-grandfather and my great-grandmother died. Before the famine they'd managed to store up some beets; they hid them in the cellar, but one of the neighbors found out and reported them to one of the commissions that toured the villages checking whether anyone was hiding food. The commission took away their beets and left them with nothing. So one after the other, the parents died of starvation. At fifteen years old my grandmother was left all alone, with no parents and no siblings. And no food.

"That was when she started walking along the berehy in

search of something to eat. She found some corn growing in one of the fields and broke off a cob. But the farmer heard, ran out with a gun, and started firing at her. My grandmother fled to the pond and sat there all day and all night, hoping no one would notice her.

"Until some kind neighbors from the other riverbank noticed her and brought her some potato skins. That saved her life. They fed her on several other occasions too. It was thanks to them, thanks to the kind neighbors and the potato peelings they gave her, that my grandmother survived the Holodomor."

3.

We're sitting at a wooden table in the vestibule, because there's a heatwave and it's a little cooler in here. Hanna Basaraba has a gentle face, framed by a dark scarf, and the pattern of her wrinkles is typical of someone who has done a lot of smiling in life. In the house there's a stove that dates back to the years we're going to talk about, and there are icons on the walls—the nearest one is of Saint George, known here as Yuri, who is dealing a blow to the dragon, straight into its open jaws.

Hanna is still smiling, this time at us. Her breathing whistles a bit, probably because of untreated asthma, but apart from that she's well.

"For my age, I'm very well," she insists. And she starts questioning Roman about everyone and everything, because despite being ninety-five years old, she can remember the names of just about every person who has ever lived in Rostivka. She asks because she cares—she'd like to know if her fellow villagers are prospering, even those who have left. "Why doesn't your mom visit me? Remind her that we're looking forward to seeing her here," she chides Roman. And later on she scolds him for the photos he took of her a year ago. "I looked terribly old in them," she sighs. "My hands are so wrinkled. If you're going to take pictures of me that come out like that, you might as well not take any." She smiles feistily.

She's happy to talk to me about the Holodomor, but since we're her guests, first we must sit down at the table for a cup of tea or coffee, and only then can we start talking about painful matters.

So here we are, drinking tea. And listening.

Hanna Basaraba's Story

There was nothing to warn us that anything quite so dreadful could happen. That summer—from what people said afterward—the harvest was perfectly good. There was already a collective farm up and running in Rostivka, but many people still had their own cows, horses, and hens in their yards. Though there was a lot of pressure to transfer to the collective farm. The communists didn't like people to farm on their own. Both my parents were already working at the collective farm—my mom helped with the cows, and my father with the horses.

Hanna Basaraba

A few months before the famine began, someone at the collective farm gave too much food to a foal, which overate and died. My father wasn't to blame at all, but it was his responsibility. So they put him in jail for several months. For sabotage.

When he was due to come out, the famine was just starting, but no one knew how awful it was going to be. Mom loved my dad very much and didn't want him to have to walk back from the city barefoot. At the time we had one cow, so Mom sold it and sent him the money to buy a pair of shoes.

Dad bought the shoes and headed home. But when he was almost at the village, bandits attacked him in the forest and killed him. All because of those shoes, which were nice, so they wanted to steal them. And so a few weeks before the famine, my mom was left with no husband and no cow, on her own with six children. All I have left of my dad is his nickname: they called him Kachany ["Corncob"], because he was small and stout like a corncob, and apparently he rocked from side to side as he walked. Here in Rostivka everyone has a nickname, and as I was the youngest, after my father's death I was called Kachanikha ["Little Cob"].

As for the famine, it wasn't as if one fine day it began and you could name a precise date. Gradually, day by day, there was less and less food. I was very small at the time, but I can remember constantly running after my mom and asking her to give me something to eat. And I remember her crying. Six children. All on her own. And less and less to eat. In the beginning we still had some hens, and they laid eggs, but then the hens disappeared. Someone must have stolen them. At the time people were fighting for their lives; no one cared anymore—a neighbor wasn't a neighbor, a relative wasn't a relative.

And then the dying began. First the weakest, the sick, and the smallest children. The less resourceful. Initially it was people I didn't know—Rostivka was a big village with more than 1,500 residents.

But then people on our street began to die. Our distant relatives. Then our neighbor Gregorko, and his wife, Alexandra.

Then we started to swell up. Everyone. It was a strange feeling.

I was lucky because I was still going to nursery school, where once a day they gave us a kind of thin soup, which we called balanda. It tasted disgusting, but that didn't matter. One hot meal each day during a famine meant a great deal. But in spite of the soup, I was so swollen I couldn't walk. All the children were like that. Normally I'd have run from our cottage to school in ten minutes, but in those days it took me an hour and a half each way. But I had to go. Because of the soup. If I said I didn't have the strength, my mother would force me out of the house. She realized that without the soup, I'd die.

With our skinny little legs, skinny little arms, and huge bellies, we all looked the same. At the time we were described as being "rachitic." Because we were so emaciated.

Now and then one of the children I played with would just disappear. They stopped coming to nursery school. Nobody ever asked what had happened. There was no point in asking. It was obvious.

The games at nursery school weren't like children's games either. We'd arrive, the teacher would say something, and each of us would sit down in a corner. Imagine a group of thirty children who aren't playing because they don't have the strength. Because they're hungry. So we'd sit there, rocking and dozing. I can remember several occasions when one of the children failed to get up again.

And then dreadful things started happening.

Two houses away from us lived a woman we used to call

Hanka "Kartoplyova" ["Potato"], because her face was round like a potato. And one day I heard someone say that she had eaten her children. She'd been driven mad by hunger. And you know what, the dreadful thing about it is that we didn't find it at all surprising. We all knew about it because she used to have children, and then, one after another, they'd vanished, but there were no bodies. All Mom told us was this: "You are never, ever to go to Hanka Kartoplyova's house for any reason at all. Whatever she might say to you, whatever she might promise, you're not to go inside."

And indeed, one day I was walking home from school with my older sister Marika, and as we passed Hanka's house she was standing by the fence and called to us. "Come over here," she said, "and I'll give you something nice." We ran off like the wind! I don't know where we got the strength, because the famine had been going on for several months by then, but we raced home; she didn't even try to chase us. She couldn't have had the strength either.

Later on Hanka Kartoplyova died, and since then her cottage has been unoccupied. No one has ever wanted to live there. Even when people came here from other parts of Ukraine to work on the collective farm, the house remained empty. News spread that a mother had eaten her children in that house. But I'd like to repeat that she wasn't a bad woman; it was just that hunger made something go wrong in her head.

The worst time was in the spring—that was when the greatest number of people died. As if they'd used up all their strength surviving the winter, and then had none left to go on living.

But that was when we had a bit of luck. There was a new

head teacher at the local school, whose name was Mrs. Sheptivskaya, and when she heard that my mom was on her own with six children, she said to her: "Hustya"—that was my mom's name—"it must be hard for you to feed your children. Come and work at the school." "As what?" "As the cook."

My mom didn't think twice. Until then she'd worked at the collective farm as a milkmaid, but you know what it's like. A cook has access to food. In times of famine, there's no better job.

The school kitchen was in the house of a family that a few years earlier had been subjected to "dekulakization," which is to say they'd been stripped of their property and sent to Siberia. My mom was given everything to make balanda like the kind I was given at nursery school. Sometimes they brought her beets, sometimes some grain, sometimes a few potatoes, whatever they happened to have. Throughout the famine I don't remember any meat; I never ate it once. But Mom used to make *galushki*—potato dumplings—and homemade pasta. The head teacher agreed that I could go to the school too, though I was only six. I remember waiting all day long for the food my mom cooked. And once the time came, I'd drink up the greasy water left over from the dumplings or the pasta and take the rest home for my sisters.

And that was how we survived.

Special commissions used to tour the villages in those days, in 1933, checking to see if anyone was hiding food. Whatever they found, they confiscated. They took away everything that could possibly be edible. Sorrel. Birch bark. They even took away candles, because in desperation people used to try making soup out of them. Some tried to boil their linen clothing and drink the broth. Our neighbor was on one of those commissions. I remember them coming to our house and inspecting every corner: the attic, the closets, the pots, even inside the stove.

Later on that neighbor lived on the same street as us. His name was Sydor. He'd bow to my mom and say good day in the usual way; he'd ask how's life, how are the children, as if nothing bad had ever happened. And Mom? What could she say to him? He was a respected communist, and he must have believed he'd done the right thing.

Those thieves who killed my dad lived on the same street as us later on too, but only after spending time in jail—the Bolsheviks had caught them all in the meantime. That's what the street was like, so what could you do? How could my mom pick a fight with them, when she was living all alone with six children?

In those days, lots of the children in our village died, but somehow my mom didn't lose a single one. We all managed to survive.

4.

Hanna has a request for me and Roman. Her first cousin Vera Mortko, who is also her best friend from her school days, lives on the other side of Rostivka. They're both over ninety and neither has the strength to walk from one end of the village to the other, and no one in either of their families has a car.

"I'd like to see her before one of us dies. Please will you take me to her? Just for a short visit," Hanna says.

We'll take her. For as long a visit as she wants.

Vera Mortko lives in a house that's covered in vines. She spends most of her time lying down by the stove, wrapped in quilts, as if with age warmth has left her. Her eyes are barely visible behind her thick eyeglasses, so for a while she stares to see who has come to visit her. But when she finally makes out her cousin's features, she hugs Hanna so tightly that it's impossible to tear them apart. Briefly, she lets go and weeps. And then hugs her again.

Hanna Basaraba and Vera Mortko

Hanna too is moved.

"How much we've been through, Vera," she says. "It's frightening to think about it."

"And we're still alive," says Vera.

"Yes, we're still alive. Tell the boys your story."

Vera Mortko's Story

I don't know how to tell you this, boys. It's beyond comprehension. No one who hasn't been through such terrible starvation could possibly understand.

But I'll try.

Just like Hanna, I was six years old when it all began. My dad was dead, like Hanna's, because he too had worked at the collective farm and ended up in jail, where he was beaten to death during an interrogation. Mom toiled at the harvest day after day, but my siblings and I had nothing to eat.

Luckily my mom made a deal with the neighbors who lived at the end of our street. They had two children, a boy of six months and a girl of eighteen months, and they had no one to leave them with when they went to work. So I took care of them, and they gave me some of the soup they were given at the collective farm. And my brother and sister grazed the neighbors' cows in exchange for a daily mug of milk each.

We too had a cow when the famine began. But one day it disappeared.

My mom started crying—I remember it as if it were today, because for a child there's nothing more upsetting than to see her mother in tears. Someone told her one of the farmers, whose name was Sak, had stolen it, so my mom went to see him. She entered the farmyard, went into the barn, and saw blood all over the floor—Sak and his sons were butchering our cow. Sak looked at Mom. Mom looked at Sak. What could she do? How could she prove the cow was ours? And even if she could, what good would it do? How could she argue with a man who was willing to let a mother and three children starve to death as long as he could make some money selling the meat?

We were all dreadfully poor then. We ate burdock or birch bark, and in the winter we dug up roots in the forest just to have anything at all to eat.

"But tell them what saved you," Hanna says. "Your mother became a cook during the famine, just like mine."

"It's true; she was employed in the kitchen at the collective farm. The manager took pity on her for being a single mother."

"Just like in my case," Hanna says, nodding. "We're the daughters of cooks. That's how we survived."

Every day my mom cooked dinner for the people working in the fields. Most of the people who worked at the collective farm survived thanks to my mom's soup. But Mom had children at home—she had to think about us as well. One day she told me: "Come and see me in the kitchen this evening, Verochka, when people are getting ready to leave work, and bring Sanya too." So my sister Sanya and I went to see our mom, who told us to hide behind the door, and when no one was looking, she gave us three small beets. "Take them home, children, and I'll make you soup."

So off we went. And I'm ashamed to admit it, but we were so hungry, and during the famine three beets was unimaginable. So Sanya and I sat down in a field, and without saying a word, we simply ate those beets.

My mom came home from the collective farm and asked if we'd brought back the beets. When she found out we hadn't, she didn't shout at us or hit us; she just started to cry so terribly. She cried and cried, and I was afraid she'd never stop . . .

And Vera starts to cry the tears of a little girl who has seen half the village die of starvation. And Hanna starts to comfort her.

"Don't cry now, Vera. It's not your fault. You were just a child . . ." Hanna says. And she pulls her cousin into her faded sweater.

"I know, Hanna, I know. But to this day I feel so bad when I think that I ate those beets. That I let down my mom when she was having a tough time," Vera says. And continues crying.

"But we survived, Vera. And we're still alive." Hanna hugs her even tighter.

"Yes. We did. It's extraordinary that we survived." Vera wipes her nose on a white handkerchief and starts to calm down. Her face is a picture of deep contemplation. And then she continues:

Before the famine, here, on my street, there were sixteen houses, with twelve to fifteen people living in each one. The place was full of children; I remember how a year before the famine we used to play outside the whole time. And after the famine? It was a graveyard. Only six houses still had anyone left alive. There were hardly any children, and most of the ones who remained didn't have the strength to live. Do you remember the cart that went around carrying off the corpses, Hanna? We were just children—children shouldn't see things like that. But twice, sometimes three times a week that cart drove by, with the men who tossed the dead bodies into it. No one had the strength to carry a corpse to the graveyard; no one had the strength to pray. I remember Mom warning me: "Don't stop on your way to school, and for God's sake don't sit down. They'll gather up anyone who's sitting or lying down—they don't look to see if you're dead or alive."

No child should ever set eyes on the things we saw.

5.

We're stopping off at one more house.

Marika Koreniuk lives on the other side of Rostivka, across the little stream that divides the town in two. She's a distant cousin of Roman's, a year older than Hanna and Vera. We can stop at her home for only a short time because she's very frail and we don't want to disturb her for long.

The house is roofed in corrugated iron, and there are work

clothes in the hall that belong to Marika's children, who are farm workers. Marika is sitting wrapped in a quilt; she comes to life only now and then.

Luckily, she brightened up on our arrival.

Marika Koreniuk's Story

The bad times began with the dekulakization, when the land and other property were taken away from the kulaks. The Soviets decided that any farmer who was just a little richer than the others must be sent to Siberia. One of these men lived here, on our street, with his family, and he was known as Uncle Ivan. His wealth consisted of a single bull that he hired out to stud. If anyone needed the bull to inseminate their heifer, Ivan would come by with it. That was all he had, just a patch of land and that bull, but that was enough for the Soviets to regard him as a kulak, so they sent him, his wife, and their three children to Siberia.

Uncle Ivan died in Siberia, and once her time in exile ended, his wife, Kalina, had no money to come home. So she picked up their youngest, eight-month-old Fedor, and started to walk, with the two older children toddling alongside her. They walked for a week, then another one, but it was tough going. The baby cried and was sick, but Kalina had to go on carrying him. Finally she could see that in a matter of days they'd all be dead. And in a flood of tears, she wrapped baby Fedor in a scarf, dug a hole, put him into it, and off she went with the other two children.

About an hour went by, perhaps less, when suddenly Kalina shouted, "Oh my God, what have we done?!" She raced back to the hole and dug out Fedor. Luckily he was still alive. She wiped the dirt from his hair. "If we're going to die," she said, "then we'll all die." They sat down and cried. And then they carried on.

And by a miracle they didn't die.

Eventually they found their way back here to Rostivka. And just a few weeks after they arrived—I remember, because we all went to see them and hear their stories—the famine began. The most incredible thing is that after coming all the way home from Siberia with Kalina, the only one of her children to survive the famine was little Fedor. He lived here later on, a few houses down from me. He died two years ago.

Our cottage was at the end of the village, on the riverbank. My stepfather—my father died not long after I was born—was extremely worried, because there were gangs roaming the villages who broke into houses searching for food, and who murdered the owners. And which cottage were they going to enter, if not the one at the end? My stepfather managed to hide a little corn, but he was so terrified of these gangs that he hid it in the attic, under the straw. The crows smelled the corn, and before anyone realized it, they'd eaten our entire stock.

So we ate frozen potatoes, like everyone else, and burdock. If you managed to survive the winter, as soon as any bud appeared on a tree, someone immediately ate it. I can't remember a single apple that year, because they were all eaten before they'd had time to grow.

But not all of us survived. My little brother Ryhorko got up one day, went out into the yard, collapsed, and never got up again. No one had the strength to take him to the graveyard, especially since it was at the other end of Rostivka. Poor Ryhorko lay there until the gravediggers came and carried him off.

6.

Before taking Hanna home, we make a stop at Rostivka's grave-yard.

I take Hanna under one arm, Roman takes her under the other, and we slowly make our way like this to the spot where several hundred former inhabitants of the village are buried.

On the right-hand side it's a normal cemetery of the kind you see all over Ukraine. The gray-blue gravestones, often with engraved or ceramic pictures of men with mustaches and women in headscarves, are overgrown with grass, and some are surrounded by metal fences. Gilded letters and flower motifs are common, and there are lots of traditional Ukrainian rushnyki tied to the crosses—they're given not just to newlyweds but also to the dead.

In the middle of the cemetery stands the "fraternal" (i.e., mass) grave of Red Army soldiers who died fighting fascism. It's cone-shaped and looks a bit like a rocket taking off, except the tip of it is adorned with a golden Soviet star. There are small benches so people can sit beside their loved ones, and the older they are, the more they think about their own relocation to a place where there's peace and quiet, there are no wars, and no one goes hungry.

The left-hand side of the cemetery is disturbing: it's over-grown with bright green bushes, here and there replaced by trees. There's burdock, nettles, plantain, clover, and fescue grasses. It's an impenetrable jungle. But why would anyone go there anyway? It's the land of the dead. The dead who had no one to bury them properly.

"This is where all those people who were brought here on

the carts were laid to rest," says Hanna. "Hanka Kartoplyova, our neighbor Gregorko and his wife, Alexandra. There are several dozen children here with whom I went to nursery school or played in the street. Hanka Ternychykha, who went to prison for stealing a few ears of corn for her children. Even Sak and his sons are buried here—remember the man who stole Vera's mom's cow? He didn't survive the famine either."

"My great-grandmother and great-grandfather too," says Roman.

"And Ryhorko, Marika's little brother. I very nearly ended up buried here with you too, children."

We stand awhile in silence.

There are no words to say in such a place.

7.

Before leaving Rostivka, Roman and I take Hanna home and stay for one more cup of coffee. This time we sit not in the hall but in the summer kitchen, a few yards away from the house.

And before we know it, all sorts of food appears on the table in front of us, including meat-filled pierogi called *vareniki*, ham-and-cheese sandwiches, vegetable salad, cake, fish, and a sort of corned beef. Just like the magic table in the fairy tale, this one too is suddenly covered in platters and dishes, and in just a few minutes there's no room left on it. While we were touring the village with Hanna, her daughter Ola was preparing all this food on her own.

I feel silly. I say there was no need to go to so much trouble, and that we didn't want to be a nuisance. But Hanna refuses to listen and simply tells Roman off again for not giving her advance warning of our visit, thus making it impossible for her and her daughter to cook us a proper lunch.

If this one isn't proper, I'm almost afraid to think what sort of lunch would be.

Roman takes the browbeating with grace, then whispers in my ear: "I deliberately didn't call ahead because I know these people. They'd want to treat us to a feast, and a poor chicken or even a piglet would have lost its life. People who survived the famine never let you leave the house with an empty stomach."

Soup made of pine needles, bark, and cones—this is what some Ukrainian students served to their fellow students in Brussels in 2019 to remind the world about the Great Famine. The students made faces and spat it out, but they took the leaflets and read about the forgotten genocide that Stalin inflicted on Ukraine. The event was organized by the Ukrainian Leadership Academy; in previous years they had commemorated the Great Famine in a similar way on the streets of Ukrainian and European cities. In addition to various activities, a food truck drove around Ukraine serving dishes like these.

But a year later, because of COVID-19, it wasn't possible to serve soup on the streets. So the young Ukrainians thought up a version to suit the pandemic—a restaurant website where you could see lovely styled photos of the foods their grandparents had eaten to survive the famine.

The contrast between dishes made of pinecones, twigs, weeds, frozen potatoes, or flax and the professional photography, food styling, and elegant tableware prompted some extreme emotions.

Valentyn Hryhorenko, who represents the Ukrainian Leadership Academy, said the initiative was the world's first Online

Restaurant of Memory. Upon visiting the site you see several dishes, with their names and ingredients and buttons marked "Check the Price."

If you click a button, you can listen to the personal story of a famine survivor.

The first dish is called Herbal Bread, which is "baked flatbread made of grated grass, kneaded in hot water with the addition of flax seeds." When you click to "Check the Price," you read: "The price of this dish is an opportunity for Ukrainians who are lucky enough to survive the hungry winter. It was easier in the spring because the weeds appeared: sorrel, goosefoot, and clover."

You can also listen to a conversation with Maria Hurbich, who survived the Great Famine as a twelve-year-old thanks to this kind of bread.

Scroll down and you find Palyanichki, which is "baked and finely chopped potato waste with grain residues." The price of this dish is "the lives of thousands of people who miraculously managed to save a handful of grain. It was often dug out of rodent burrows, because for a few ears of corn from the field you could be shot."

Hlibtsi is "crumbled and baked straw with millet and buckwheat chaff and hemp seed." The price of this dish is "millions of Ukrainians who survived thanks to substitutes: dried straw, rotten watermelons, and potato peelings. They literally sneaked food away from the animals."

And so on.

The young people who took part in the project and who commented on the photos and dishes online emphasized that often it was the first opportunity they'd ever had to hear the personal stories of their own family members from the time of the Great Famine. But they were also surprised at how much the famine has permeated the lives of their families and of subsequent generations.

"It's still trailing behind us almost a hundred years on," says Oleh, one of my Ukrainian friends. "My family is in the habit of stocking up on immense, absurdly large amounts of food, as if another famine could come along at any moment. And when my wife became pregnant, she had a recurring dream in which she had nothing to feed her children. It was only recently she realized she was having the nightmare that her grandmother experienced in real life."

POSTSCRIPT

Two weeks after we took Hanna to visit her, Vera Mortko died. We witnessed the final meeting of the cousins who miraculously survived the Great Famine.

IV

A Meeting in the Mountains

Stalin's Eating Habits

1.

He lays a hand on my arm. He looks me in the eyes, and then, resignedly, he looks off toward the mountains. Then at me again. "I killed a man, Witold, do you understand?" Again he looks away, at the sky; clearly, talking to me is not bringing him the kind of relief he might have been hoping for. "He was standing next to me, roughly as far away as my brother is now." And he points at his brother, who is sitting quite close by. "And I shot him dead, you see?"

Then he waits for me to say something.

I don't know what to say. And I don't know how to enter into the mood of this conversation. It's 2009 and in the place we're sitting, just a year earlier, the Russian invasion of Georgia was under way. I'm wondering how to get myself out of this pickle.

I'm on my own, drunk, among some Georgians the size of oak trees; we're surrounded by mountains I can't name. A while ago they told me they're descended from princes—as I already know, here in the Caucasus there's often someone claiming to be royalty.

But then they started telling me that their great-uncle was Stalin's brother—that's an advance on the usual story, because although everyone in Georgia is proud of Stalin, I've never met any of his cousins before.

Especially since I know that Stalin's brothers died as soon as they were born.

But now they're telling me about the Russian soldiers they killed during the recent war between Russia and Georgia. Four big, beefy guys, with necks like tree trunks.

It's all too much for me. I'm trying to devise an escape plan.

But before I can make a move, one of the men lunges at me. He pins me down. And holds on.

2.

He couldn't stand cooking. When he was a child, his mother had various jobs. One of them was as a cook. Supposedly that was why for the rest of his life Joseph Stalin hated the smell of food being cooked, and had all the kitchens serving his dachas and houses built at a distance—which was true of the dacha in New Athos that I visited in Abkhazia.

When he and his comrades were exiled to Siberia by the tsar, they agreed that they would share all the duties equally— the cooking, the cleaning, and the procurement of food. But it soon became clear that Stalin had no intention of cooking or cleaning. He just went hunting and fishing.

Yakov Sverdlov, who was in exile with Stalin, was particularly angry with him. "We were meant to cook the dinners ourselves," recalled Stalin years later. "At the time I had a dog, and I named him Yashka, which naturally displeased Sverdlov, because he too was Yashka [the diminutive of Yakov]. After dinner Sverdlov always washed the spoons and plates, but I never did. I ate my food, put my plates on the floor, the dog licked them, and everything was clean."

Toward the end of their exile, when they were living with a third communist, Lev Kamenev, whenever it was time to wash the dishes, Stalin would flee the house.

After the revolution he ate with his wife, Nadezhda Alliluyeva, at the Kremlin canteen, which in those days had the reputation of being one of the worst in Moscow.

The French writer and communist Henri Barbusse visited Stalin shortly after Alliluyeva's suicide and said of his living conditions: "The bedrooms are as simply furnished as those of a respectable second-class hotel. The dining room is oval in shape; the meal has been sent in from a neighboring restaurant. In a capitalist country a junior office clerk would turn up his nose at the bedrooms and complain about the fare."

According to Vyacheslav Molotov, who headed the Soviet diplomatic corps, Stalin's one and only culinary extravagance in those days was a bathtub full of pickled gherkins.

3.

Let's go back to my meeting in the mountains.

It all started innocently enough. I was in Gori, Stalin's birthplace, in the beautiful mountains of central Georgia. I was driving around the picturesque neighboring villages to find the local wine producers that used to supply the Kremlin cellars—the only wine Stalin drank was Georgian.

"Wine producers" sounds very grand. In fact, every self-respecting farmer in Georgia has some vines and reliably makes fantastic wine, as well as a sort of brandy, often 70 percent proof, known as chacha. It was a cottage industry of this kind that I was looking for.

The Georgians' boundless hospitality made my work impossible—because how can you get any work done when everyone you visit brings out the wine and the chacha and has to treat you before they'll answer your questions? After half an hour you're too well oiled, and besides, the day is still young, the nature is beautiful, your host is friendly, so why on earth do any work? And then once we'd had a drink, every single host told me that a plane used to fly from Moscow just to fetch Stalin's wine. What's more, every other host swore he had documents to prove it, and two of them even showed them to me, though first of all, they were in Georgian, and second, I was too tipsy to understand them or remember anything about them.

So I'd been having a jolly time driving around Gori for several days when I encountered the first of the Tarkanishvili brothers. He was in his off-road vehicle, just leaving the allotment he'd inherited. He had a bit of a paunch, and he was wearing a cap with the logo of an American basketball team. When he heard what I was looking for, he told me, in broken Russian, to call him that evening.

"You won't regret it," he said. "My family has a better story about Stalin than anyone else. In all of Gori."

I didn't need to be told twice.

4.

The following evening the brothers drove me into the mountains. They tossed into the back of their pickup truck a sheep that they'd butchered for shashliks. On the way all four of them started talking over one another:

"As a true son of our land, Stalin created a 'little Georgia' for himself in Russia. And did what he could to be surrounded by Georgians. Best of all, family."

"Your family won't betray you because they know that if they did, they'd have nowhere to come home to."

"That's why he kept all his sidekicks, those Molotovs and Khrushchevs, on a short leash. They knew that one false move and *blam*! You're gone, grand Mr. People's Commissar. Only the Georgians had peace."

And so our journey flew by. On the way the gentlemen told me about their sports successes: one was a wrestling trainer, another trained weight lifters. They managed competitors at the international level.

By the time we reached the mountains, we were very well acquainted and fairly well canned, and the brothers finally decided to tell me about Stalin.

"For many years it was a secret—our father told us the story of Uncle Sasha, but he always stressed that we weren't to repeat it to anyone . . ."

"Which was pointless, because in Georgia everyone knew anyway . . ."

"Our great-uncle Alexander, or Sasha, was Stalin's brother. Don't look at me like that! He was his brother. Boys, he doesn't believe us . . ."

"He will soon. Listen, Witold. Stalin's mother worked for our great-grandfather as a cook. And once or twice he and she . . . well, you know, they did what guys and gals do. When he found out she was pregnant, he married her off to the illiterate cobbler Vissarion."

"Vissarion knew how to write! But he drank like a fish."

"I heard he couldn't count to three. Whatever the case, he had no idea what was going on. And when he realized, he took to beating the kid badly—really badly."

"Little Stalin was always running away to spend time with our great-uncle Sasha, who was the same age as him, and who was also the son of our great-grandfather. They became friends, and many years later Great-uncle Sasha became Stalin's cook and food taster at the Kremlin. Well, look at that—he still doesn't believe us."

It's true. I didn't believe a single word.

5.

For many years Stalin, following Lenin's example, didn't attach much importance to food—those men of the revolution were sustained by something else. Just like Lenin's wife, Nadezhda Sergeyevna Alliluyeva was clueless about cooking. Whereas Stalin himself knew how to make pretty good shashliks—he'd learned that at home in Georgia.

But when Alliluyeva committed suicide in 1932—some say she couldn't take it when she realized her husband had deliberately starved Ukraine—Stalin wanted nothing to do with shashliks or any other food. He became withdrawn and sank into a depression. Like others in the government he ate at the

Kremlin, in the canteen. For the children who remained with him, the state hired a cook, apparently a rather average one.

Many years later Vyacheslav Molotov recalled that the food cooked for Stalin "was very simple and unpretentious." In the winter he was always served meat soup with sauerkraut, and in the summer, fresh cabbage soup. For a second course there was buckwheat with butter and a slice of beef. For dessert, if there was any, cranberry jelly or dried fruit compote. "It was the same as during an ordinary Soviet summer vacation, but throughout the year."

The brothers went on to tell me several stories about their great-uncle, and then about the 2008 war between Russia and Georgia. The oldest one, Rati, really did lunge at me. But it turned out he just wanted to hug me and raise a toast to Poland's president, Lech Kaczyński—the Georgians adore him because he defended their country against Russian aggression. For them, the brothers told me, Kaczyński is as great a hero as Stalin.

The next morning, once we had sobered up enough for one of them to be able to drive, they drove me back to Gori. We said goodbye with less enthusiasm, as you do when you have a hangover, but we promised one another we'd be friends for the rest of our lives. And although I haven't seen them since, I remember our meeting with great fondness. But for many years I filed away the story about the great-uncle who cooked for Stalin along with the myths and fairy tales that people sometimes tell me on my travels.

I was very much mistaken. Great-uncle Sasha really did exist. More than that, he genuinely revolutionized Stalin's eating habits; he got him out of the depressing Kremlin canteen and reminded him of the wonders and vitality of Georgian cuisine, as well as the virtues of the Georgian feast with friends. Stalin made use of these lessons to the end of his days.

Was he really the great-uncle of the four brothers who treated me to lamb shashliks that night? That I don't know and am likely never to find out—I have tried to find them again, to no avail.

But let's start at the beginning.

V

Beauty and Beria

Stalin's Cook and His Wife

1.

His hair was combed back; he wore fashionable tapered pants and patent leather shoes. In the 1920s Alexander Egnatashvili was the

Alexander Yakovlevich Egnatashvili

king of Tbilisi society. If anyone stepped on his toes, he didn't think twice about lashing out—for many years he'd been a wrestler, and he had even performed at the circus in Moscow as a strongman.

But if he took a liking to someone, he was generous, willing to share a joke and a drinking session.

Before the revolution, which spread from Petrograd down to the Caucasus, his father, Yakov, had a chain of restaurants—several in Gori, several in Tbilisi—as well as a grocery store and a wholesale wine company. At one of the restaurants he employed Keke Djugashvili, a beautiful but indigent woman from Gori. He was godfather to the two sons she'd supposedly had with her husband, the cobbler Vissarion, but as both children died soon after birth, when Keke and Vissarion produced a third son, Joseph, they chose someone else to be the godfather. People gossiped anyway, saying that the three boys were not actually Vissarion's but those of the enterprising innkeeper.

However, when Georgia became part of the Soviet Union, entrepreneurs like Yakov became enemies of the people. The new government regarded him and all other capitalists as an ulcer on the healthy body of Soviet society. Yakov lost all his businesses. He still sent his son Alexander—Sasha for short—to open a restaurant in Baku, the capital of Azerbaijan, and by doing so he might have saved at least part of his commercial fortune. Sasha hardly slept at night, and even learned to speak Turkish and Azerbaijani, but it was of no use. Eventually the Bolsheviks treated him like a capitalist there too.

So he went back to Georgia.

Fortunately for him, Lenin soon introduced the NEP, the New Economic Policy, under which people were allowed to run small businesses. The enterprising Sasha didn't need to be told twice. He quickly began to rebuild his father's empire.

He did it mainly by persuasion, on top of which he had the right conditions: he was regarded as one of the strongest men in Georgia. He soon opened four restaurants and a wholesale wine company. Two of the licensed premises adjoined the

Soldier's Bazaar, where furniture, shoes, bedding, and all sorts of craftwork were sold, and where skilled workmen gathered for hire. While waiting to be hired, the workmen passed the time drinking wine and chacha, which were sold straight from the barrel by a barman named Grisha and served with fried liver, shashliks, fish, pickles, radishes, and bread. A shot of vodka and a snack at Grisha's cost five kopecks.

The second bar alongside the Soldier's Bazaar was named the Golden Anchor, and quite by chance, it was also run by a man named Grisha. "One day Grisha was having scrambled eggs and tomato for breakfast. Suddenly Sasha appeared and asked him if scrambled eggs were on the menu," recalled Ivan Alikhanov, who was Sasha Egnatashvili's future stepson. "It wasn't. So Sasha whacked Grisha on the head with a frying pan and said, 'If it's this good, it should be on the menu.'"

Apart from the two facilities at the bazaar, Sasha had two others. Located on the edge of town, the Darial offered its guests some unusual attractions. It was run for Sasha by a man named Stepko, who liked a joke, and who was also rather generously endowed. According to Alikhanov: "When the *tamada* [toastmaster] wanted to make fun of new guests, he'd ask Stepko to serve them the 'pièce de résistance.' Then Stepko would put his penis on a plate and cover it with greens."

But the real apple of the enterprising Georgian's eye was a restaurant named By the Kura (referring to the river), which as well as having a liquor license offered rooms for hire by the hour. No wonder that apart from the tipsy clientele, equally tipsy prostitutes used to hang out there.

In the late 1920s Sasha Egnatashvili made a fortune almost overnight. And he was madly in love with Liliana Alikhanova, a beautiful German who lived in his building and whose husband, a rich local man named Ivan Alikhanov (the father of the Ivan Alikhanov quoted above), had brought her home with him from a vacation in Thuringia. She'd been working there as a chambermaid and was barely eighteen when she arrived in Georgia with Ivan, leaving her whole life behind. To make sure his family would not object to his marrying a chambermaid, Ivan married her off to an impoverished German baron, then got her a rapid divorce, which allowed him to bring her back to Georgia as a German baroness. As a result she was quickly accepted by the elite, and their home became one of the leading salons in Tbilisi.

Liliana Alikhanova

Liliana liked the resourceful Sasha too, especially as her husband was seriously ill, and she was finding life with three children difficult under the Bolsheviks, whose language she never mastered. Sasha would invite her and the children on vacation, organize trips to the seaside, and bend over backward to win her affection, even though Ivan was still lying in bed in their shared apartment; despite his ill health, Ivan knew perfectly well what was going on.

This unusual situation came to an end with Ivan's death.

Soon after, Sasha and Liliana were married. And they had the honeymoon of their lives. Ivan Alikhanov Jr. recalled with delight how much energy and life Sasha brought into his family. He showered the boy's mother with gifts. He took the children, both his own and Liliana's, to wrestling matches at the Tanti Brothers' circus. Thanks to these expeditions with his stepfather,

Alikhanov had a lifelong involvement with professional wrestling, first as a competitor and later as a trainer.

Sasha and Liliana both loved to cook. They went shopping once a week, and this was an event in itself. Sasha would make a fuss, haggling and inspecting each individual tomato, apricot, or fish. Despite this, the tradesmen loved haggling with him, and with good reason: he always left the bazaar with two wicker baskets piled high.

They took one basket home with them. And Sasha took the other one to the former Palace of the Governor of the Caucasus, where Stalin's mother, Keke Djugashvili, lived. It was Sasha's father, Yakov, who had made his son promise to take care of his former housekeeper. Many years after the alleged affair, Keke, now wrinkled and wearing the headscarf typical of old women in Georgia, still mattered to him. Although she was the leader's mother, her pension was only enough for a very modest life. Stalin used to write her effusive letters, but he hadn't been to see her for years. Although Sasha's gifts often made her feel embarrassed, the groceries he brought were essential.

In those days Keke was a sort of adopted grandmother to little Ivan Alikhanov. She often stopped by their apartment to play lotto with his mother.

Occasionally, if he happened to be in Tbilisi, Yakov Djugashvili, Keke's grandson and Stalin's son, would visit them. For the gossiping tongues of Tbilisi, his first name was yet more evidence that Yakov Egnatashvili was the leader's real father—for according to Georgian tradition, the firstborn son should be named for his grandfather.

2.

Liliana and Sasha's idyll ended with the scrapping of the New Economic Policy.

"When a pig is fully grown, you have to slaughter it"—this is how Ivan Alikhanov characterized the government's new policy toward private entrepreneurs. It resulted in private businesses being hit by constantly rising taxes. "As soon as you had paid one tax, another was imposed, and this was repeated until there was nothing left to pay with. As a result, the NEPmen [as those who ran private businesses under the NEP were called] ended up in jail."

To save her husband, Liliana sold off all the family mementos left to her by her first husband—silver tableware, a gold watch, and jewelry. All for nothing. Eventually, Sasha couldn't pay one of the series of taxes and was imprisoned. The recently rebuked NEPmen were given long sentences. Though no one knew it at the time, many of them would never get out of prison.

Liliana didn't wait to see what would happen; she ran to tell Keke the news. Together they went to see the head of the Georgian communists, Filipp Makharadze. When he said he could release Sasha, but only if someone else took his place, Stalin's mother volunteered without hesitation. "I'm not allowed to arrest Stalin's mother," said Makharadze, spreading his hands. But seeing their determination, he agreed for Sasha's brother Vasily, known in Georgian as Vaso, to replace him in prison.

As soon as he was released, Sasha lost no time. He raced off to Moscow, where through Georgian contacts—probably through Yakov Djugashvili—he managed to reach Stalin. They talked late into the night. Stalin not only annulled Sasha's sentence for not paying his taxes but also gave him the kind of job that is only assigned to trusted people: Sasha became the chef for the Central Committee of the Communist Party's first holiday home at Foros in Crimea. The leader also wrote a letter to Lavrentiy Beria, then head of the Communist Party in the Transcaucasus, to say that all the charges against Egnatashvili were to be dropped.

From then on, Sasha's entrepreneurial and organizational skills were to serve the Party and the state. And also the NKVD, the Soviet secret police, whose functionary he became on the spot.

"In this extraordinary way," writes Ivan Alikhanov, "from being a burned-out Tiflis restaurateur, my stepfather suddenly reached the top of the Kremlin nomenklatura, the so-called Stalinist inner circle."

But in this barrel of honey there was a spoonful of tar. Its first name was Lavrentiy, and its last name was Beria.

3.

If anyone stood in his way, he enjoyed torturing them. He'd pull out their fingernails. He allowed his thugs to rape arrestees' wives in front of their husbands.

There have been few characters in the history of the world as unambiguously evil as Lavrentiy Beria, organizer of the Stalinist purges, the executions, and the Gulag. Millions of people lost their lives on his orders.

He was ruthless in pursuit of his objectives. Take the story of Nestor Lakoba, head of the Communist Party in Abkhazia and a friend of Stalin's. For many years Lakoba was Beria's mentor. But when Lakoba became close to Stalin, Beria began to undermine his position. He did it gradually but tenaciously, until in 1936 Stalin gave him the green light for Lakoba's assassination. Beria himself dined with Lakoba at the supper where he was poisoned, and watched to the end as his former friend died. Later on he personally tortured Lakoba's wife and killed his teenage son.

If he recognized anyone as his opponent, he didn't rest until he had annihilated them. The fact that Sasha Egnatashvili, whom Beria's apparatus had deemed guilty, had managed to wriggle out of prison, get all the way to Stalin, and alter his own fate was something that Beria regarded as a personal insult.

This was the kind of man whom Sasha was up against.

It is difficult to say if he knew this from the start. But he certainly knew that working so close to Stalin was a profession unlike any other.

In Stalin's environment, every day involved fighting for his life.

Sasha must have performed well as manager of the dacha in Crimea, because eighteen months later he was summoned back to Moscow, where the Party entrusted him with his next task: to supervise Joseph Vissarionovich's newly built dacha in what was then the Moscow suburb of Kuntsevo, as well as the adjoining farm, which included a dairy, a vegetable garden, and a henhouse. Like Lenin, Stalin wanted safe, healthful food over which his bodyguards could maintain control.

Construction of the dacha began following the suicide of Stalin's wife, and it was designed by Miron Merzhanov, the architect responsible for almost all the Generalissimus's villas, including those in the Moscow suburbs, in Crimea, and in the

Caucasus, such as the villa in New Athos, Abkhazia. The house was permanently guarded by 150 men; there were six telephone lines connected to it. To improve security, seventy thousand trees were planted around it, and artificial hills were made to shield the house from the road. On Kuntsevo's extensive grounds were several other buildings for the staff. Sasha Egnatashvili and Liliana moved into one of them.

Depressed by his wife's death, Stalin found there a safe refuge, including a rose garden where he liked to work, an orchard including lemon, apple, and pear trees, and even some watermelon patches.

Sasha employed in the kitchen a Georgian named Metreveli, who came from the Racha region, famed for its good chefs. "He paid Metreveli twice the maximum salary for a head chef, but on one condition: he was not to steal," writes Ivan Alikhanov. "Sasha explained to us that as a rule, cooks steal food. And if the cook is dishonest, all the employees will follow suit. The cost of the goods saved by guaranteeing honesty was far more than the head chef's double salary."

Sasha also employed Valentina Istomina, a girl of eighteen who until recently had worked at a factory in the capital; for some reason she had come to the attention of the security service and had been chosen as Stalin's housekeeper. Eventually she was to be a key figure in the aging dictator's life: she not only cooked for him and served him but also became his lover.

Liliana's children, who had moved to Moscow for their studies, used to visit Sasha and Liliana at Kuntsevo every week, which reminded them, at least for a while, of their golden years together in Tbilisi. Although their life was completely different now, the couple still loved each other very much. For her children's visits, Liliana would fry sirloin steaks, bake potatoes, and prepare plenty of jars of pickled mushrooms, gherkins, and tomatoes, as well as Georgian sauces: *tkemali* (made of plums) and *adjika* (made of tomatoes and peppers). As in the past, Sasha helped her in the kitchen. The food they cooked for their children was not much different from the fairly simple diet that Stalin still ate; for instance, for supper on the leader's fifty-fifth birthday his guests were served cabbage soup and veal stew. But the delicacies from Kuntsevo could be eaten only there. In this regard Sasha was an exceptional stickler: the children were not allowed to take a single jar of food back to Moscow.

Sasha managed the farm so well that in addition to providing the food for Stalin and his guests, he also sold some of the agricultural produce, above all strawberries, to the nearest grocery store.

He liked to oversee everything in person. Whenever a calf was born, he was the first in the barn. When harvest time came, he walked shoulder to shoulder with his employees. He also pitched in in the kitchen: many a time he stood alongside Metreveli and the other workers he came to employ as the dacha grew in size.

Sasha often prepared Stalin's meals personally, sometimes with Liliana at his own home. Nor did he forget about the leader's mother, Keke; he wrote her letters and persuaded his brother to take care of her. In 1935 he wrote: "My dear spiritual Mother, yesterday I went to see Soso [Stalin's childhood nickname] and we had a long chat. He has put on weight. He joked a lot."

Sasha was a demanding boss, but seemingly a fair one. Every day after work his employees met up to play the accordion and sing, often into the early hours.

But at the same time, Sasha was an officer—in those days a general in the NKVD—and certainly not a spotless figure. His colleague in the service, Stalin's head of security Nikolai Vlasik, was constantly being accused of rape, abuse of power, and even stealing food. Stalin fired him from the service several times, including once when the leader took it upon himself to calculate his own expenses and found that apparently he was consuming ten kilos of herring per day (most of which was being stolen by Vlasik), and on another occasion when some caviar went missing. Such accusations were not generally leveled at Sasha, or at least they never led to any repercussions.

Sasha did have a weakness for infidelity. But this did not stop him from loving Liliana more than life itself.

4.

Once Sasha had become permanently established within Stalin's entourage, he asked Stalin one day if he ever missed Georgian cooking.

"Feed me," Stalin reportedly replied.

So Sasha and Liliana boarded a train and traveled to Tbilisi, where they packed two railcars full of supplies: sheep, turkeys, barrels of homemade wine, and even a *tone*, which is a Georgian bread oven. Sasha also took two of his former employees back to Moscow with him: Grikula, who had worked at his wholesale wine company and was now to be in charge of Stalin's wine cellar, and Pavel Rusishvili, from a notable Georgian family, whom he had known forever because Pavel's father had sold wine to Sasha's father's restaurants; as soon as he arrived in Kuntsevo, everyone took to him and called him by the diminutive Pavelek. At first Pavelek joined the bodyguards, but when he froze opening and closing the security barrier in the cold weather, Sasha took pity on him and transferred him to the household staff, where he became a butcher and later a chauffeur, delivering to the Kremlin meals prepared for Stalin in the kitchen at Kuntsevo.

Sasha's visit to Georgia brought about a genuine gastronomic revolution, first in Stalin's eating habits and then in cooking throughout the Soviet Union.

Eventually, Stalin became so nostalgic for Georgia's culinary traditions that he set about transplanting them to Soviet ground. Before long at his table there was a tamada—the Georgian master of ceremonies who raises toasts, invites dinner guests to speak, and generally manages the *supra*, or feast. At first this role was performed by one of Stalin's political personnel, but in time he began to appoint his favorite professional actors.

He also realized something that the Georgians had known for centuries: the Georgian supra is an opportunity for the host to show off his wealth and power, for a rich man to intimidate poor ones and bring them even more firmly under his thumb.

Soon these ideas were implemented at the Kremlin dinner table. It would no longer be modest. Like the tables of rich Georgians, it would be dripping with wealth, overloaded to demonstrate, even in difficult times, the role, weight, and power of the country capable of producing such a lavish spread.

But all this was yet to come. For the time being, Liliana personally took care of raising the turkeys. They would prove more useful than anyone might have imagined, because in 1937 doctors prescribed Stalin a diet whose main ingredient was turkey liver. There weren't enough turkeys at Kuntsevo, so—according to Ivan Alikhanov—Sasha "drove his Cadillac around the Moscow region in search of those birds." To dispel any doubt that the head of Stalin's dacha at Kuntsevo really did have an official Cadillac, his stepson included a photograph of his mother with the vehicle. Sometimes Sasha drove it, but it was usually his personal chauffeur, Nadaev, who did.

The kitchen's change to Georgian cuisine brought Stalin great joy. Sasha grew even closer to him. Did the chef yet know how dangerous it was to be so close to Stalin? Or that anyone who flies too close to the Sun of Nations might get burned?

Meanwhile, throughout the Soviet Union purges were under way, organized by Lavrentiy Beria, who had been permanently transferred from the Caucasus to Moscow. More and more of the people who had built the foundations of the state ended up in NKVD torture cells at the Lubyanka, in prison camps, or in front of a firing squad. Writers, officers, painters, and the intellectual elite of various ethnicities were shot, including Belarusians, Tatars, Ukrainians, and Poles. Anyone who had been or was still close to Stalin knew that a death sentence could be passed at any moment. But Sasha deluded himself that his friendship—and probable kinship—with the leader was stronger than politics.

At Kuntsevo the employees still played the accordion at night, while the beautiful Liliana crushed sugar into the turkeys' corn pellets to swell their livers.

5.

In September 1938 Nikolai Vlasik, Stalin's chief of security and Sasha's friend and frequent guest, became head of the First Department of the Main Directorate of State Security. Sasha was appointed his deputy in charge of administrative affairs and given the rank of major. They remained within the structure of the NKVD but were directly subordinate to Stalin.

Beria was also at the peak of his career, having become head of the NKVD in 1938. He was in charge of the mass deportations of ethnic minorities from territory occupied by the Soviet Union.

Even at peaceful Kuntsevo it was increasingly obvious that the world situation was changing for the worse. World War II was under way in Europe. In 1939 Stalin had made a pact with Hitler under which they agreed to divide the spheres of influence between them, but the tension was palpable even within the leader's immediate circle.

Sasha's duties increased. He cooked for Stalin less often, but now he was responsible for something far more important: the closer war came, the more the leader feared for his life. Sasha was to ensure that the food placed on Stalin's table was safe for him to eat.

He performed this task with total dedication, usually testing the food himself. This won him a nickname that is the Russian equivalent of "guinea pig": *Krolik*—"the Rabbit."

He traveled to Georgia to buy wine. Stalin could not eat anything that had not passed through Sasha's hands—and throat. Even the fish that was served to Stalin had to come from the farm run by Sasha; for this purpose the soldiers dug pits to form two ponds that were stocked with carp. Stalin's favorite fish was herring, but it couldn't be raised in a pond.

Sasha could see that the situation for Germans in the Soviet Union was getting more dangerous. He wanted to protect Liliana, the love of his rather bumpy life, and so with a heavy heart he tried to persuade her to leave for Germany. But she wouldn't hear of it. In the first place, she had no one to go to. Her parents were dead, and her more distant family had no desire to reconnect with a relative who had married a wild Georgian. Second, she knew that by leaving she would expose her sons and also her beloved husband to great danger.

So Liliana wrote a letter to Stalin. She admitted that her husband had been encouraging her to leave the USSR, but she had not agreed. She wanted to stay in Russia and serve the country that had adopted her.

Stalin did not reply, but Liliana stayed put. However, Sasha knew he must use all his cunning to save his wife, especially since Beria was one of those closest to Stalin and he plainly hadn't forgotten the humiliation of being forced to release Sasha from jail.

For his part, Beria knew that Sasha was too close to Stalin for him to launch a frontal attack. Sasha was with Stalin at all the most important moments, including the visit of Hitler's foreign minister Joachim von Ribbentrop, with whom the USSR had signed the nonaggression pact, and important meetings that took place at Kuntsevo.

Liliana was quite another matter. Stalin often made use of wives to blackmail their husbands and keep them on a short leash. In 1939 the wife of Stalin's secretary, Alexander

Poskrebyshev, was arrested. The wife of Mikhail Kalinin, who was nominally head of the Soviet state, spent eight years in a prison camp. Kliment Voroshilov, marshal of the USSR and people's commissar for military affairs, had to defend his wife against the security police with pistol in hand. He was the only one to succeed in protecting his spouse from arrest.

Sasha was aware that, especially as Stalin's alliance with Hitler could not last forever, Liliana could be next.

6.

Although Sasha and Liliana lived on the grounds of Stalin's dacha, Stalin visited them only once, in 1938. He did so without warning, and the terrified Liliana hid behind a curtain. "The hostess shouldn't hide," Stalin told her, half in jest.

He was accompanied by Beria, who knew Liliana from Tbilisi, where as a local Communist Party functionary he had requisitioned her apartment. But although he must have remembered her, he introduced himself as if they were meeting for the first time.

This did not bode well.

Their reason for calling on Sasha and Liliana was the visit of an unusual guest who was staying at the couple's house for a few days. He was Date Gasitashvili, a cobbler from Gori who many years earlier had been an apprentice to Stalin's father, Vissarion. Sasha had met him in Georgia and brought him home as a surprise for Stalin. Stalin was delighted. When he asked if he could help Date in any way, the only thing the cobbler wanted his top-ranking compatriot to do was to sing with him. "It's a good thing Sasha found me or I'd have died not knowing what had become of you," Date said to Stalin at dinner, which raised a laugh—at the time, portraits of the leader hung everywhere.

The gentlemen poked fun at each other for a while, and after one of these jokes, Date threatened to remove Stalin's pants and spank his butt until it was "as red as that flag of yours."

Amazingly, Stalin was thrilled. Thanks to the old man, he was briefly taken back to his childhood.

The leader also had a short conversation with Liliana, found some distant kinship between the Georgians and the Germans, and then summoned all the Georgians who happened to be on the grounds of Kuntsevo to Sasha and Liliana's house to take part in a small, improvised supra. It seems that the old cobbler's visit managed to dispel the clouds from above Sasha's and Liliana's heads.

"I'd like to think that Stalin visited our house to soothe the increasing friction between my stepfather and Beria, and that he wanted to show Beria his positive relationship with Sasha's family," Ivan Alikhanov wrote many years later. "But it could also be that, in keeping with the logic of those troubled times, the purpose of the visit was to incite hatred between the people around him. If that was the case, the goal was achieved. The visit became a reason for Beria to dislike my stepfather even more. We all paid a high price for it, my mother more than anyone."

7.

In June 1941 the Russians heard a speech on the radio by the head of Soviet diplomacy, who announced that without declaring war, Hitler's troops had attacked their country. Most of the population was filled with patriotic feelings, and they were sure the war would last only a few months. Few people wondered why Molotov was delivering this speech, rather than Comrade Stalin.

Meanwhile, Stalin was too shocked to say anything. For months, as Joseph Goebbels wrote, he had been behaving like a rabbit hypnotized by a snake. Though all the intelligence he had gathered told him to expect an attack, for a long time he hadn't believed Hitler was really planning one. When it happened, he wasn't able to defend the country against the Wehrmacht.

On the second day of fighting, the Soviet Union lost more than two thousand airplanes, while the Germans lost only sixty-one. By the fifth day, the LVI Panzer Corps had made it halfway to Leningrad without encountering any great resistance along the way. In the first three weeks of fighting, two million Red Army soldiers were killed. Several Soviet armies fell into a German ambush at the first Battle of Smolensk; another three hundred thousand Russians were taken prisoner in this way.

The Soviet Union was entirely unprepared for war. It paid a heavy price for the Stalinist purges among army officers: between 1937 and 1939, forty thousand of them were arrested, and fifteen thousand of those were executed. The victims included three of the five marshals of the Soviet Union, fifteen of the twenty-five admirals, and the vast majority of the army commanders too.

People in Stalin's entourage began fighting for the lives of their relatives. Sasha himself would remain with Stalin throughout the war, but he sent Liliana to Kuybyshev, which the Soviets were preparing as a substitute capital city in case Hitler took Moscow. It made sense—Kuybyshev was far away from the front, and also from Beria. But in addition, thanks to the outbreak of war, Russian Germans were being persecuted all over the country. Some had lived in Russia since the days of Catherine the Great, while others had come to serve at the courts of successive tsars. More than thirty thousand people of German origin were deported from Leningrad alone.

Liliana too was put in prison.

But Sasha believed he would be able to rescue her.

The war was now in full swing. The Russians were still suffering losses; the Germans had captured Stalingrad, with only some small Soviet bridgeheads still holding out. In the north the Germans had encircled Leningrad, which Hitler decided to defeat by starving it rather than by attacking it. Although the Germans came close to Moscow, they would never manage to capture it.

At this time Sasha was working relentlessly. He hoped that if he could prove his unswerving loyalty to Stalin, he could save himself and his wife.

MENU
◇◇◇

Georgian Walnut Jam

This is the Georgian jam that Stalin's mother, Keke, used to send her son via Sasha Egnatashvili, straight to the Kremlin. Be sure to use young walnuts that have been picked before the shell has formed.

2¼ pounds (1 kg) young (green) walnuts
5 cups (1 kg) sugar

1 teaspoon lemon juice
Pinch of vanilla powder

First, soak the walnuts for 2 days, remembering to change the water every 3 to 4 hours.

Drain the water and rinse the walnuts in cold tap water, then soak them again in fresh water for another 2 days.

On the fifth day, bring a large pot of water to a boil, add the walnuts, and cook for 10 minutes, then drain them in a colander.

Add 2½ cups (600 ml) of water to the pot and stir in the sugar. Bring it to a boil, skimming off the froth with a spoon. Add the lemon juice, vanilla, and finally the walnuts.

Remove the pot from the heat. Once the jam is completely cool, bring it to a boil again. Repeat twice more.

VI

A Baker in Besieged Leningrad

Tamara Andreyevna, a portly woman of just over ninety, is the sort of person who may be unique to this part of the world—strong and determined, someone who has survived war and famine and is not afraid of anything on earth, but has never stopped being warm, kind, and obliging to the whole world. We have friends in common who have arranged for us to meet. We shake hands, and the taxi I have ordered pulls up. The driver is a young man from the Caucasus; men like him travel all over Russia in search of work because it's hard to find in their republics. He has a sallow complexion and a trimmed beard, and instead of the air freshener that most drivers attach to the rearview mirror, he has a miniature Quran.

"Salaam alaikum, brother," Tamara Andreyevna says to the driver. "Where are you from? Ingushetia? I like the bread there—*churek*, made of corn flour and kefir. Now switch off the meter, because you're making this journey for free. And switch off the GPS too—you're in my city, and I'll guide you."

The confused Ingush glances at her, then at me—he doesn't

seem amused by the idea of driving for free, and I would prefer to pay him, but Tamara Andreyevna warns me: "Don't answer back, Witold. We're in Leningrad, and I survived the blockade of this city. And that means I have my privileges."

Before we reach our destination, my newly met ninety-year-old questions the Ingush about where exactly his family is from (then gets him to show her on a map) and me about where exactly my family is from (this too will not happen without a map), then shows us both where the corpses of people who died of starvation were thrown during the siege of Leningrad, and finally where the bakery she worked at was, thanks to which she managed to survive.

"Well, brother, perhaps you're not going to take any money from me?" she asks the Ingush at the end of our journey.

He isn't. And he says that whenever she needs to go somewhere, wherever it might be, she's to call him first.

1.

We clamber up the stairs to the sixth floor. But since it's a prewar apartment house, the floors are tall, and I feel as if we've climbed to the eighth floor. Every two or three steps Tamara Andreyevna has to stop because her legs ache, but her good mood never abandons her.

"Until I turned eighty I shuddered at the thought of those stairs," she says. "But then I realized that as long as I can get up them, I'm still alive. All my life I've been very active—opera, theater, reading group—so I've gone up and down them as many as five times a day. And that's why I'm still fit. If I'd lived on the first floor, I'd be dead by now."

Finally we manage to get to the very top: there's nothing above Tamara Andreyevna's apartment but the roof, and above that there's nothing but the sky, and up there is our Creator and Savior, in whom Tamara believes deeply. My hostess puts the kettle on for tea and starts to tell me the story of the toughest years ever experienced by the city, by her and her family, and by Russia.

"To begin with, Witold, in June 1941 it all seemed quite unreal. What war? We were enjoying the white nights, everyone was out in the streets, the girls were kissing sailors. A twelve-year-old, as I was then, notices such things, so I remember it well," she says, and looks at me as if to make sure I know what a twelve-year-old girl might notice. I have no idea, but I believe her every word. She pours boiling water over our tea bags and continues:

I also remember wondering quite seriously if it would all be over by the end of August, and we'd go back to school as normal. My dad had been to the Finnish war just over a year earlier, and he'd been away from home for only four months, but I was sure, I have no idea why, and please, Witold Miroslavovich—here's the tea, here's the sugar, here's some strawberry jam—please, don't ask me why I thought we'd deal with the Germans faster than the Finns.

The mood was excellent. Everyone wanted to fight against Hitler, and everyone, absolutely everyone, was sure the Germans didn't have a chance against us.

My God, what fools we were.

But then how were we to know how quickly the Germans would move deep inside Russia? They never mentioned it on the radio. Even when we lost a city, they only talked about "extremely heavy fighting," but no one ever said we'd lost a city. It was quite a while before people learned what to make of those messages. "Heavy fighting" meant we were in retreat. "Very heavy fighting" meant we'd lost a battle, and it had usually happened several days earlier.

And then came July, and August, and there was nothing to suggest that the war would be over quickly. The men were being called up for the army. Some people, including children, were evacuated. More and more information kept reaching us about the cruelty of the Germans: here they'd executed defenseless civilians, there they'd tormented people. The "heavy fighting" was happening closer and closer to Leningrad.

In July they introduced ration cards for bread, but no one was expecting famine, so often people didn't buy the bread. Though some had already begun to suspect something. In our communal apartment building we had a neighbor from Ukraine whom we called Uncle Ostap. And Uncle Ostap and his wife bought as much bread as they could, when it was still very cheap, and dried it in the oven and made rusks. People laughed at them, but Uncle Ostap said that less than ten years earlier they'd survived the famine in Ukraine and they didn't want to go through the same thing a second time. Our janitor, Uncle Fedor, told him to stop because the NKVD might come and arrest him for spreading defeatism. But Uncle Ostap didn't stop, and the NKVD didn't come to see him.

If this were a stage play, Witold, I'd say the danger increased very gradually.

My mom and I were summoned to the edge of the city to dig ditches that were supposed to hold back tanks. Even at that point it still seemed unreal. What tanks? What Germans? The Red Army will never let them get this far! But we did the digging. Everyone had to do something to defend the Fatherland against fascism. Upon hearing that the Wehrmacht had shot a young girl somewhere, my brother Piotr volunteered for the Red Army. He must have falsified his birth certificate, because he was too young—he was only sixteen. I remember talking to him before he left. How proud I was that he was going to fight for the Fatherland. My brother impressed me so much.

I never saw him again.

Dad worked at city hall, in the municipal services department, and before 1941 he managed a group of men who cleaned the city. He was the first to understand that the war wouldn't end soon. One day he came home from work in despair and told my mom: "Leningrad has no provisions. What we have is enough for two months, maybe just a month and a half. If the Germans surround us, there will be famine."

Could our neighbor Uncle Ostap have been right? Maybe we should make rusks too? But no one had the mind to do it. At the time people said the Germans would want to capture the city as fast as possible. No one imagined they would encircle us and keep us under siege for two and a half years.

Both of my parents had known hunger in the past, during the civil war and the first few years of the Bolshevik governments. Mom had told me before that people ate crows in those days, and she herself had survived because someone had given them four horse hooves, which my grandmother had used to make a viscous soup. But you know what it's like, don't you? When your parents or grandparents tell you how they survived famine, and you've grown up in a country where you have white bread for breakfast every day and at school you have a two-course lunch with compote to follow, you simply don't believe it. You think: that was an aberration, nothing like that will ever happen to me.

Well, that was what I thought too. That August in Leningrad, famine still didn't seem like a real prospect to anyone.

But we found out the most important facts about those months only after the war. For example, that the Germans were already encircling us, but food from Leningrad was still going to Moscow. Or that Stalin wanted to send us trains with aid while it was still possible, but Zhdanov, the head of our communists, refused. He wanted to show that the city of Leningrad could manage by itself. Even when the Germans were already at the tollgates, he was more concerned about his own career than about people's lives.

I also remember the start of the first air raids, and how all the children in our communal building—in those days we lived in a communal apartment not far from Yusupov Palace; there was a toilet in the corridor, a shared kitchen, and children all over the place—they all raced to the windows. It's dangerous, said our parents, someone will get hit by shrapnel. Of course we should have run off to the shelters. But in the early days few people did that. My dad didn't even interrupt his dinner. As if we wanted to treat the Germans with disdain.

At that point you could still buy food in the stores, but things were becoming scarce, and very quickly. I remember Mom spotting a large, ten-pound jar of black caviar. It cost as much as she earned in a month. We left the shop, and I remember my mom saying that prices had to stabilize, that caviar couldn't be so expensive. But then we walked around the city and we saw that there was already nothing left in the stores.

That day we couldn't make it back in time to buy that jar, so the next day we set off first thing. Luckily it was still there. Mom bought it, and we carried it home together, terrified of breaking it.

And I'll tell you, Witold, that jar of caviar saved our lives.

The German air raids became more and more frequent. And even then, in September, when we already knew things were very bad, the authorities kept trying to persuade people that Leningrad had enough provisions to last for two years. How many people could have had the chance to escape the city if they'd known the truth? How many lives could have been saved?

But at that point no one was concerned about human lives. Their concern was not to surrender the city. Because Stalin and the Politburo decided that whatever happened, we wouldn't surrender Stalingrad or Leningrad.

2.

On September 8, the Germans closed their blockade of the city. That day too Badayev's warehouses burned down, where the city's food was stored. There was a smell of burning meat in the air. I started crying; perhaps that was the first time it got through to me that the war wasn't going to end and we had some really tough weeks and months ahead of us. But my brave mother said I mustn't snivel, there were four of us—my brother was at the front, but we didn't yet know he was dead—and that we were sure to manage.

At roughly the same time, my mom volunteered for our building's brigade that threw incendiary bombs off the roof. It was a very difficult and dangerous task. If a bomb fell on the roof of the building, Mom had to use a special stick with a sharpened metal tip to knock it down, in the space of around ten, maybe twelve seconds. Otherwise the roof would catch fire and the whole building could burn down.

Each apartment building in the old city had a brigade like this. I was very proud of my mom for doing something so brave. Again, it was a child's stupidity, but I was waiting for a bomb to fall onto our roof for real and for my mom to throw it off, then we'd all praise her, she'd get a medal, and I'd be even prouder of her.

Both my parents were working, my brother was at the front, and at about this time more food ration cards were introduced, so I used to go and do the shopping. I remember how from day to day it got harder and harder. People squeezed past each other, pushed their way into the lines, and fought. At that point they still had the strength to fight—a couple of months later no one would.

And then, in late October, quite unexpectedly they opened my school. What a joy it was to see my school friends! Almost every day our classes were interrupted by German air raids. We all went down into the shelters in an orderly way, and our teacher, Anna Trofimovna, simply carried on with our lessons there. I remember an unreal scene when the sirens were wailing and we could hear the sound of bombs falling nearby, but Anna Trofimovna went on telling us about the Italian Renaissance. At the time I thought, that's the perfect way to die—listening to stories about Michelangelo.

But none of us died, or at least not that day. The school went on operating throughout the entire blockade, though later on I stopped going.

Every day at school we were given a plate of warm soup, which meant a great deal, because in November they reduced the food rations. Until then, working people had received 250 grams [8¾ ounces] of bread each day. Children and those not working received 125 grams [4½ ounces]. Look at this, Witold, I'll cut you a slice of bread so you can understand how much that is. You see? Three skinny little pieces. And on top of that the bread was half-filled with cellulose. I'll tell you what they added to the bread a little later.

Anyway, there were days when it was impossible to get even that.

The famine began. And people I knew started to die. Our neighbor from the floor below. My father's brother. And finally Uncle Ostap, who had prepared those rusks for himself but contracted dysentery, and no rusks could help him with that.

I was saved by the soup at school. And at home we were saved by the jar of caviar my mom had bought by a miracle. And a box of glue my father bought. It was good glue, made of fish oil—no one makes that kind nowadays. It was strange to eat, but after a few days of hunger it didn't matter to me what I ate—I'd fill my stomach with anything we managed to find. Every day Mom gave each of us two spoonfuls of caviar with our bread, and she made aspic out of the glue. At the nearest store, not far from Griboyedov Canal, you could still buy mustard, for some reason. And if you didn't think about the fact that the aspic was made of glue, you could just about swallow it with that mustard.

People were getting increasingly desperate. Some used to go to the spot where Badayev's food warehouses once stood, gather earth into pails, mix it with water, and try to separate out the sugar. Just to get at least a few calories.

And then my father was given a new task at city hall. He and his four staff members had to make the rounds at the apartment buildings, asking the janitors which apartments housed someone who might die. If they found a corpse, they took it to the cemetery. At first they had a horse and cart for that, but then the horse disappeared—someone must have butchered it for the meat—and they had to pull the cart themselves. In the winter, they swapped it for a sled.

But in the winter they didn't have to tour the apartments anymore. People were dying in the streets. They'd leave their house and never come home. Near our house, I saw in Griboyedov Canal the corpse of a small boy of about eight. Maybe he went down for water and didn't have the strength to scramble back up? I don't know. But I do know that we quickly got used to seeing things like that.

3.

Dad was miserable at his new job. He worked very hard and with dedication, but he came home tired and downcast. I think he was the only one of us who understood the scale of what was happening. And he was scared we'd be next, and that all of Leningrad was going to die.

I remember a day when I took my place in line for bread, but I wanted to check if there was enough for everyone, so I walked a few dozen yards up to the store entrance. Just then some

German bombers flew overhead. The woman I'd been standing behind was killed on the spot. Why wasn't I? Why was I so lucky, but she wasn't? I don't know. I ask myself and God this question every day.

But even so, with every passing day it was becoming clearer to us that we wouldn't survive the winter. I could tell that I was getting a little weaker every day.

The hardest time of all was February, the coldest month. Especially since we had already burned everything in our household stove, a so-called burzhuika, including part of the floor and most of the furniture. No one had enough strength to leave the house. I stopped going to school, and when Dad got back from work, he barely had the strength to get upstairs to us on the third floor.

That was the hardest time—until in the course of a single week I lost both my parents.

First my father was called up to serve, and five days later he went to fight. And a few days after that my mom fell down the stairs, broke her pelvis, and had to go to the hospital. Amazingly, the hospitals were still functioning, and there was even some food there. Many people's lives were saved by a stay in the hospital.

So I was left alone, without my parents, without firewood or food, in five-degree weather. I didn't have the strength to go and visit Mom, who was lying there all alone and couldn't do anything for me either. I remember one day when I sat on the windowsill and couldn't move. I was simply waiting for death.

Then, in my delirium, I dreamed that a woman was leading me across the roof of our building. I followed her, and she kept smiling at me gently, until we were both standing at the edge of the roof. At first I thought it was my mother. I looked at her.

"Are we going to jump?" I asked.

But then I saw that it wasn't my mother; it was the Mother of God, just as I had seen her once in an icon at my Catholic friend's house. "No, my daughter," she said, "you're going to live."

I protested, saying: "But I have nothing to eat, I have no firewood, everyone around me is dying. I won't survive!"

But she smiled again. "You're going to live," she repeated.

I know this story is hard to believe, Witold, but a metaphysical experience is understandable when so many people around you are dying. Soon after, I was woken up by Aunt Tola, our janitor Uncle Fedor's wife, who had come to our apartment to check if I was alive. She'd brought me a piece of bread. She scraped the remains of the caviar out of the jar and gave me two or three spoonfuls—not more, she said, or your guts will get twisted. Then she trudged off to her husband to discuss what could be done with me. They were good people; Fedor was in the brigade with my mom that cleared the roof of bombs. They had two sons—one died before the war, and the other, Igorek, two years my junior, was the apple of their eye.

Uncle Fedor had a cousin who worked at the local bakery. He went to talk to him, told him there was such and such a girl, her brother and father had gone to war, her mom was in the hospital. They wrinkled their noses, because in the famine years anyone would want to work at a bakery, but Uncle Fedor had his ways. They gave me two days to get on my feet, and then I was to report to work.

So off I went. I remember not being able to tie my shoe-laces, and at first I was amazed that in spite of my terrible hunger my foot had grown. Only later did I realize that nothing had grown—I was just swollen from hunger.

I had to leave the house at two in the morning, because that's what it's like to work in a bakery. It took me a long time to walk there—from my house, near Nevsky Prospekt, normally it would have taken me fifteen minutes, but it took me over an hour. The moment I entered the bakery, though, I found myself in paradise. It didn't smell of bread in there, surprisingly, but of engine oil, because they had no other kind, and they had to grease the oven with something. But the very sight of the flour, the very sight of the white baker's aprons, the sight of the tins—all this had a soothing effect. So there's bread? That means the world is still turning. Maybe somehow we're going to survive it all.

I was greeted by the senior baker. He had white hair combed back and a gray apron covered in flour.

"Vyacheslav Ivanovich," he introduced himself.

"Tamara Andreyevna."

"All right then, Tamara dear. Shall we get started?"

"Yes!"

Vyacheslav Ivanovich took me to the place where the other bakers were working. I was given the same sort of white uni-form and cap as they had, and I was informed that there was no stealing—all the loaves were counted, the flour too—and that the penalty for stealing was execution. I introduced myself to the other workers, they shook my hand, and I got down to work.

My job involved pouring the dough into metal molds. It was

dull and laborious, the same thing over and over without a break for hours on end.

But there's one thing you have to know, Witold. During the blockade, the bread in Leningrad wasn't the kind you're familiar with. I've already told you the city only had provisions for a month or so. In the winter they tried to deliver various goods to us across the frozen Lake Ladoga, which was our only connection with the rest of the country, but the Germans bombed the vessels and most of it didn't arrive. So our specialists made dough for bread out of whatever could be found. The base was flour, both oat and rye, but powder made of pine needles was added to it, ground flax residue, ground tree bark, cellulose, and everything else they brought us from the main depot. It didn't smell great, as I've already said, and we didn't even have cooking oil, but even so I was delighted. Bread is life, Witold— in a place like besieged Leningrad, you could definitely feel that. From the time I started working at the bakery, I felt I had turned away from death toward life.

For the first few days my work comrades—that's how we addressed each other, "Comrade"—taught me what to do and turned a blind eye if I couldn't keep up. But after a week I was working in sync with them. We knew people's survival depended on us, so all of us, absolutely everyone, put their heart and soul into the work.

I felt so good at the bakery that I didn't want to leave. Anyway, why waste energy? After a while, getting there took me half an hour. Going home was another half hour. But we had to conserve our strength; there was no point in throwing it away. So the ones who had families went home for the night.

And I slept at the bakery.

Sometimes as I walked through the city, I saw people who had set out to go somewhere and died on the way. Sometimes one of their relatives took them to the cemetery on a sled, but it was rare for anyone to have enough strength. Instead, the dead lay there until the city dealt with them. I'd walk along and see people standing in line for their piece of bread, and I'd wonder why I was so lucky. Why did I have a job at the warm bakery, why could I get a bit more bread? What law explained why fortune had smiled on me?

Until one day, all of a sudden, the spring came. And I hardly recognized Leningrad! Those who had survived the winter began to come outside. Day after day, absolutely every piece of ground came to be occupied by people cultivating vegetables of some kind—carrots, cabbage, radishes, turnips, kohlrabi. Beets, parsley, lettuce. Every inch was taken up by some sort of crop, including the little park beside Saint Isaac's Cathedral, the Summer Garden, and the Field of Mars. At the larger areas under cultivation, they put up sentry boxes like the ones hunters use, often with an armed policeman inside. And the whole area beside the Orthodox cathedral was sown with cabbage.

The seedlings and seeds were brought from Moscow and other cities by special airplanes. They were distributed to every district. You could also get them at the Botanical Museum, which offered talks to explain which wild plants were safe to eat. (In fact, there were no weeds in the city: no couch grass, burdock, or nettles. Nor were there any birds, or dogs, or cats. Everything that could be eaten, people had eaten that winter.)

I could feel the life returning inside me. If we had survived the winter, we'd be much better prepared for the next one!

On the First of May, Labor Day, one of the most important

days in the communist calendar, the parents who worked with me brought their children to the bakery, and each child was given a sweet bun. We baked them specially at dawn using white flour, which at the time was an unimaginable delicacy. Vyacheslav Ivanovich had made a special trip to the other end of the city to get it.

Except that I didn't get a bun.

How I cried, Witold! Some of those children were older than me! But I was a worker there, not the child of a worker. It didn't occur to anyone to think of me.

Vyacheslav Ivanovich saw that I was crying. He came up to me with his grandson, Pasha, and told the little boy to share his bun with me. Pasha wasn't willing, but his grandfather made him, so he tore off half his bun for me. I felt awkward eating it, but I forced myself.

It was the most delicious thing I'd eaten since the start of the war.

4.

Not long ago my son showed me a picture of a Finnish baker from Leningrad. His name was Daniil Ivanovich Kyyttinen. He worked hard—we all worked hard in those days—but he never put a crumb of bread in his own mouth. He died at the bakery of starvation in 1942. My son asked if I remembered him. "Son," I said, "I can't remember my own coworkers from those days, let alone someone who worked at a different bakery! He died at work? Maybe because he was a Finn, they watched his hands more closely than they watched the others?" After all, there were Finnish troops blockading Leningrad as well as the

Germans, so he can't have had an easy time here. Or perhaps he just had that sort of character? They said "Don't take anything," and he didn't. I don't know. I've never heard of any other baker who died of starvation.

It's true that there were those who never put a single crumb in their mouths. But there were also those who made a profit out of the blockade. After the war I went to visit a friend from school, Irina. We used to share a desk, and we liked each other, so she and her mother received me very warmly in their sitting room: "How are things, Tamara? How's your mom?" and so on. So I'm sitting there, and I look at the walls: valuable paintings. I look at their fingers: gold rings. For a while I couldn't help wondering how it was that a single mother, less than a year after the blockade, was so well off that she and her daughter could be wearing gold rings. But when I realized the truth, it made me tremble all over.

Irina's mother worked as a preschool teacher. And every day at the preschools, just like at my school, right through the toughest months of the blockade they served soup. Of course if you have access to food you're always going to find a way to siphon off a little. You give each child a spoonful less—and you've got a whole bowl of it. And at that time you could go to the bazaar, and in exchange for a loaf of bread or a bowl of soup, you could get a gemstone or a gold ring. People were giving away everything for food.

My friend and her mother had rings of that kind. I left their house as soon as I could; I said I had a headache and had to get some fresh air.

Irina is still alive today. We used to see each other quite often, but I no longer wanted to talk to her. Although she was just an accountant at a factory, she was always going on foreign vacations or buying herself furs, and each of her three sons built himself a house. They made so much money out of that soup during the blockade that the third generation is still living on it.

Yes, Witold. I'd like to forget about it, but I do remember that not everyone behaved like a human being during the blockade. At the bakery too there were women whom I used to see after the war with lots of rings on their fingers. Drivers who distributed the bread, sales assistants in stores that sold it—I saw plenty of these people later on with gold teeth, with lambskin coats. When did they carry off the bread? How? Where did they take it? I have no idea, but they must have had their ways. Later on, under communism, you could only talk about how brave everyone in Leningrad had been and how they'd helped each other.

Well—not everyone.

It's even sadder when I remember the days when we had to add powdered stone to the flour in order to make the bread. And let me remind you, the bread ration was 125 grams [4½ ounces].

But there were also people like that Finnish baker.

And then there were our authorities. While he was still working, my father sometimes had to go to the Smolny Institute, where the city authorities had their headquarters and where Andrei Zhdanov—the man who had failed to prepare the city for famine—ruled the city. My father told me that in the canteen at the Smolny they had everything, as if there were no blockade: chops, potatoes, chicken. You couldn't take anything out of there, but inside you could eat. As everyone in

Leningrad said at the time, airplanes flew in from Moscow bringing Zhdanov brandy and sausages.

5.

Our soldiers broke the ring of German troops around Leningrad only in 1944, after two and a half years of the blockade. That was roughly when my mom came out of the hospital. She knew I was alive, because I had been sending her messages via friends. She hugged me. She kissed me. By now we both knew that Dad had been killed at the front—a letter came to say he'd died a month and a half after he was called up. We wept together, and then we went home and lived in an incomplete family for several years.

The saddest thing, Witold, is that I was never a child again after that. I stopped being one when I was twelve, when I had to cope with everything on my own. By the time the Germans were beaten, I was almost fifteen. I was completely grown up. At one time I had dreamed of going to college and becoming a doctor. But in those days I had no such opportunity. I went to work at a store, where for many years I was a salesclerk. Then I worked in the office at a cooperative grocery, working with bread on a daily basis again, but in a different way.

Now I know far more about how difficult a task the experts had in the days when I worked at the bakery. Because a whole team of specialists worked on what to add to our bread. Do you know, for example, why an extract of pine needles was added? Because it's highly effective against scurvy. And although we were hungry, no one suffered from scurvy.

But I have a lot of questions too, Witold. Why, for instance, through the whole of the blockade did the Leningrad Zoo continue to exist? People were dying of hunger, but every day the hippo at the zoo was being fed dozens of pounds of food. Did feeding a hippo really matter more?

I still have the jar of caviar that saved my life. Do you want to see it? Here, I keep thread in it, needles, buttons, and scraps of material that will probably never be of any use, but it's a pity to throw them away.

My mom and I never found my brother, Piotr. But three years ago I saw a program on TV featuring a professor who was researching the fate of Soviet prisoners of war. He said he had a whole list of those taken prisoner on the outskirts of Leningrad, and he'd be willing to share it with interested families.

I asked my son to get in touch with him, and it turned out my brother's name was on his list. All I know is that he was taken into captivity and that he worked as a POW in a mine. He was probably killed in that mine. It was heartbreaking, because for a while I had hoped that maybe he'd survived and we might see each other again before I died. But no. Such things do happen, but very rarely.

Sometimes I can't get to sleep at night because I'm thinking. About my dad. About the children from our communal building. About Vyacheslav the baker, about Aunt Tola, who was so kind to me, and about all the people who died in Leningrad during that dreadful blockade, over whose bones we walk here every day. And then I weep into my pillow, Witold, because what else can I do? Once I cried almost all night, and when I finally fell asleep, I dreamed about my brother. It was a strange dream, because although I knew I was dreaming, I was talking to him as if he were a real person. And I said: "Piotr, I feel so sad when I think about all of you. I'm so sorry you're not here." And he

Tamara Andreyevna

replied: "Don't cry, Tamara. You didn't survive just to weep, but to go on living for the rest of us."

So I go on living.

To this day, once, maybe twice a year I dream that I'm twelve years old again and I'm walking on the roof, with the Mother of God ahead of me. And I always ask her, "Is it time?" And she always shakes her head no. Not yet. I know that one day she'll nod her head yes. And then we'll hold hands and fly off together over Leningrad, to my loved ones, whom I miss every day.

MENU
◇◇◇
Blockade Bread

Every year to commemorate the victims of Leningrad, bakeries all over Russia organize a campaign titled "Let's Bake Blockade Bread." One of them, in distant Ulan-Ude, posted a recipe on the internet—apparently it came directly from one of the Leningrad bakeries.

Pinch of yeast made from timber waste
1½ cups (150 g) coarsely ground wheat or rye flour
½ cup (50 g) oat bran from horse fodder (this has nothing in
*   common with bran as we know it; the first in Leningrad*
*   came from suburban stables)*

1¾ ounces (50 g) pressed sunflower seed cake
Corn flour (in Leningrad, the baking industry workers collected
    the remains of it at factories by shaking it out of sacks)
½ cup (50 g) ground pine bark flour

First, add the yeast and some water to a bowl. Leave the yeast to rise.

Preheat the oven to 425°F (220°C). Mix the remaining ingredients into the yeast mixture and knead the dough. Form the dough into a loaf, and bake for 30 to 40 minutes.

Altogether the blockade of Leningrad lasted for more than nine hundred days. One of its saddest testimonies is the "menu, for after starvation, if I'm still alive," which sixteen-year-old Valentina Chepko wrote out on a piece of paper in the toughest winter of 1941. It is preserved in the Museum of the Defense and Siege of Leningrad.

First course: soup—potato and mushroom, or pickled cabbage and meat.
Second course: kasha—oatmeal with butter, millet, pearl barley, buckwheat, rice, or semolina.
Meat course: meatballs with mashed potatoes; sausages with mashed potatoes or kasha.

She finishes her menu with the words, "But there's no point in dreaming about this, because we won't live to see it!" She died in February 1942.

VII

Exhumation

Cooking in Wartime

1.

We meet early in the morning, as soon as the sun has risen high enough.

Each man brings a bucket and spade, and the stronger ones, like Andrei—who has a large belly and suspenders holding up his pants, which is why his friends call him Obelix, from the French comic book series *Asterix*, and who (as I'm about to find out) works on a construction site in Norway but is here on vacation—are lugging an engine for a pump, as well as the pump itself. We'll need it, because today we're going to be working in some ponds.

There are fifteen of us—fourteen Russians and me—in Estonia, three or four miles from the Russian border.

I'm carrying an axe—it'll be useful, because on our way

we'll have to clear the forest—and two of the other guys are carrying chainsaws. Our manager, Pavel Varunin—Pasha to his friends—is carrying a metal detector.

"We'll be looking for medals, pants buttons, and belt buckles," he says.

I'm going into the forest with them to dig up the remains of Red Army soldiers from World War II, and I'm trying to get my head around it. After all, these are the same soldiers who trampled all over Estonia and neighboring Latvia and Lithuania, and half of Europe from top to bottom, and who in my country are remembered mainly for looting and raping.

Not to mention the fact that once they had invaded Estonia, they occupied it for another forty-six years after the war ended.

But to do them justice, I can also see them as soldiers who were often still in their teens, or at most their early twenties, and who—as children do—believed everything they were told by Soviet propaganda and Joseph Stalin, the so-called Sun of Nations. And they dropped like flies, because Stalin had far-reaching plans for world conquest and it was all the same to him if five, fifteen, or twenty-five million of his soldiers died. So here, somewhere in this earth, lie all those Sashas, Grishas, Mikhails, and Seryozhas, whom no one remembers because they were killed too young to have left a permanent mark in anyone's memory, and whom for years on end no one had the opportunity to find.

On this 125-mile stretch of road from Narva to Tallinn lie more than one hundred thousand of them.

That's eight hundred corpses per mile. Every two yards there's another one. It was these young men who defeated fascism with their courage and tenacity. I can't forget about the bad things they did, but I'm trying to remember their achievements as well.

I'm going with Pasha's group because I want to find out what the places they fought and died in were like. And what they ate, of course. I want to see up close what their eating conditions were like, where the field kitchens stood, and to find out as much as possible from people like Pasha about the everyday life of the Red Army soldiers.

We're near the village of Kuningaküla, which the Russians used to call Knyaz-Selo. If we were to turn left, we'd reach Kuremäe, where Pühtitsa Dormition Convent, an Orthodox monastery, is located—a tiny bit of Russia for the three hundred thousand Estonian Russians who remained here after the collapse of the USSR. The monastery features huge firewood stacks, barrel-shaped like matryoshka dolls.

If we were to turn right, we'd reach the Narva River, which marks the border between Estonia and Russia.

But we're going straight. Into the dense undergrowth.

Pasha Varunin is head of the local Russian organization Kamrat, which for many years has been exhuming Soviet— and not just Soviet—soldiers on various military fronts that saw action during World War II and then organizing funerals for them, with an Orthodox priest, flowers, grannies in headscarves, veterans festooned in medals, and plangent singing. The organization is based in Narva, capital of the Estonian Russians—or, if you prefer, the Russian-speaking Estonians.

Anyone who goes to dig with Pasha instantly becomes a friend. "In 1944 there was fierce fighting here, because Narva was the gateway to Estonia, and Estonia was the way into Scandinavia and control of northern Europe," he says. "Stalin thought

Narva could be captured in two weeks. But the Germans fought back so ferociously that the Red Army still hadn't been able to get into Narva by the time it entered Poland and Romania, although Narva is fewer than one hundred miles away from Leningrad."

But before Pasha really gets going, we're fetching out our axes and saws, because nature here is truly wild, and to go deeper into the forest we have to clear it. There's a stream running behind the trees—we must chop down some of the trees to make a primitive bridge and then cross it.

2.

I'm chopping down trees with Seryozha, an engineer from the Narva area who works at a local oil shale mine. Pasha has told us to stick together, because Seryozha's grandfather Vyacheslav Antonovich fought on the Ukrainian front during the war and was in charge of the food supplies.

"Our shale deposits are one of the reasons why the Germans refused to let Narva go," says Seryozha, out of breath, as he hands me the axe. "They used it to make fuel for tanks and submarines. The mines begin six miles from the city. Five from where we are right now. But I've heard you're interested in food. That's just like me. My grandfather was the most important person in my life. I used to listen to his stories."

"So tell me how they ate at the front!"

"Each Red Army soldier had a mess tin in his kit, and a tobacco pouch or a cigarette case. They also had spoons, but no forks; only the Germans had an ingenious folding object, one half of which was a fork and the other a spoon. The Red Army men liked these fork-and-spoon things so much that they often searched for them on the bodies of dead Wehrmacht soldiers."

"They stole them?" I ask.

"They didn't steal them, they took them," Seryozha says indignantly. "You can't apply our standards to what people did while fighting at the front. We find Soviet weapons and mess tins among the Germans as well; they took things from our men too. Though the Germans had better mess tins: they were oval, handier for carrying. Both sides also looked for food on the corpses, because they were often hungry."

"Why was that?"

"Either a food transport hadn't arrived or the villages had nothing left to provide rations. My granddad mentioned that right from the start, in June 1941, the Germans applied a scorched-earth strategy: they took away all the food the peasants had set aside. It would have worked if their Blitzkrieg had succeeded and they actually had reached Moscow by the fall. But since the war continued for another three years, it rebounded on them. They ended up retreating into starved territory. Though that did not apply to this particular part of the front. Here it was our men who were hungry, not the Germans."

"And what did the soldiers eat on a daily basis?"

"The basic diet was so-called *kulish*: soup made of millet with some meat or lard added. There was also borscht, cabbage soup, and goulash: buckwheat, usually overcooked, with meat. But the staple food was bread, made of whatever the army baker could get. Usually that was rye flour, though sometimes they got corn flour from the Americans, and the cooks had to rack their brains to think what to do with it. According to Ministry of Defense guidelines, a soldier should have plenty of bread, meaning 800 grams [28 ounces] a day in the warmer months and 900 grams [32 ounces] in the winter. He should also get a pound of potatoes, 300 grams [10.5 ounces] of other vegetables, 170 grams [6 ounces] of grain or pasta, 150 grams [5 ounces] of meat, 50 grams [1.8 ounces] of fat, and 35 grams [1.3 ounces] of sugar."

"Did they get it?"

"No. In practice, the amount of food a soldier received depended on which front he was fighting on and what the supplies there were like. The Red Army men, at least at the start of the war, when they were mainly retreating, often died hungry. They got 200 to 300 grams [7 to 10.5 ounces] of bread, which was baked daily by field bakeries, and also soup, usually fish or vegetable. If they were lucky enough to be fighting in a unit that had been sent American canned food, they also got a can of beef, usually to share among three of them. The officers additionally received—again, in theory, but we need some sort of measure—40 grams [1.5 ounces] of butter or lard, 20 grams [0.7 ounces] of cookies, and 50 grams [1.8 ounces] of canned fish. The generals were a separate caste. They were brought sausages and wine. But do you know what saved the ordinary soldiers?"

"No, I don't."

"The forest. Like this one here. My granddad told me he taught the soldiers how to make soup from nettles: all you needed was two potatoes and a small bonfire, and anyone could make it for himself in a mess tin. Or when they were walking across terrain where there were lots of snails, they roasted them on the bonfire. I once copied my granddad's recipe for that soup: we'd spent all day at a pond like the one we're going to. Everyone was hungry. No one had brought any sandwiches, but the guys did have a few potatoes to bake in the embers. I said, 'Give me those potatoes and half an hour.' And I made nettle soup just as my granddad had. They were all amazed! Ever since, I've regularly treated them to dishes he told me about. I make salad out of ground elder. I've made kulish several times. And by trying the sorts of foods they ate in those days, we can feel even closer to them."

3.

We've forced our way through the bushes and across two streams. My legs are covered in scratches. But finally we're at the pond that Pasha was aiming for.

The Russians communicate without using words; it's clearly not the first time they've been on an expedition like this together. One lights a bonfire and two more fire up the pump, which starts to suck water from the pond and spit it out a few yards away. Everyone else gets down to digging.

And that includes me. I pick up a spade, and yard by yard, deeper and deeper, I search for the remains of soldiers who were killed here. I'm digging almost shoulder to shoulder with Pasha, and, panting, he explains all the secrets of this place.

"The front came through here several times, so we can never be entirely sure if we're going to find Germans or Russians. Anyway, plenty of other nations fought here too, because volunteer battalions came from all over Europe. We pay no attention to nationality—we bury all the remains with respect. But we never know if we're going to find anything. Sometimes in a pond like this one, we find the remains of several dozen people, because during the war, throwing corpses into the water was the easiest way to dispose of them. But sometimes we dig all day and find nothing. The main thing is that we try. If I were in that situation, I'd like to think that someone would at least try to find me and give me a proper burial."

Suddenly my spade latches onto a long, black object that looks like a section of bicycle inner tube.

"What's this?" I ask, knowing it's not an inner tube.

"A boot sole. From a felt valenka," Pasha says, adding: "Now we know our guys are lying here, because the Germans didn't wear valenki. Dig carefully—there'll be more."

Indeed, after two prods with the spade I find another valenka sole. Soon I have a whole collection.

I try to think for a while about these boys, surely younger than I am, who came to rest forever in their clumsy footwear here among these trees. But it's all happening too quickly, because when Pasha comes out of the pond to collect the soles from me, Andrei—the fat guy who carried the pump—shouts: "Booooone! Pasha, I've got a bone!"

Pasha and I both come running.

He has found a piece of collar bone.

4.

We're having a breather to cool down after Andrei's find. We're all feeling moved. I take advantage of this short break to return to my conversation with Seryozha.

"Seryozha, so who cooked during the war?"

"Cooks who'd had special training," he says. "One of my granddad's tasks was to teach them how to take advantage of the natural gifts of the terrain they were in. The Ministry of Defense even issued a special book about which herbs, leaves, and weeds could be useful in cooking. It included a recipe for a salad made of ground elder, for instance, which is a weed, but a very healthy one, and it grows everywhere. It also explained how to find and make use of sorrel and wild garlic, and how to grind acorns to make coffee. How to use knotgrass, burdock, mallow, or wild cucumber. The point was that the cooks didn't have to wait with their arms folded until the supplies arrived, because sometimes they were late, and sometimes they had no way to reach the front."

"So how did they do the cooking?"

"They had field kitchens. The guys and I once dug up one of those mobile stoves. It had two boilers, with a firebox underneath them. The original pots were even preserved inside the boilers. We gave them to the local museum; they're putting together a display about what soldiers ate at the front. And how they ate. But I'll tell you, as far as field kitchens are concerned, we had one big advantage over the Germans. Their kitchens still moved on wooden wheels and couldn't cope with having to speed up. It's all right for infantry, because they don't go fast, but for mechanized troops it's a problem. But in keeping with a decree issued by Voroshilov in 1936, our field kitchens had rubber tires."

"And how did they eat?"

"Usually before dawn and after dusk, so the smoke wouldn't give the kitchens away. The Germans used to drop bombs on the kitchens, because they knew that when people are unable to eat, their morale collapses."

5.

After Andrei has dug up the first bone, we all become much more cautious. Now we know the pond is full of human remains. We're up to our ears in them, all in a mass grave.

This makes a vast impression on me. But I can see that even Pasha Varunin, who has been involved in this sort of operation for twenty-five years, is moved.

He and his pals have brought a white sheet with a diagram of the human skeleton drawn on it. They arrange on top of it all the bones that they succeed in finding, large and small.

Two hours later we have dug up several ribs, cervical vertebrae, tibias, foot bones, pelvic bones, and probably a shoulder.

Suddenly my spade knocks against something hard. Although I know where I am and what we're looking for, my hands start to shake. I can see a white object, with at least ten other small white objects attached to it. They look like little pearls arranged in an uneven row.

I've found a human jawbone. To be precise, an upper jaw.

I call Pasha right away; he comes with the bucket and very carefully rinses my find in water. He washes each tooth separately. The jaw is well preserved. The soldier to whom it belonged had no teeth missing, and judging by wear and tear, Pasha estimates that he was about twenty-five.

He hands me the jaw to place at the very top of the skeleton drawing. Before I do that, I squeeze it hard for a few seconds. Who were you? What was your name? How old were you? Where were you from? Did you have time for a last thought when the bullet hit you? Or perhaps you didn't even notice your own death?

I place the jawbone on the white sheet.

Soon after, in the same spot, Pasha finds some pieces of skull.

6.

Over the days that followed, Pasha and his group found the remains of more than eighty Red Army soldiers. The soldiers were given a collective funeral in July 2020, buried in three coffins in an anonymous soldiers' grave not far from the forest where I helped to dig.

Only one of the soldiers could be identified. He was Ivan Zakharovich Artemyev. A medal for bravery, number 1225454, was found on him, and also a Party membership card. He received the medal in June 1944; a month later he was dead.

At the time of his death he was twenty years old. In Demidovo, near Smolensk, where he was from, his family was located. Once the formalities were completed, he was returned to his native village for his eternal rest.

MENU

◇◇◇

Carrot and Inonotus Tea

Grate a carrot and dry it out in a frying pan, without adding oil. Brew as you would ordinary tea. You can add a pinch of powdered inonotus, a parasitic fungus that grows on birch trees. In Poland it is considered poisonous, but the Red Army soldiers believed it gave them energy and helped them combat parasites, and it adds a slightly tart flavor to carrot tea.

Just remember that you drink it at your own risk.

VIII

The Feast at Yalta

1.

Airplanes carrying the president of the United States, Franklin D. Roosevelt, and the British prime minister, Winston Churchill, land at Saki military airport. There to greet them is Vyacheslav Molotov, the Soviet minister of foreign affairs, the same man who six years earlier had signed a pact with his German counterpart, Joachim von Ribbentrop, dividing Europe and guaranteeing they would never attack each other.

It is February 1945. Molotov and Stalin are going to divide Europe again.

The Wehrmacht is on the defensive on every front. The Allies are close to the Rhine, Berlin is being bombarded again and again, and less than two weeks ago the Red Army captured Łódź and also liberated the Auschwitz concentration camp. Seventy delegates from three countries are heading for the tents pitched beside the airport for tea and snacks, and the tables are groaning with red and black caviar, smoked sturgeon, and desserts for which the imperial kitchen was once famous. The ailing Roosevelt goes to bed, but Churchill savors the caviar and Crimean champagne.

And this is just the start.

Stalin already knows what sort of impression richly laden tables make on his guests and highly appreciates the role of a well-designed meal in diplomacy. After the conference in Tehran, he gave Roosevelt a splendid, three-foot-long sturgeon; the American wasn't entirely sure what to do with it, but those who witnessed the gesture would remember it for many years to come.

Here in Yalta, Roosevelt will be presented with a large Soviet turkey, the kind that Sasha Egnatashvili has been raising for Stalin for the past thirty years. Everything that's going to appear on the dining tables in the next few days has been organized by Sasha, the Kremlin's expert at achieving the impossible. It could hardly be otherwise—he was the one who reminded Stalin that in Georgia, if you want to impress someone with your wealth, you invite them to stay. And now in Crimea, which only seven months ago was in the hands of the Germans, and from which the NKVD has deported two hundred thousand Tatars in only two days, Sasha is organizing extraordinary feasts for hundreds of people day after day. Everything is always served on time, always at the right temperature, and always beautifully presented.

Sasha is probably the only man capable of organizing the culinary side of the conference at Yalta to such a high standard. But behind the perfectly prepared dishes lies a great tragedy. As he cooks for the guests at Yalta, Sasha is still fighting for the life of his wife, Liliana.

2.

The main negotiations conducted by the heads of state are held at Livadia Palace—where tsar Alexander III died and where Nicholas II found out, to his misfortune, that he would be tsar of Russia.

Recently the cooks at one of the Yalta restaurants situated near the palace re-created the menu from those extraordinary days. The dishes included turkey in quince and orange juice, fried herring from Kerch on the Black Sea served with potatoes, neck of pork with forest mushrooms, wild game, sturgeon in aspic, and of course huge buckets of caviar.

Special bakeries were established on the spot to operate exclusively during the conference. Three thousand sets of knives, forks, and spoons were brought in, of which more than four hundred were made of silver.

And in the negotiations, Stalin got everything he wanted.

Sasha earned himself a medal, as well as a financial reward. The innkeeper who had started in Tbilisi by whacking his employee on the head with a frying pan full of scrambled eggs had now planned every aspect of cuisine for the world's most important people. The conference at Yalta was the cherry on top for his professional life. In September he would also be nominated as a general and would get a beautiful new uniform.

But from this moment on, his life would only be in decline.

It is hard to say when exactly Sasha found out that his

beloved wife, Liliana, was dead. But what he didn't know until long after the event was that Beria had murdered her four years earlier, at the very start of the war—she was shot before the siege of Leningrad had even begun.

3.

For Beria, killing Sasha's wife did not eradicate the grudge he bore against the Georgian. In fact, Sasha's success during the Yalta conference wound up working against him.

The vengeful head of the NKVD continued to tighten the noose around Sasha's neck.

In 1948, three years after Yalta, Ivan Alikhanov came to Moscow for a wrestling competition. He took the opportunity to visit his stepfather but found him in a very poor state. Sasha was a shadow of his former self; high blood pressure and diabetes had left him bedridden. There he lay in his general's uniform, with cotton padding behind the collar and cuffs. In every room of his apartment there was a thermometer, which he checked obsessively to make sure the temperature was kept at 70 degrees Fahrenheit.

Sasha lived in central Moscow, opposite the City Council and above the Georgian restaurant Aragvi, an unusual place on the city's culinary map because it was a favorite of Beria and his NKVD agents. Parties were held there for agents leaving the service, and foreign intelligence officers puzzled over how to persuade one of the regulars to collaborate with them. As a distinguished NKVD general, Sasha had the right to go there for meals on subscription.

Stalin sent him doctors from the Kremlin, but Sasha had

seen too much in his life to trust them. He covertly brought in a private doctor and got his medicine from an ordinary pharmacy; he was afraid that at the pharmacy for state officials he might be given poison.

He cooked for himself. He didn't trust even Nuria, the illiterate Russian woman who had been his housekeeper in the days when Liliana was still alive and had worked for him for more than a decade.

"On the day I was there, Alexander Yakovlevich made boiled turkey liver for lunch," notes Ivan Alikhanov of his stepfather, whose strange behavior he goes on to explain: "After working at the Lubyanka for more than seventeen years, he evidently knew a great deal about the laboratories where all kinds of poison were produced and applied, and about various methods for poisoning, through food, medicine, or the temperature, or gas. That was why he had to maintain a constant temperature in the rooms, and that was what he needed the padding for. My stepfather was mortally afraid of Beria."

This was the man who had devoted his life to Stalin and was probably his half brother too, who took care of every detail, fed him like a mother, and tested his dishes before he ate to make sure he could never be poisoned; who lost his beloved wife and then slowly died in pitiful circumstances, fearing his own shadow.

Beria had cut Sasha off from Stalin and from Kuntsevo, and it is entirely probable that he was just waiting for a convenient moment to complete his revenge. Meanwhile, Sasha was missing Liliana. As soon as he saw his stepson, he started talking to him about his mother.

As he spoke of her, he sang the romantic song "Come Back, All is Forgiven."

In the fall of 1948, not long after Alikhanov's visit, Sasha Egnatashvili stopped eating.

Alikhanov thinks his stepfather was trying to get Stalin's attention. As if he were hoping he could turn back time—that when Stalin heard what was happening to the man whom he called his brother, he'd take him back to Kuntsevo and care for him.

But nothing of the sort happened. Sasha died on the last day of 1948.

His family took his body home to Gori. As Alikhanov gazed at the body in its coffin, he couldn't believe it belonged to his stepfather, once one of the most powerful people in Georgia.

There in the coffin lay a wizened old man.

"On December 31, 1948, after a long and difficult illness, loyal son of the Bolshevik Party and of the Soviet Fatherland General-Lieutenant Comrade Egnatashvili Alexander Yakovlevich died," Soviet citizens read in the newspaper *Pravda* two days later. "In the person of Comrade Egnatashvili, the organs of state security have lost a talented and tireless worker, wholly dedicated to the service of our Fatherland. He shall live on in the memory of all who knew him as a Bolshevik chekist, loyal son of our nation, and modest comrade." The obituary was signed, "A group of comrades."

4.

The Soviet Union had won the war, but in the process it had lost more than twenty-five million citizens—more than any other country.

After the war, Stalin felt increasingly old and exhausted.

Turkey liver was no longer enough for him. He supplemented his strength with vast amounts of food. He ate like a man possessed.

At one time, that had been quite unthinkable for this ascetic Georgian. But Anastas Mikoyan, one of the Generalissimus's closest colleagues, recalled that after the war, Stalin "took a deep plate, mixed two soups in it, and then, according to a custom I knew from my own village, he crumbled bread into the hot soup and covered it all with a second plate—later on he ate the whole thing. Then there were appetizers, main courses, and a lot of meat."

But Stalin's teeth were so rotten that he could eat only the softest meat or overripe fruit. Although his belly continued to get bigger, he would mock the gluttony of others.

Over the course of these meals, which often descended into alcoholic revels, the fates of nations and the lives of millions of people were decided. Once again according to Georgian custom, Stalin would tell the carousers to drink until they dropped. And although he drank little himself, he kept a close eye on the others the whole time; if anyone avoided drinking, he rebuked them. Then he forced everyone to dance—that was his other way of humiliating his closest colleagues.

Stalin died eight years after the war, after pissing his pants. That day, a young cook named Vitali Alexeyevich arrived for his morning shift. But Valentina Istomina, Stalin's longtime housekeeper who was originally hired by Sasha Egnatashvili, stopped him in the doorway. She told him the leader was dead, and that Beria had started to execute everyone who worked for him. She led Vitali to a side exit where a car was parked, and he managed to escape.

After Stalin's death, Beria took charge of the country and, to everyone's surprise, proved far more liberal than his political patron. He released some political prisoners and was ready to talk to the Western countries about the unification of Germany.

But his former comrades couldn't forget the years when he had commanded the Soviet apparatus of terror. After one hundred days he was accused of treason and killed by a group of conspirators, one of whom was Nikita Khrushchev. This small, barrel-shaped apparatchik from Ukraine, who was jointly responsible for the Great Famine, took the reins of power. Now at the forefront of change, Khrushchev delivered his "secret speech" to Party members, in which he identified the errors of Stalinism.

For many years Khrushchev's so-called lichnik, or personal cook, was Alexei Alexeyevich Salnikov, a KGB lieutenant-colonel (every Soviet leader's personal chef, starting with Sasha Egnatashvili, had a military rank in the NKVD or KGB). Salnikov recorded that Khrushchev ate breakfast at around six in the morning. It usually consisted of two slices of black bread toasted in a frying pan, as well as yogurt served in small glass jars (sometimes mixed with tvorog, which is similar to curd cheese).

Between meals he drank natural juices: orange, grape, black-currant, or plum.

For dinner Khrushchev was very fond of Ukrainian borscht with dumplings. Between meals he and his family loved to chew on rusks, usually imported from Ukraine. As for official receptions, Khrushchev liked alcohol, but the older he became, the less he drank. The Kremlin ordered special glasses to be made for him at one of the glassworks; they had thick bottoms, and although they looked like fifty-milliliter shot glasses, in fact they could hold only thirty milliliters.

Lieutenant-Colonel Salnikov was witness to many historical events, such as Khrushchev's famous speech at the United Nations in 1960, when the Soviet leader banged his shoe against the lectern. Salnikov was also present in Abkhazia when Khrushchev heard the news that the apple of his eye—the space flight project—had finally been realized: Major Yuri Gagarin had flown into outer space and safely returned to Earth.

MENU
◇◇◇

Turkey in Quince and Orange Juice

At Yalta's farewell dinner on February 10, 1945, the British, Soviet, and American leaders ate salted herring, sturgeon in aspic, sea perch in champagne sauce, and haunch of wild goat. There was also roasted grouse and partridge, suckling pig steaks in a baby radish sauce, and the star of the conference—turkey in quince and orange juice.

For dessert: ice cream and beautifully decorated petits fours made of sponge and marzipan.

1¼ pounds (0.5 kg) quinces
Oil, for frying
8¾ ounces (250 g) turkey meat (just the livers can be used,
*   as the dish was made for Stalin)*
Salt

Pinch of curry powder
3½ ounces (100 ml) fresh orange juice
2 whole walnuts, chopped

Cut the quinces into slices. Heat oil in a frying pan. Sear the quince slices on both sides, then remove from the frying pan.

Using the same oil, brown the turkey meat. Add the salt and curry powder and cook for 5 more minutes.

Add the quinces to the meat, mix in the orange juice, and cook over medium heat for 6 to 7 minutes.

Before serving, sprinkle with the chopped walnuts.

IX

Gagarin's Cook

KOROLEV: Your food is in the tubes—breakfast, lunch, and supper.

GAGARIN: Check.

KOROLEV: Got that?

GAGARIN: Yes.

KOROLEV: Sausage, candy, and even jam to have with your tea. Got it?

GAGARIN: Check.

KOROLEV: Altogether you have sixty-three tubes. You'll come back awfully fat . . .

GAGARIN: The main thing is the sausage, for chasing hooch.

KOROLEV: You monster. They're recording everything, you rascal. Ha ha ha.

April 12, 1961: a dialogue recorded in the final minutes before the takeoff of Vostok 1—*humankind's first flight into outer space.*

Sergei Korolev was the brilliant chief designer for the Vostok program, the father of Soviet space science; at the time his identity was top secret.

Yuri Gagarin was just about to become the first man in space.

"I arrived at work, just like every other day. My boss turned on the radio. We listened. And they reported that the first man had flown into outer space. His name was Yuri Gagarin, and right then he was orbiting the Earth."

Directly after college, Valentina Borisovna started work as a food technologist at the Moskva restaurant, one of the best in the Soviet capital in those days.

"And then what?" I ask her.

"I was dumbstruck. It was so beautiful, unimaginable! A little later, we saw through the restaurant windows a group of young people walking to Red Square with placards to celebrate this success. I was very young at the time, and my boss could see I couldn't sit still, so he let me go and join them. Who'd have thought that just two years later I'd be making food for the cosmonauts?"

"When Gagarin made his flight, I was still in college," says another of the women I'm speaking to, senior specialist Ludmila Vasilyevna Mukyanov, "and I'd gone to help the workers at a collective farm. I was sitting in a potato field when the president of the Komsomol ran by, shouting: 'There's a man in space! Gagarin! Our guys have launched a Sputnik!' It was on my birthday. As if specially for me, I thought."

Only my third interviewee, Viktor Frantzevich Dobrovolsky, doesn't say what he was doing when the rocket launched into space. He's not allowed—all his life he has worked on projects that are confidential or top secret. We can only imagine where he was and what he was doing that day. But it definitely had something to do with space food.

Because we're talking at the Birulevsky Experimental Plant, the research institute where the food for Russian space missions has been produced since the 1960s.

To arrange a meeting with these three people, my colleague Maria Pistunova and I wrote to various authorities for almost two years. For decades the plant was classified; even now, when many Soviet secrets have been revealed, the cosmonauts' diet remains largely confidential. So we kept being bounced from one authority to another.

And just when it seemed that there was no hope of my coming here as a foreigner, something—though we have no idea what—fell into place within the Russian space bureaucracy. So here we are: drinking coffee, eating chocolate, and chatting.

Meanwhile, in the next room six women are packing food into little bags that will soon make their way into orbit.

1.

The commander of one of the units fighting against the Germans in Soviet Belarus was facing a tough situation. A woman had come to him with her baby son slung on her back and was demanding that he welcome them both into his detachment.

"And what are you going to do in this unit?" asked the commander.

"I'm going to feed you," answered the woman. "I'm a very good cook. My grandma taught me."

"But what about the kid?" asked the commander, scowling. "War has no place for a six-month-old baby!"

"My husband abandoned me, despite the war," replied the woman. "And I've had enough of begging people for help. If you won't help, I'll tie the child to my belly and throw myself under a train."

The commander could see that the woman was desperate. He wasn't going to argue. Let them stay, he thought—his men could do with some food made with a woman's touch. They could all be killed at any moment, so having a kid here wouldn't make much difference.

And so Faina Gavrilovna Kazetskaya, a Belarusian, became a Soviet army cook. With her son slung on her back, she walked with the unit all the way from Ukraine to Königsberg. The boy's name was Kim, in honor of the KIM (Young Communist International) youth movement.

When she wasn't cooking, Faina was constantly on the go. She learned to repair vehicles, transfer telephone calls, and even paint buildings. She wasn't afraid of any job, and she did everything with her baby son in tow. When she was seriously wounded in the fighting to take Königsberg, little Kim became the field hospital's mascot.

But when the war ended, Faina had nowhere to go. The husband who had abandoned her had a new family in Belarus. Her parents were dead.

Luckily a friend from the army got a job near Moscow, in a place named Monino, where the headquarters of the Soviet air force was located. Faina went with her, and to her joy, she too got a job. As a cook.

She must have excelled, because in 1960 she was offered a

transfer to a place then named Kilometer 41, an elite secret military unit that was just being formed.

"It was a beautiful place," she recalled. "There was a birch grove nearby, large meadows and fields. Later on the town of Star City was established there."

So Faina became a cook for what would be the first contingent of Soviet cosmonauts.

2.

The forefather of space exploration in the Soviet Union was Konstantin Tsiolkovsky, a Russian (later Soviet) self-educated scientist. More than a century before Elon Musk was born, he was talking about cities on other planets.

For many years he was the sort of mad scientist who goes around with holes in his shoes, doesn't eat, and is misunderstood by society. But in the 1920s and 1930s his work started to break through to the general public—and to visionaries—throughout the Soviet Union. Among them was Sergei Korolev, a boy from Zhitomir, Ukraine, who ever since he'd seen an airplane for the first time at the age of ten was obsessed with aviation—and, once he'd read Tsiolkovsky's book, he was obsessed with space flight too.

As a student at the polytechnic, Korolev quickly proved to be an unusually gifted designer. He soon joined a team that, on Soviet military chief Marshal Tukhachevsky's orders, was working on the development of modern weapons.

But in 1937, during the Stalinist purges, Tukhachevsky was accused of espionage and executed. And everyone who collaborated with him was punished. Korolev was sent to a labor camp, where he spent six years. He was released thanks to the intervention of another legendary figure, Andrei Tupolev, who designed or codesigned more than a hundred airplanes, and who in the Stalinist era was also unjustifiably imprisoned.

After the war, both Korolev and Tupolev finally had their glory days. For several years they worked together. Korolev went on to design intercontinental missiles, and in the mid-1950s he became head of the top secret Soviet program for the conquest of space.

3.

The first living creatures in space, or at least the first we know about, were fruit flies, which in 1947 the Americans sent to a height of 66 miles.

The first more complex organisms were dogs, sent by the Russians.

"Korolev realized that before space technology had advanced enough to be able to send a man into space, they had to check if it was at all possible," says Larissa Filina from the Memorial Museum of Space Exploration in Moscow. We're meeting in an unusual place—the house that the Soviet authorities gifted to Korolev in the early 1960s in recognition of his work. "Dogs and monkeys were considered," she continues. "Monkeys are very similar to humans, but dogs are more obedient, so they decided to use dogs."

Korolev worked on sending dogs into space with the biologist Vladimir Yazdovsky. They learned a great deal from their work with dogs, and the conclusions they reached often went beyond merely technical or biological observations.

"The first observation was that mongrels and strays fare much better than purebred dogs," says Filina. "They're strong—for generations they've had to survive—and they can wolf down anything and it won't do them harm. A nice-looking domesticated lap dog wouldn't be able to cope in space."

Korolev would use these experiments as the basis for selecting the first cosmonaut.

But before that point was reached, soldiers from the unit where the scientists worked made regular expeditions to the Spartak Stadium in Moscow to catch some of the stray dogs that wandered the area.

From homelessness to space flight . . .

"There are many interesting stories to tell," says Filina. "Such as the time some of the strays bit a guy and he ended up in the hospital. Another time they brought back a bitch, fed her, shut her in a box, and that night she had puppies. Instead of taking care of a prospective cosmonaut, the whole base ended up nursing her babies."

The first dogs to fly into space, in 1951, were named Tsygan and Dezik. They were followed by Chaika and Lisichka, Pcholka and Mushka—altogether seventy-one quadrupeds (according to the Cosmos Museum near Yaroslavl). The most famous of all was Laika. She flew the highest, and was the first living creature to be sent into orbit. But after a few hours' flight, the temperature in the cabin rose so much that she was boiled alive.

"Laika's mission was always going to end in her death," admits Filina. "She had an automatic feeder, which gave her a meal every few hours. The final, tenth one contained poison."

Yet the most important flight for both Soviet space exploration and humankind involved Belka and Strelka: after orbiting the Earth in a rocket in 1960, they safely returned.

"Thanks to which," Filina says, "our engineers now knew it was possible to send a man into orbit."

4.

Korolev learned a lot from his adventures with flying canines. Like the stray dogs, prospective cosmonauts came from homes with, let's say, complicated histories. They were not the well-bred children of officers, but boys who had been through the mill and coped with adversity.

"First there were twenty of them," says Gagarin's biographer Anton Pervushin, who is a walking encyclopedia of knowledge about the Soviet conquest of space. "The best pilots of the time. The conditions they had to meet were these: very good fitness; height below 180 centimeters [6 feet], because a taller man wouldn't fit in the rocket; maximum weight 70 kilograms [154 pounds]; and a pleasant appearance. Frankly speaking, the first cosmonaut had to be handsome."

"Why was that so important?"

"That was something they'd learned from the dogs," Pervushin tells me. "Belka and Strelka, the first dogs to come back, became celebrities. When Strelka had puppies, Krushchev took one as a gift for President Kennedy's daughter. They could all see that space exploration had incredible potential for promoting the country."

The military unit where Faina Kazetskaya cooked was growing at lightning speed.

"At first the canteen was in a small wooden cottage," Faina

said many years later. "The kitchen had a wood-burning stove. In the first few months there were only five pilots, which meant very little work. But later on there were ten, then twenty. At that point we were given modern cooking facilities."

Faina was also given two assistants.

As a teenager, her son was surrounded by first-rate soldiers and scientists—future heroes. He began to dream of following in their footsteps. Not wanting to cause him grief, his mother hadn't told him the truth about his father—that he had abandoned them at the hardest possible moment. Instead she told him that his father had been a hero, like those young men. She pretended he'd been killed at the front, saving other men and fighting against fascism. The boy took the bait. When he finished school, he went to the air force school in Monino.

Meanwhile, the young pilots who had started training for space flights nicknamed their cook Mamania.

"They were still kids, all under thirty," she recalled. "But I was born in 1918. I was already over forty. On average I was twenty years their senior."

The pilots did treat her a bit like a mother. Yuri Gagarin had great respect for the cooks: Ivan Gorchayev, his father-in-law, cooked at sanatoriums and restaurants in his native Orenburg.

"All his life Gagarin was the leader in everything he did," says Pervushin. "There's a picture of him from technical college, with the basketball team. They're all tall and burly, and one is noticeably smaller. Of course it's Gagarin. And of course he's the captain."

"He was very funny, but he also knew how to be serious if the situation required it," recalled Faina. "One time Valery Bykovsky came in to breakfast, but instead of eating he started playing billiards. I could see what he was doing, so I went up to him. 'Why don't you want to eat, sonny? Don't you like the food? Tell me what you'd like and I'll make it for you.' And he replied: 'I don't want anything.' Then Gagarin went up to him. He gave him a good dressing-down. 'Mamania said you're going to eat, and that means you're going to eat. To the table, quick, march!' Did he obey him? You bet he did!"

Faina sometimes took supplementary training courses at the Metropole restaurant in Leningrad; she wasn't a professional who'd been to cooking school. But she soon noticed, as did her bosses, that for these young men, cut off from their families, her lack of formal training was a plus. They didn't want the sort of food you'd get in a restaurant. They preferred home cooking.

Over time, the unit started up its own auxiliary farm with pigs, hens, cows, and a vegetable garden. Just like the farms that had provided for Stalin and Lenin.

"Onions, parsley, cabbage, carrots—we had all our own produce," Faina recalled. "We had so many green vegetables that there were always bowls of salad in the corridor. Anyone who felt like it could come and eat as much as they wished."

In the beginning there were so few prospective cosmonauts that Faina did her best to cook each of them his favorite food.

"Pavel Popovich was fond of Ukrainian borscht. I knew how to make it because I'm from Podolia. Once I'd made it, they all asked for it to be a permanent item on the menu. Gagarin loved fresh milk. He could drink a whole liter of it in one go. The problem was that fresh milk can upset your stomach. For pilots that's very dangerous. So the girls and I had to work out how to boil the milk for him without it losing its flavor."

Andriyan Nikolayev, a future cosmonaut from Chuvashia, liked his republic's national dish, hupla, a round pie stuffed with potatoes and meat. So Faina sat up all night and learned how to make it.

"I don't remember any of them ever complaining. But I do remember them having sessions in a pressure chamber, where they had to sit without moving for a long time, so we cooked more vegetable dishes for them as the healthier option. Carrots, cabbage rissoles, omelets, and vegetable soups: borscht, solyanka [sour soup], cabbage. And lots of pickles."

But although the cosmonauts adored Faina's cooking, her dishes couldn't be taken into space. At that point no one knew how the human body behaves in a weightless environment; the cosmonauts were given food that had been ground to a pulp in special tubes, so there'd be no crumbs or scraps floating around the spaceship.

"While they were exercising at our training center, they were brought that food in tubes from Moscow so they could get used to it," recalled Faina. "They didn't like it. They used to come here afterward and sneak into the kitchen. 'Mamania,' they'd say, 'give us some potatoes. They can be yesterday's, but let them be real.' Not that the space food they were given wasn't good. The bread, for example, was very tasty—it tasted like the bread my granny used to bake. I was amazed they managed to make it so good. But meat and potatoes out of a tube couldn't possibly taste good."

The cosmonauts' training program was exhausting. They spun in a device that subjected them to a load factor similar to what they might experience in flight. They did parachute jumps at night and in the rain. They had to learn what to do if the canopy didn't open right away. But the worst experiment involved being shut alone in a soundproof cabin—for ten days.

"Those exercises were very tough," said Faina. "They worked under constant stress, because they all wanted to be the best, to be the first to make it to outer space. And then they'd come to me, and I'd feed them as best I could."

5.

It seems Gagarin won that coveted spot with his smile.

But there may have been another, even more superficial reason.

"His main rival was also his best friend. His name was Gherman Titov. Apparently he scored highest on all the tests, and did very well physically too," says Anton Pervushin. "But how would it have looked if less than twenty years after the victory over Germany, the Soviet Union had sent into space a man whose name was 'German'?"

What's more, Gagarin had personally experienced some very tough times during the German invasion. When the front passed through his village on the outskirts of Smolensk, there was such great famine that little Yuri stole some leftover food from the German soldiers' garbage can. As he later told the story, he and his brother dug some old, dried bread crusts out of it. His mother was a milkmaid. His father was a carpenter who had built a house for the whole family himself—but during the war it was occupied by a German officer, and for two years the Gagarins lived in a dugout.

A few months before the first human space flight, Gagarin and Titov went to Baikonur in Kazakhstan, from where the Soviet

Union had sent the dogs into outer space, and from where it would soon launch the first cosmonaut. There the men passed from Faina's hands into those of another cook, Maria Kritinina. Brought up on the Don River, this twenty-five-year-old would feed two generations of Soviet cosmonauts before their space flights, and would become a legend of Baikonur cooking.

Together, Gagarin and Titov watched the launch of yet another rocket to carry dogs into space. Before their eyes, the rocket exploded.

They both knew that one of them would board the next rocket.

Finally, on the day before the flight, when they heard that Gagarin would be flying, both men put on a brave face. Only many years later did Titov admit how much bitterness he felt.

An hour before the flight, Maria Kritinina tried to press a few onions on Gagarin, so he'd take them with him into outer space.

"They're ours, they're good for you," she told him in a confidential tone. "Who knows what's really in those tubes . . . ?"

But Gagarin merely replied with a smile. He knew he'd be carefully searched before the flight—after all, everything he was to take with him into space had significance, for both science and politics. There was no chance of smuggling a single onion onto the rocket.

6.

Let's return to the Birulevsky Experimental Plant, where those tubes for the cosmonauts were produced.

"I came here from the air force," says the director of the

plant, Viktor Frantzevich Dobrovolsky. "I was involved in studying food for pilots there as well, and I wrote my dissertation on it. It was a natural path: 'Do you know anything about feeding people who are exposed to great g-force? Come and join us,' they said. The space program was the most prestigious. It meant emoluments, foreign trips, and expeditions to rocket launches. We were the elite of Soviet food technology."

"That's right. But now no one wants to work here," says Valentina Borisovna, spreading her hands. "That's why they keep us on when we should have retired long ago."

Indeed, it's hard not to notice that everyone sitting at the table is in their seventies or eighties.

"Young people today take things for granted," says Dobrovolsky. "We worked hard and with dedication, without concern for money, because we were focused on ideas. That's how it was in the Soviet Union: ideas came first. We planned what food we'd send out with the first of our people to fly to the Moon. We discussed very seriously what food could be grown on other planets and how, and what plants should be sent out first to avoid polluting the soil on Mars, for instance."

"I came here for the Mars project!" adds Ludmila Vasilyevna. "I was so pleased we'd be making food that would fly there. But these days an applicant comes along to work here as a cook, and it's all the same to her if the food she makes will be eaten by people in outer space or not. She just wants to get a thousand rubles more, and if she goes to an outlet selling kebabs or blinis, she'll get it."

"But here we are, boring you with our problems, when you want to find out as much as you can about the first cosmonauts," says Dobrovolsky. "So allow me. Gagarin's flight was of course a breakthrough for humankind. But in terms of food, it was uninteresting. He was in space for only an hour and forty minutes."

"Yes, as Tsiolkovsky had predicted," adds Ludmila Vasilyevna.

"That's right." Dobrovolsky nods. "But he never said anything about food. And Gagarin didn't have to eat in space at all, because he wasn't exactly going to starve in less than two hours. However, Korolev wanted to know as much as possible about the behavior of the human organism in outer space. Until then they had known nothing. That's why Gagarin was given distinct orders to eat a meal in a state of weightlessness. And what exactly he ate, my colleagues can tell you. Ludmila Vasilyevna was the first of us to come and work here . . ."

"In those tubes Gagarin was given exactly what the fighter pilots had been given before him," says Ludmila Vasilyevna. "He was given more than sixty tubes because Korolev wasn't sure they'd succeed in bringing him back right away. They contained all the foods that we were supposed to test for the pilots in those days."

"Now we have more than three hundred." Dobrovolsky smiles, because this is largely to his credit. "In those days we only had a few dozen. The set he chose for that day included vegetable soup, chicken liver pâté, and blackcurrant juice."

"According to some sources he also ate chocolate cream," I say. "Is it true?"

"We don't know for certain," says Dobrovolsky. "But he did have cream, so who knows, maybe he tried it. That cream was a novelty. A gift from our food technicians for the first cosmonaut, to give him a little treat. Today you can buy that sort of cream in any store, but in those days it was nowhere to be found."

"Gagarin ate in a state of weightlessness. It was the first meal eaten by man outside of the earth's gravity," says Ludmila Vasilyevna.

"We can move on to other topics now, but do you have any more questions about Gagarin?" asks Dobrovolsky.

I have two.

First I ask about Gagarin's famous, recently declassified conversation with Korolev shortly before takeoff. In it he mentions sausage, and says he'll eat it as a chaser. So the question is: What was the sausage meant to be a chaser for?

But Dobrovolsky says it was all a joke. There was no sausage, or anything to chase.

"In fact, they took a serious approach to the topic of alcohol," he says. "It was the first space flight in human history. There's no question anyone would have given him or allowed him alcohol. Or sausage."

So I ask my second question: If they had failed to bring Gagarin back, did he—like Laika the dog—have poison in the final, sixty-third tube?

"Please don't joke about such serious matters," Dobrovolsky replies, though I wasn't joking at all.

7.

Gagarin landed near the village of Smelovka, not far from Saratov. The story goes that the first thing he saw upon landing was a cow's rear end. People from the local collective farm fled in terror at the sight of him. The first person to have the courage to speak to this strange alien was Rumia Nurskanova, then five years old.

"My granny was terrified it was an American invasion," Rumia said in 2021. "But when the alien spoke in Russian, I offered him some milk from a can."

Gagarin thanked her and said he'd filled up on food from tubes in space. Once reunited with the cosmonauts' doctor, he was advised to eat an apple.

"Meanwhile, my father ran up and told Gagarin that he'd landed on soil where the best potatoes grow," Rumia said. "And so one thing led to another, and they made a deal that Gagarin would come back after the harvest to try them. And we'd host him. He promised me and my granny that he'd come and visit us, for potatoes with cream and pickled gherkins. Ever since, when we've planted potatoes in this part of the field, we've always said we're planting them 'for Yuri.'"

The remains of Gagarin's tubes were snapped up by the locals.

8.

Gagarin soon became a celebrity. And a Soviet export commodity. Wherever he went, he was greeted by hundreds of thousands of people.

After his visit to Japan, trade between the USSR and Japan increased fifteen times over.

But the first cosmonaut started to feel like a monkey in a cage. So whenever he could, he broke away. The photographer Boris Golovnya, Gagarin's friend who traveled half the globe with him, recalls how in Tokyo they lost the KGB agents accompanying them at every step (the agents were there to protect Gagarin, but also to make sure he didn't do anything unpredictable) and went first to an electronics fair, then for a beer.

"Just when we thought we'd managed to break free and were on our own, a black car drove up to the bar. The window opened, and a gentleman in plain clothes saluted us. Then he asked Yuri to please return to the hotel, because he was going off duty and wanted to get some sleep before the next day's work."

Gagarin had another adventure in London.

"Elizabeth II invited him to breakfast at Buckingham Palace," says Anton Pervushin. "So they went in, sat at the table, and there was lots of cutlery: forks, spoons, knives, fifteen of everything, as in a palace. But Gagarin wasn't fazed by that sort of thing. He told the queen he was an ordinary village boy who had eaten everything with the same spoon all his life. And that he had no idea what to do with all these forks. The queen burst out laughing. Apparently she told him that although she had grown up in a palace, she wasn't sure herself what to do with all those utensils. Gagarin did exactly the right thing: he was himself, Yuri, the boy next door who became the first man to fly into space, and now he smiled broadly and wanted there to be peace on earth."

But the longer Gagarin wore the mantle of the first cosmonaut, the more he started to lose his way. He really was a shy village boy who dreamed of flying, not of traveling around the world in a golden cage. So he escaped into alcohol—and sex. On a trip to Crimea, he paid a visit to a young female doctor. Suddenly there was loud knocking at the door. It was his wife, who'd been told by a well-wisher where to find her husband. Gagarin jumped from a second-floor window and hit his head.

The next day the Soviet newspapers reported that the heroic cosmonaut had been injured saving a drowning child.

9.

After Gagarin's historic mission his friend with the dubious name, Gherman Titov, finally flew into space.

"While Gagarin ate food in space because he had orders to, Titov ate because he was genuinely hungry," says Anton Pervushin. "He ate three dishes: vegetable soup, pâté, and black-currant juice. The next day it was traditional Russian borscht. He was given large portions, more than two thousand calories, but after landing he was sorry he hadn't eaten more. It turned out that the g-force in space is so great that cosmonauts need three thousand calories. So Titov was the first man to eat a proper meal in space. And the first to urinate. It's rumored that he wanted to do more than that, but he didn't want to go down in history as the first man to take a crap in outer space. He held out until after landing."

So this honor fell to Valery Bykovsky, the man who had refused Faina Kazetska's breakfasts at the cosmonauts' canteen. In June 1963, he spent five days and nights alone in outer space. Even if he'd wanted to hold out until landing, there was no chance of it.

At the same time, the first woman in space went on her mission. Her name was Valentina Tereshkova, and she was an ordinary textile worker from Yaroslavl who after work had learned to parachute jump as a hobby. On hearing about Gagarin's flight, she wrote a letter to Nikita Khrushchev, offering herself up as the world's first female cosmonaut.

"Khrushchev was impressed by her determination," says Anton Pervushin. "She was selected from among five candidates."

While Valery Bykovsky was the first person to defecate in space, Tereshkova was the first to be sick in orbit.

"I was poisoned by the food," she said apologetically upon her return. "That bread was very dry. I wanted black bread, potatoes, and onions."

After landing, Tereshkova ate ravenously.

"She stuffed herself—she was fed the potatoes and onions she'd missed so much. They also gave her *kumis* [fermented mare's milk], and by way of thanks, she handed out tubes of space food," Pervushin relates. "This went against all the medical recommendations, because the cosmonauts were supposed to refrain from eating until the doctors had examined them. Korolev was furious, because in terms of research her flight was totally useless. A great success was trumpeted, and that couldn't be denied. But thanks to Tereshkova's insubordination, no woman went into outer space for the next twenty years."

10.

Although it has been officially explained, to this day Gagarin's death is shrouded in controversy. Could his favorite cook have had a hand in it?

The last time Faina Kazetskaya saw Gagarin was the night before the plane crash that occurred on March 27, 1968. Star City had grown to a medium-sized town and a dozen cooks worked around the clock in the canteen, but Faina was still in charge of feeding the cosmonauts. And they still treated her like a mother.

"I was on shift the night before Gagarin's death," she recalled more than thirty years later. "At about one in the morning the duty officer called me: 'Faina, four people are about to arrive, including Yuri Alexeyevich.' A few minutes later a car stopped outside the canteen, and indeed, Yuri was in it. He greeted me, but when I started to set the table, he protested. 'Mamania, don't set the table. Just make sandwiches. We'll come fetch them at five o'clock.' 'Why's that, boys?' I asked. 'Have something hot!' 'Thank you, but we don't have time.'"

The next morning Gagarin had a flight scheduled with his instructor, Vladimir Seryogin. Minutes before they went out to board the plane, the cosmonaut remembered his favorite snack.

"Have you got any milk, Mamania?" he asked.

She took a bottle from the fridge. She wanted to heat the milk, but Gagarin, laughing, drank a cold mug of it in one gulp. Both pilots ate their sandwiches and left.

Afterward, the waitress who set the table for them recalled that Gagarin had forgotten to collect his dinner voucher, so she ran to give it to him.

"At noon I finished my shift and wanted to go home," said Faina Kazetskaya. "But at the checkpoint they told me to go back. That was when I was first told, 'Gagarin and Seryogin have been killed.' I was to wait in the canteen for the investigators."

Soon afterward, several military men came into the cosmonauts' canteen.

"They started riffling through everything—even the contents of the garbage pails were taken away in sacks," said Faina. "They interrogated us: What had Gagarin eaten, what had he drunk? . . . It was very hard for me to speak. Not out of fear. But I couldn't believe Yuri was dead. How could that be? One minute the man was there, a good man, and now he was gone. Our pilots often crashed. But not Gagarin! We all wept."

Faina was told often that pilots shouldn't be given fresh milk straight from the cow, because it can cause loose bowels; did she have trouble speaking for this reason? Did the commission that investigated Gagarin's death consider the fact that it could have been caused by something as prosaic as a glass of milk? It sounds improbable, but on the other hand, pilots often have only a split second to make a decision that could determine whether they live or die. Was that the case here?

No one knows. The archives on the death of Yuri Gagarin, including the statements made by Faina Kazetskaya, are classified.

Faina only ever gave one interview.

11.

The longer the space flights continue, the more ambitious the tasks put before the team at the Birulevsky Experimental Plant.

"Today we have the sum total knowledge from several hundred flights," says Dobrovolsky. "What's more, since the end of the Cold War we have been able to compare our knowledge with that of the Americans. Instead of competing, we exchange experiences. I don't want to sound immodest, but where space food is concerned, Russia is still the world leader. When a Russian flies to the International Space Station, he always has to take several extra cans of food, because it's well-known that the others will pinch it off him."

"Our cosmonauts are given containers full of food, including rations for sixteen days and nights," explains Ludmila

Vasilyevna. "No breakfast, lunch, or dinner is repeated in this time period. We've also moved away from the tubes: they turned out to be impractical, and food of that consistency during longer flights meant that the cosmonauts had to learn to chew their food all over again. Now they're given canned food. Only mustard and honey fly in tubes these days."

"The food the cosmonauts get is the healthiest possible," stresses Dobrovolsky. "We sign contracts with factories and farms that produce fruit and vegetables without pesticides specially for us. We prefer to give the cosmonauts a natural diet to avoid any potential risk to their health posed by chemicals in outer space. We have very strict monitoring. But we also monitor ourselves—effectively, because in sixty years we haven't sent a single microbe or parasite into space. If someone were to have a stomach complaint up there, it would be a disaster. We have to prevent that from happening down here before they leave."

"In addition to the main container, they get an extra one too," adds Valentina Borisovna. "The first has food that's made according to our specifications. But for the second they can order their favorite items. They can choose tvorog [similar to curd cheese] with nuts, fruit juices, and kissel [a fruit dessert], for instance. They can even have chocolate or soured milk."

"The technology has advanced a long way," says Ludmila Vasilyevna. "Today the cosmonauts are given either canned food or vacuum-packed dried food. You just have to pour boiling water over it, and your meal is ready."

"The procedure has been the same since the 1960s: we meet with each cosmonaut and give them various things to try," explains Dobrovolsky. "They evaluate each meal, giving it marks from one to five. We try to make sure they get only the food they've marked the highest. But sometimes a cosmonaut orders food from us, only to order something completely different a few days later. It's curious, but tastes change in space. We don't know how to explain it, but it's true. Someone might not be able to bear eggs on Earth, but in space he'll refuse to eat anything else. And then he returns to Earth, a few days go by, sometimes weeks, and everything goes back to normal. Why is that? We can't explain it. Not yet."

"Almost everyone likes the taste of onions in outer space. We can't explain that either," says Ludmila Vasilyevna. "But of course, when the cosmonauts are in a small space, eating onions is not necessarily the best idea. So we've been working to develop onions that won't give off odors. The first attempts have already flown into orbit."

"The cosmonauts' favorite food is stroganoff," adds Dobrovolsky. "And a fish known as Polish-style zander. With eggs, butter, and lemon juice. I have no idea why it's called 'Polish-style' zander. But the cosmonauts also love pureed peas, solyanka, tomatoes in sauce, caviar, cabbage soup made with sauerkraut, rassolnik [pickled cucumber and barley soup], *kharcho* [Georgian soup with meat, rice, and walnuts], and borscht. Many dishes have been added to our menu since cosmonauts from fraternal countries started flying; for each one we have tried to prepare a surprise from their national cuisine. So from the Hungarians we still have goulash, from the Bulgarians moussaka, which we call meat-and-vegetable gratin. Only your *bigos* [a Polish traditional dish of meat and sauerkraut stew], which we made for the Polish cosmonaut, Mirosław Hermaszewski, didn't catch on."

12.

To this day the family of Rumia Nurskanova, the five-year-old who was the first to talk to Yuri Gagarin after he landed, plants potatoes to mark the landing of the first cosmonaut.

"We know he's not coming back, but we got used to doing it. For us it's a special day. We made our promise, so we do the planting," Rumia told a TASS reporter.

For his services, the state gave Sergei Korolev a house in Moscow. These days the building serves as a branch of the Memorial Museum of Space Exploration, where I met with Larissa Filina. After our interview, she shows me around the villa.

"The cosmonauts come here after their flights as if they're visiting a temple," she says. "When Gherman Titov was still alive, he used to come here just to meditate. He always walked around the house in socks. My older colleagues told him he didn't have to take off his shoes, but he would just smile."

In the kitchen the original equipment has been preserved, including the stove, the sink, and even the curtains.

"Korolev liked stuffed cabbage with cream, stuffed marrow, and buckwheat with fresh onion and pork fat," Filina says. "But his favorite snack was black bread with a thin coating of mustard and a slice of Ukrainian pork fat, which we call *salo*. He could eat it nonstop."

Korolev died two years before Gagarin, of a heart attack. His years in the labor camps had ruined his health; on top of that, the constant stress brought on by his work wore out his heart.

Maria Kritinina, who cooked at Baikonur, encouraged successive cosmonauts to take an onion into space with them.

Eventually Piotr Klimiuk from Belarus did just that, but instead of eating it, he planted it in water. During his week in space the onion grew several inches of green leaves, which the satisfied Klimiuk added to his food. After him, other cosmonauts began smuggling in an onion from Kritinina. She worked at Baikonur from the time of the first dog flights right up to the Gorbachev era and perestroika. In 1986 she returned to her native village on the river Don. She died in 2013, a few days before the anniversary of Gagarin's flight.

Though nearing the age of eighty, Ludmila Vasilyevna, the senior specialist at the Birulevsky Experimental Plant, would like to see the day when she plans a menu for a mission to Mars.

"We'll have to develop entirely new technology," she says. "Currently, our dried food has a shelf life of one year. For Mars we'll need to invent products that keep for three or four years. That will be a fascinating process. I'd love to take part in it."

MENU

◇◇◇

Baikonur Borscht

This unique recipe for borscht, served to the cosmonauts at Baikonur, was recorded by Olga Gopalo, a journalist writing for *Komsomolskaya Pravda*, who visited Maria Kritinina in 2013.

10½ to 14 ounces (300 to 400 g) pork and veal
3 or 4 potatoes

Vegetable oil, for frying
2 onions
1 carrot
2 bell peppers
2 bay leaves
2 tablespoons tomato puree
1 teaspoon sugar
10 to 14 ounces (300 to 400 g) cabbage
Garlic
Dill
Parsley
Salt and black pepper

Place the meat in a large pot and cover it with cold water. Bring it to a boil, then reduce the heat to low and cook until the broth is cloudy.

Meanwhile, heat a frying pan. Add enough oil to coat, then sauté the onions, carrot, bell peppers, bay leaves, and tomato puree. Stir in the sugar.

Add the sautéed vegetable mixture to the broth, then add the cabbage, garlic, dill, and parsley. Bring it to a boil, then turn off the heat. Cover with a lid only when the borscht has cooled, because the droplets that form on the lid will spoil the flavor of the dish.

OVERHEARD IN THE KITCHEN

While Gagarin was still alive there was a palace coup at the Kremlin: Nikita Khrushchev's comrades ousted him from power and sent him into retirement. His place was taken by the younger, jovial Leonid Brezhnev, who definitely abused alcohol.

Gagarin's death spawned many legends. One of them is that somehow he angered Brezhnev, who gave orders for him to be killed. One of the most extreme myths is that Gagarin was never actually in outer space, and had to die so he wouldn't give the game away.

The more reasonable stories involve a fighter plane that broke all the rules by descending to a low altitude in poor visibility without contacting the control tower and flew just a dozen yards away from Gagarin's plane, throwing it off its flight path.

In 2011 the Russian space agency Roscosmos officially closed the inquiry into Gagarin's death, putting all the blame on the pilot and the incorrect performance of a simple maneuver. But many Russians believe that the circumstances of the first cosmonaut's death have not been properly explained. What circumstances? For instance, the fact that the original inquiry was completed unusually quickly, and that the commission investigating the crash gave orders for the plane in which Gagarin and his instructor had been flying to be cut into pieces, sealed, and buried in barrels.

When the wreckage was found, it turned out Gagarin's hands were still gripping the control column. The searchers discovered not only the two pilots' bodies but also their personal belongings, including Gagarin's wallet, which held his driver's license and a photo of Sergei Korolev. In his jacket pocket they found the dinner voucher he'd been given by the waitress after he left the canteen.

Meanwhile, under Brezhnev's regime the Kremlin's dining tables reached their apogee. Never again would such lavish meals, feasts as rich as in the days of the tsars, be eaten at the Kremlin.

The great irony was that the man now in charge at the Kremlin was not particularly fond of the food served at those splendid banquets. Why not? Let's have his cook tell us about it.

X

The Kremlin Chef

Viktor Belyaev's Story

The first time I saw Leonid Ilyich Brezhnev was when I was sent to the Kremlin as a young kitchen boy to help at a reception marking the thirtieth anniversary of our victory over fascism. As I looked at him, I thought I was watching television. I couldn't get my head around the fact that I, Viktor, a boy from Izmaylovo, was really cooking for the head of state and his guests.

Later came Gorbachev, Yeltsin, and Putin. I cooked for them all; if you woke me in the middle of the night, I could tell you what each of them liked best. When Richard Nixon visited Gorbachev [in 1986], he had all my dishes photographed, and each evening he dropped by to say hello to me. Margaret Thatcher ordered an unimaginable number of my pancakes. And your Polish leader Edward Gierek always brought me Polish sausage, because no one made such good sausage in the entire Soviet bloc.

Where should I start, Witold? Maybe from the beginning. With the young man from Izmaylovo I used to be, who had nothing at all but aspirations.

1.

Izmaylovo is now part of Moscow, almost in the center, but when I was a child it was still on the outskirts, and it was known—as it still is—for the fact that tsar Peter the Great spent his childhood there. There are beautiful churches, monasteries, and monuments dedicated to him. There's a stream he swam in, and streets he walked down. If you live in a place like that, you soak up history like a sponge. And as a boy, my aim in life was to do something connected with history.

I decided to go to the technical college near my home in Izmaylovo for a degree in archive studies. I thought I would study old documents, read books, and do other equally interesting things.

But you need to know that I was brought up without a father, with just my mom, grandma, and grandpa. When I was four years old my father was jailed for "being a hooligan"; supposedly he'd stolen something, or beaten someone up—I don't know, I never got to the bottom of it—but Mom didn't want to know him anymore, so I didn't know him either. The central figure at home was my grandpa. He was tall, with hair as black as a raven's wing, and he was a war veteran: he'd added two years to his age, or else they wouldn't have accepted him in the army, and he'd gone all the way to Berlin on one leg—he'd lost the other one while fighting at the Battle of Smolensk.

Even for times of war, when there were plenty of heroes, Grandpa was exceptional. A military doctor—a Pole, in fact—made him a prosthesis from a piece of wood. They wanted to send Grandpa back to Moscow, for how could a lame person march with the army? But he insisted, flatly refusing to go back to Moscow, and taught himself to walk on that leg so well that if you didn't know, you wouldn't notice he had a fake one. When he got home, he had a whole iconostasis of medals, including the Order of Alexander Nevsky and three others for the Great Patriotic War. He had so many medals he could have hung them on his back as well as his front.

And one day my grandpa, who was a very practical person, asked me: "Viktor, where are you going to go to school?"

"To the technical college," I said, "for archive studies."

"And what are you going to do after college?"

"Well," I said, "I'll sit in an archive and read old documents with a magnifying glass."

Grandpa looked at me, shook his head, and said: "That's not a serious profession. And a man should have a serious profession to be able to feed a family."

And with that, the conversation ended. At least for the time being.

Grandpa was in the habit of hanging all those medals on his coat lapels once a week and going to the local bar for a beer or two. And it so happened that not long after our conversation, they opened a new bar near our home. Grandpa went, had his two beers, and was leaving, when in front of him he saw a sign: COOKING SCHOOL, OPEN DAY.

Oh, he thought to himself, that's interesting. He went up to the school, stood by the door, and just then along came one of my future teachers, Valentina Petrovna Minayeva. She looked at my grandpa and his medals and asked: "So how about you? Do you want to sign up for school in your old age?"

"Not me, but my grandson," replied Grandpa.

And she was so taken by this that she gave Grandpa a tour

of all the various nooks and corners and showed him everything at that school.

When Grandpa left, he headed for the store. He bought two chekushki, meaning 250-milliliter [8¼-ounce] bottles, of vodka. He came home, put them on the table, opened one, and drank it. Then he said: "Viktor, I went to the cooking school. Two years of study, with one week of practice for every week of theory. Then you become a cook. And all your life you're well fed with your nose in the snuff"—that's a Russian idiom meaning, you'll live well and be rich.

My mom started to cry. "Just don't go into the food trade! They'll teach him to steal, he'll go to jail!" [Author's note: In those days there were frequent prosecutions of food factory managers who, having access to produce, were tempted to steal some and sell it on the black market.]

And Grandpa replied with a proverb: "To pluck a little from a lot isn't stealing. It's fair distribution."

And he winked at me.

I liked that proverb very much. Whether I liked Grandpa's idea, I wasn't yet sure. But it was hard to argue with him, so I withdrew my application from the technical college and transferred it to the cooking school.

The school was wonderful. It had very high standards, and to this day I still make use of the things they taught me there. Because they taught us everything: how to butcher a carcass, how to cut up poultry, even how to cut up wild game. Also a little bookkeeping and a little food technology. Lots of knowledge, fantastic teachers. And indeed, as Grandpa had said, we had a week of theoretical classes at school followed by, right from the start, a week of practical work at a restaurant.

But after the first month of practical work I was exhausted and wanted to give up. They'd sent me and a colleague to the Cheryomushka restaurant, where for the first two weeks we did nothing but clean boiled eggs. What for? So they'd look nice. They probably had no idea what to do with us, so they gave each of us a thousand eggs to scrub.

After those two weeks my classmate and I plucked up the courage to go to the boss and say: "There's just one thing. We were supposed to learn to cook here . . ."

So he told us to wash the dishes and the pots as well. The frying pans were half filled with grease. The pots were huge vats, big enough to hold several hundred liters. It was dreadful work.

So we complained at school. And our teacher, Valentina Petrovna, came to see what those practical lessons of ours were like. When she saw us with those frying pans, pots, and eggs—because no one had let us off cleaning the eggs—she made a big fuss to the restaurant manager. She threatened to end the relationship with the restaurant if they didn't teach us the profession.

So the manager transferred us to the salad team.

It was my first serious exposure to cooking, and I can't say I was instantly filled with great love for my profession. It was certainly better than cleaning eggs and vats. But I didn't think chopping up lettuce, cucumbers, and tomatoes was something I could do for the rest of my life.

2.

After a year at school, they started sending us out to really good places for our practical work. In those days the culinary map of Moscow wasn't as complicated as it is now. There were five top restaurants: the Metropole, the Ukraina, the Moskva, the Praga, and the National. That was all.

I ended up at the Praga.

It was a stylish restaurant, with white tablecloths, elegant waiters, and a superb kitchen, located in the center of Moscow on the famous Arbat. Our waiters were legendary. The head waiter was a man named Grigoryev, who in a single evening served only three or at most four tables. People made reservations several months in advance just to be served by him. He was handsome and elegant—everything about him was sleek and smooth. He could give perfect advice on what to eat. And he also took a lot of care to make sure the kitchen did everything to the highest standard for his clients. He would watch the chefs' hands to see if they fried things in butter, if they weighed the food out correctly, and so on.

I got on well with the staff there. And when I graduated from school with a red diploma [top marks], the boss offered me a job. I agreed very willingly. But I still wasn't entirely sure if I wanted to be a chef or not.

I didn't know it yet, but the waiters and chefs from those five good restaurants were often employed at the Kremlin for various large receptions. But I was about to find out. As soon as I started the job there was a major event celebrating thirty years since the victory over fascism. At the Kremlin, as ever, there was going to be a reception to mark the occasion, and the boss said he was adding me to the group of chefs who would serve at it.

My legs gave way beneath me, Witold. "Where? Me? To the Kremlin? But I don't know a thing!" But the boss just smiled.

"Calm down, Viktor," he said. "You'll learn. You have to start somewhere."

At the time I was very young. Let me remind you, a year earlier I'd been washing eggs at a restaurant in the suburbs. And now suddenly—the Kremlin. But never mind: the boss had said I was going, so there was no arguing. They dressed me nicely—we had starched white outfits and chef's hats—and off we went.

The reception was enormous. What did we cook? I can't remember, but on that occasion I just helped the senior chefs, mainly chopping, washing, or stirring the pots at most, and when the waiters got tired of carrying the plates they recruited me to help them.

Until suddenly the bodyguards came crashing into the kitchen. "Nobody's to leave!" they shouted. We looked through the door, and there were Brezhnev, Kosygin (who was the premier then), and all the members of the Politburo.

I couldn't get my head around it: was I watching TV, or was I really seeing this? I glanced at the other chefs to check if they could see it too. And I found that none of them was even looking in the direction of the politicians. For them it was a day at work like any other; they'd seen our Politburo in the flesh many times before, and they knew they'd often see them again.

3.

The Kremlin is the Kremlin, but now that I'd finished school I was called up for military service. I was sent to join the border force, who guarded our northern border: from Naryan-Mar, a town in the Nenets Autonomous Okrug, to Mys Shmidta, a small village in Chukotka, from where—if you look carefully—you can see Alaska, and where the Arctic Ocean begins.

Our detachments were subordinate not to the Ministry of Defense but to the KGB, and through it, to the USSR Council of Ministers. What was the difference? From my perspective, it was mainly to do with food. An ordinary Soviet soldier was issued 200 grams [7 ounces] of butter per day, but a border guard got 500 [1¼ pounds]. It was the same with all the other rations. We also had better-quality barracks and slightly better uniforms. The Soviet authorities took the best care of us they could.

I flew to Vorkuta, where I was to start service in the Separate Arctic Border Detachment. And there, as happens in the army, first you're trained by the sergeants. My sergeant found out about my episode at the Kremlin and sent me to the commander. I went along, wondering what it could be about. Would they hit me? Shout at me? But the commander said that as I had cooking skills, it was a pity not to make use of them. And he immediately added that although we had good rations, we had very poor cooks. The men were from every Soviet republic, but they had no idea about cooking. He said he'd be happy to provide a plane so I could spend a year touring all our posts and teaching everyone to cook.

"Sure I will," I said, "just tell me when, what, where, and how, and we'll be off."

And off I went. My cooking lessons took me to places where normally I'd never have gone in all my life, not at any price. There are no roads and no trains; you can only fly in by helicopter. If I had a ruble for every polar bear I've seen, I'd be a rich man. Plus thousands of seals, and landscapes to take your breath away. It's like that because in the far north, nature has only twenty-four days to produce any crops. Throughout the year it's very harsh, but on those days, Witold, it's madness. If in that time you stick a spade handle in the ground, something will sprout from it. There are tons of blueberries—it looks like a great purple carpet. Raspberries and mushrooms too. Until I arrived, in all those places they only made use of the fresh fruit on those twenty-four days when they grew.

So I showed all the cooks how to freeze as many of those blueberries and raspberries as they could, and then they could have compote all year round. At each post I advised them to put up a greenhouse, to make the growing season last a bit longer. I don't know if they took heed of my advice at every place, but at headquarters in Vorkuta they did. As far as I know, the greenhouse is still there to this day.

I also asked the captains of the ships that sailed to us from abroad to bring seeds. As a result, we had delicious peppers from somewhere on the Mediterranean, tomatoes from Holland, and cucumbers from Scotland. They all grew in our greenhouses. Not throughout the year, of course, because it was too cold there, but from just twenty-four growing days, suddenly there were three, almost four months with a supply of fresh vegetables, and that was a big change.

I also taught the cooks to butcher deer carcasses—see what good schooling I'd had? They'd even taught me that sort of thing. We ate reindeer too. But the greatest wealth of those lands is fish—sturgeon, grayling, whitefish, muksun. They have so much of it you just can't imagine. Never in my life have I eaten better fish. Muksun has such delicious flesh that you can serve it up without cooking it and eat it with a spoon.

In that year I toured twenty-two posts. Sometimes they took my advice, sometimes they didn't—you know what the attitude to food is like in the army. But it was one of the finest adventures I've ever had. It was there that I first felt I really did want to be a chef, that it was my path in life, and that I liked it. I realized this in very prosaic circumstances. We could build greenhouses, and we could freeze blueberries, but sooner or later the severe northern winter would start to make itself felt. We had sacks full of carrots, beets, and potatoes, but they'd freeze, and then they tasted awful. The cooks before me had simply poured water over them and served them up to the soldiers. After all, a soldier will eat anything.

But I didn't want to do that. I took those potatoes, peeled them, sliced them, and soaked them in milk overnight. The next day I smeared butter on top and put them into the dukhovka [a kind of stove] so they'd bake nicely. And once they had, I broke some eggs on the surface and served the gratin to my comrades.

They all started asking where I'd gotten fresh potatoes from—after all, no ships had come in. "They're not fresh," I replied. "It's just that the cook prepared them properly for you."

They looked at me, at first in disbelief and then in admiration. And that was the first time I ever felt I could be a chef.

4.

I came home from the army, and at the Praga restaurant they received me with open arms. But it was clear to everyone that I wouldn't be there for long, and that I'd be going to work at the Kremlin.

To everyone except me, that is, because I didn't think much of myself as a chef.

Even so, it really did happen. It turned out that Alexander Fedorovich, the uncle of one of my teachers, was made the Kremlin's food manager—I couldn't possibly have expected that one day I would replace him in that post. He asked her if she had any capable graduates, and she named me—it was rare for anyone to graduate with nothing but top grades, but I'd managed to do it. So Alexander Fedorovich invited me in for a conversation.

"Do you have a wife, young man?" he asked.

"No," I replied. "But I have a girlfriend."

"After two years here you'll get a nice apartment. It'll be perfect if you want to get married."

In those days you waited far longer than that for an apartment, so it was a serious reason to accept. I didn't think about it for long.

But before I started the job, I had to wait two months until the secret services had vetted me properly. I filled out a questionnaire, and then they checked to see if I was telling the truth. I had a problem, which was what to write about my father, who had been in jail, but someone suggested I put that I didn't know him and wasn't in touch with him. Apart from that, I had to say if anyone in my family had been repressed in the Stalinist era, if anyone had been a German POW during the Great Patriotic War, or if anyone lived abroad.

Luckily in my case there was no issue with any of it.

I took the opportunity to ask Mom and Grandpa a few things, and it turned out that my forebears on their side of the family had been very rich; they had traded in food on a grand scale, and even had their own barges. My great-great-grandfather's house stands in the city of Skopin to this day, and it's now the local history museum. All this greatly interested me—as I've already told you, I adored and still adore history.

But the real elite were the family of my father, whom I didn't know. They turned out to be direct descendants of Alexander Danilovich Menshikov, who was Peter the Great's right-hand man.

Luckily at the Kremlin, either they didn't check quite so far back or they weren't bothered. I got the job.

When I arrived I was still a child. And the Kremlin kitchen has always been a place with unusual personalities. There were people still working there who had cooked during the Great Patriotic War, people who remembered Stalin and Khrushchev, people who had seen and experienced a great deal in that kitchen.

But no life story can compare with that of Timofeyevich. I only ever saw him once, but I'll never forget his face or his slightly stooping figure. Timofeyevich was a legend because he was born at the Kremlin, and in the days of the tsar. Behind the Kremlin walls, on the site where the State Kremlin Palace now stands, there was once a large complex of churches. Timofeyevich's father was a deacon in one of them, and his mother washed the dishes in one of the kitchens. In those days the servants lived right inside the Kremlin, so he was born there. As a small boy he came to help his mother at work, so the chefs taught him to cook. And there he remained. He survived the revolution and he survived the war, cooking the whole time. He only moved out of the Kremlin in the 1940s, because at that time no one could live there, but the management gave him an apartment right beside it. He used to walk home.

My good friend Zhenya Grishin once cooked crayfish with him for a banquet for Russian moviemakers. It was some sort of important occasion because there were five hundred of them, so several thousand of those crayfish were needed. They were still cooking them late at night when at some point Timofeyevich glanced at his watch and said: "Zhenya, go home or you'll miss the last subway. I'll finish off these crayfish for both of us."

So Zhenya went home. Meanwhile, Timofeyevich finished cooking the crayfish, turned off the oven, and . . . died. In the morning they found him by the oven. Like a real chef, first he'd finished the job. The man who was born at the Kremlin died at the Kremlin.

5.

To start with, I worked in the so-called spetskukhnia ["special kitchen"], where we provided the service for Kremlin receptions. We cooked a lot of food for very large numbers of people—there could be as many as a thousand guests. Once I'd finished my work, I'd seek out someone who needed help. My colleagues were very pleased to have my assistance, and by offering it I learned a great deal from them.

I can't say I had a particular guru in those days. I'd learn a bit by watching one chef, and a bit more by watching someone else. I became familiar with more and more interesting recipes. For instance, in the confectionery department we made bite-sized pierogi. That was one of the showpieces of Kremlin cuisine: hundreds of tiny handmade pierogi. It made a great impression on the guests, because you don't have to be an expert cook to notice how hard they are to make, and there were vast numbers of them at the receptions.

We also made rasstegai, which are like pierogi, but stuffed with fish in sweet pastry. They had three little holes in them, and after they were baked, crispy pastry, like for making angel wings, was braided on top. It looked beautiful, but it took so much effort and precision that what can I say? For three years I couldn't do it, until finally something clicked into place and I got the knack.

I learned all sorts of culinary tricks. Take borscht. It was always made the day before the reception, because it could keep for a few days without going bad. Except that after twenty-four hours, it loses its color. So we made a special dye: you grate a beet, pour water over it, add lemon juice, and boil it. If you add it to the borscht, the color returns instantly.

The most interesting times were when the leaders of important countries came. The Polish first secretary Edward Gierek was very fond of me. He always brought gifts specially for me, not just something they'd put on the plane in Warsaw. One time he brought me a handmade shirt from somewhere near Kraków, exactly the right size. I wanted to thank him, so I learned to make bigos. But he said to me: "Viktor Borisovich, I have Polish food every day of the week in Warsaw. Here I'd like to eat your food."

So we had an agreement that whenever he came, his bodyguard would come to see me and say: "The boss would like chicken Kiev." Or sturgeon "monastery style." Or chicken tabaka. And then I'd quickly make him whatever he fancied.

I remember that he loved wieners. He could eat four of five of them for breakfast. At the Mikoyan Meat Processing Plant, the biggest in the USSR, we had a whole production line that made gourmet wieners specially for the Kremlin. They were truly delicious, and we used to cook them for breakfast with peas.

When Gierek was due to visit, a few days in advance my boss would say to me: "Oh, that *Pole of yours* is going to be here." The rule was that if you worked well with one of the foreign leaders, and if they liked your cooking, you were assigned to them for good. And I did work for Gierek many times.

The only food item the Poles brought with them were sausages. I don't know how they're made, but I've never eaten such good sausages as in Poland. I once told Gierek that, and they started bringing good Polish sausages not just for me but for the official meetings too.

So I have pleasant memories of my relationship with Gierek. Though I never once worked for his successor, Wojciech Jaruzelski, because another chef was responsible for him.

6.

As I was generally popular at work and had a good reputation, after a year or two I was made an offer to become a lichnik. What's that? It's a personal cook for one of the country's VIPs. The division of labor at the Kremlin, as in many other kitchens around the world, was that one presidential kitchen chose the menu and cooked for all the guests at a reception. But a second kitchen cooked for the country's leader and the VIPs, and it was manned by the lichniki, or personal chefs. These were highly trusted people; in Russia they were employed directly by the KGB and vetted in every possible way. Not even the Kremlin employees were allowed to enter their kitchen, because the

head of state's food was one of the most strictly guarded secrets. No one should know the system involved or the identity
of the lichniki. It was all to do with security.

Being a lichnik was a highly prestigious role for a cook. It
meant you cooked superbly and they trusted you. But luckily,
although I was still young, I knew enough to steer clear of becoming a lichnik. Why was that? In the first place, we wouldn't
be having this conversation now. For the rest of his life, everything a personal chef does has to remain confidential, and he's
not allowed to talk about it.

Second, for the rest of his life he's banned from leaving the
country.

Third and finally, the lichnik has a firm position as long as his
boss is in power. After that he can't work at the Kremlin anymore and is sent off to other tasks. Why is that? I don't know.
Someone decided that would be better for security. I knew all
the lichniki. I've also met people who cooked for former general
secretaries—one of them even became my friend and mentor.
But allow me to approach all this as a historian, Witold, chrono-
logically.

So although I didn't become a lichnik, I often worked for
Leonid Ilyich Brezhnev, both at the Kremlin and at his private
dacha. It was the stagnation period, when Brezhnev was increasingly unwell and was the target of many jokes. Well, that's
the truth—the Kremlin was ruled by old men in those days.
And they may have slept through the moment when it was high
time to introduce reform.

But I only knew them from the culinary side, which gave me
no cause for complaint. They ate modestly; they had no unusual tastes. At the dacha in Zarechye, where Brezhnev lived,

his wife, Viktoria Petrovna, was in charge. She cooked very well herself. She liked to cook, and she didn't want to give it up just because her husband was the head of state. She had a housekeeper, but they cooked together. For example, she used to make excellent vareniki with walnut stuffing—I wouldn't know how to make those. And they always had blackcurrant liqueur, made by the lady of the house. They served it to special guests.

After every large reception—and receptions were held at the dacha for as many as a hundred people—Viktoria Petrovna would come down to the basement, where the kitchen was, to thank us. Several times Brezhnev himself came too—apparently in the past he always had, but by the time I started work he was old and sickly. He was very friendly, shaking hands with everyone and saying thank you. We'd each drink a glass of the famous liqueur, then we'd tidy up and cars would drive us back to Moscow.

The receptions in Brezhnev's day were very lavish—the tables groaned with food, and it was always the best food. Can you imagine how we cooked, if all the best chefs were brought in to the Kremlin from throughout the country? At the time we probably had the best professional kitchen in the world.

Although there were often hundreds of people at the receptions, only a few of them were under strict protection. The general secretary of the Central Committee of the Communist Party, the premier, the minister of defense, and seven others. That was the so-called First Table—they each had their own lichnik and a separate kitchen under KGB supervision. They even had their own supply chains and their own separate farms, and no one was allowed to know where their supplies were from.

In the spetskukhnya, we cooked for everyone else.

The First Table even had their own special waiters, highly trusted people. Brezhnev always wanted the Kalinichenko brothers, Vasily and Nikolai, from my former restaurant, the Praga, to work for him at the receptions. He was constantly calling from the Kremlin to ask for them. They were the kind of waiters you don't come across nowadays. They had both been in the profession since the end of the war, almost forty years. In Moscow in those days there was a special school for waiters, which lasted two years. A good waiter shouldn't tell you any personal stories, share his private life, or draw attention to himself at all. He should approach you, bow, and remain in the shadows but be at your beck and call. I was once witness to a conversation between President Vladimir Putin and former president of Ukraine Viktor Yanukovych. At some point Putin dropped his napkin and automatically, without breaking off the conversation, leaned down to pick it up. But the napkin wasn't there anymore.

Because there was a good waiter.

The Kremlin dining tables have a whole history of their own. We had an entire school of food and table decoration—dozens of people worked at it. The knowledge that had accumulated since the days of the tsars reached its peak under Brezhnev. There'd be beautifully decorated sturgeons on those tables, silver-plated bowls filled with black and red caviar, Kamchatka crab salad, and all sorts of meats and fish.

But in fact two general secretaries in a row, Khrushchev and Brezhnev, were from villages or small towns in Ukraine. Where would they have seen sturgeon in the countryside? Or caviar, or Kamchatka crab? They weren't accustomed to these dishes, and if you're expected to eat things like that every day of the week, they don't taste good at all!

And many times I witnessed a situation where there'd be a reception for six hundred, the tables piled high with food, and each place set with knives and forks. But Brezhnev would be sitting there annoyed, scraping one of his eight forks across the plate. Because there was nothing there for him! Absolutely nothing on the table that he'd have liked or wanted to eat.

Before this sort of reception, the lichniki would come to us to go over the menu and see what we'd be cooking. One time one of them came along, looked at Brezhnev, and said: "He won't eat anything. But as soon as the reception ends, he'll call and ask for fried potatoes. With sausages or soured milk."

And so it was. The reception would end, Brezhnev would be driven home, and the first thing he'd do would be to call the chef to ask for fried potatoes with soured milk. Or herring, or pickled cabbage, depending on his mood. I saw it several times myself after receptions at his villa. The guests would leave and Brezhnev would call and say, "Fry me some potatoes."

That man was the leader of the biggest country in the world. He could have had any food he wanted—caviar, sturgeon; he could have had a bear shot the next day or a muksun fetched and baked—but all he wanted was a few potatoes with a drop of soured milk. And a shot of vodka.

They had an interesting way of preparing soured milk for him. They baked it in clay pots at a temperature of 60 or 70 degrees [Celsius, between 140 and 160 degrees Fahrenheit], until it went brown on top. Brezhnev's lichnik had to go to Ukraine specially to learn this method from some old women. But that was the only food-related quirk of the man who ruled one fifth of the Earth's surface. Not too demanding, wouldn't you agree?

7.

If Brezhnev had a passion, it wasn't fine dining but hunting. Sometimes he went to the Białowieża Forest, where there was a small hunting lodge. But he usually went to Zavidovo, just outside Moscow. There's a stream there, a nice nature reserve, and so much wild game that the local lake is even named Kabanovy Lake, meaning "Wild Boar Lake."

Whenever Brezhnev went hunting, we knew there'd be game meat to cook. He never came back empty-handed. His bodyguards said that when they counted up the game at the end of the hunt, he always parceled it out: take this boar to the premier, this one to the head of the trade unions, and this one home for me. He loved goulash made with wild boar and mushrooms.

He sometimes went hunting alone, with no one but his bodyguards and a forester, but occasionally he took half the Politburo with him. A chef was needed to cook for them while they hunted. They usually made wild boar or venison goulash, but they brought the meat with them from the Kremlin, because there was too little time at the hunt. I went on one or two of these hunting trips, and I cooked that goulash too. If Brezhnev wanted to show someone his respect, he cooked them a hunter's *kulish* himself—it's a soup made of millet with wild game meat.

People remember him as an old man festooned with medals; there were jokes about having to use a crane to seat him on the tribune. But he was good to us chefs—we saw him as a friendly, modest, jovial man.

MENU

◇◇◇

Ukha

The recipes and the ones that follow were given to the author by Viktor Belyaev.

3 potatoes

½ carrot

1 parsnip

2 onions

1¼ pounds (0.5 kg) cod

1¼ pounds (0.5 kg) halibut

1¼ pounds (0.5 kg) sea perch

4 bay leaves

2 teaspoons salt

Black pepper, to taste

1 leek

2 tablespoons dill

4 or 5 saffron strands

4 lemon slices

Cut the potatoes, carrot, and parsnip into strips and finely dice the onions. Cut the cod, halibut, and perch into large chunks. In a large pot, bring 8 cups (2 L) of water to a boil, then add the cut vegetables. Reduce the heat to medium and cook for 10 to 15 minutes, until the potatoes are parboiled. Add the bay leaves, salt, and pepper and cook for another 3 minutes.

Add the fish and the leek and cook for another 10 minutes.

Toward the end of the 10 minutes, add 1 tablespoon of the dill and the saffron. Just before serving, add the lemon slices and the remaining tablespoon of dill.

MENU
◇◇◇

Lamb Rissoles with Cheese

10½ ounces (300 g) lamb
1 egg
1 or 2 garlic cloves, crushed
3½ ounces (100 g) white bread cubes, soaked in water
Salt and black pepper
2 tablespoons grated cheese, such as mozzarella

Mince the lamb and place it in a large bowl. Add the egg, garlic, bread, and salt and pepper. Stir well to combine and then pass the mixture through a meat grinder.

Mold the resulting mince to form an even number of rissoles. Sprinkle half of them with cheese, then top these with the remaining rissoles to hide the cheese.

Heat a frying pan, and fry the rissoles until soft.

MENU
◇◇◇
Sea Breeze Layer Cake

1¼ pounds (0.5 kg) onions
Olive oil, for frying and soaking
2¼ pounds (1 kg) pollack
Salt and black pepper
1 can seaweed
4 boiled eggs, finely chopped
1 cup plus 2 tablespoons (250 g) mayonnaise
1 bunch fresh parsley

Slice the onions into large rings. Heat a frying pan, then add enough oil to coat the pan. Fry the onion rings until golden. Remove the pan from the heat, douse the onions in oil, and set aside for at least 2 hours.

Move the onion rings to a mixing bowl. Reheat the oil-filled pan over low heat, then place the fish in the pan along with the salt and pepper and cook gently for 15 minutes, or until softened. Remove the fish to the bowl with the onions and mix well to combine. Add a coating of mayonnaise on top.

Now deal with the seaweed. Mix it carefully with the finely chopped boiled eggs and place on top, as the next layer. Once again, coat it all in mayonnaise.

In a glass serving bowl, place a layer of the fish-and-onion mixture. Spread about 3 tablespoons (40 g) of the mayonnaise on top.

Repeat with more fish-and-onion mixture and more mayonnaise, making five layers. Add one more layer of fish. For the sixth and final mayonnaise layer, chop the parsley and mix it with the remaining mayonnaise, then decorate the top of the layer cake with it.

Place the bowl in the refrigerator for at least 3 hours to allow the flavors to infuse.

OVERHEARD IN THE KITCHEN

Viktor Belyaev is likely to have the best memories of Brezhnev— it was in Brezhnev's day that the Kremlin's chefs were the most highly appreciated, the tables featured the most lavish spreads, and the policy of "overawing with food" was at its peak in the entire history of the USSR.

Other employees from the Kremlin's kitchen speak of it the same way Viktor does. Longtime senior-ranking chef Alevtina Georgiyevna Kerina, a KGB junior officer, recalled how during a visit to the United States she cooked wild boar steaks stuffed with foie gras, and how with other cooks she prepared a culinary showstopper—pheasant decorated with its own feathers. "We roasted the bird, made it a pedestal out of bread, then stuck its feathers in one by one. The guests at the reception took them all as mementos," she said many years later.

Kerina also made "fish tanks" for these banquets: she'd pour some thick stock into a transparent dish; make water lilies, algae, and crayfish out of lettuce and vegetables; and place at the bottom a large cooked sturgeon decorated with shrimp, olives, and lemon slices.

To serve the famous Russian caviar at a reception in Washington, DC, the chefs put up a special tower-shaped stand, which they surrounded with fresh flowers and then topped with a large bowl full of caviar, as it was once presented at the Kremlin.

Beautiful? For sure. The problem was that the Soviet Union couldn't afford those Kremlin luxuries anymore. The sturgeons, the caviar, the Kamchatka crabs, even the Olivier salad served all over Russia exceeded the country's resources—as did the entire Soviet arms industry, which consumed the lion's share of the nations's assets, and the equally costly space exploration industry. Although both programs competed to be the world's greatest, they were greatly underfunded.

There is probably no better example of how the Moscow overlords wasted money than the Kremlin banquets. Especially because they took place during periods when ordinary citizens of the USSR could sense an imminent crisis. There are reasons why Brezhnev's era is known as the age of stagnation. The decline of his power came at a time when Soviet people were increasingly faced with empty store shelves, and so-called sausage trains started traveling to Moscow: crowds of people poured into the capital from the provinces to buy food and essential goods, because there was next to nothing in the stores where they lived.

Brezhnev also made a foreign policy mistake that cost the

Soviet Union a great deal of money and a lot of prestige. The campaign to provide "fraternal aid" to Afghanistan, which was supposed to involve replacing one group of communists with another that was more obedient to Moscow, developed into a bloody ten-year war against the mujahideen.

Like many events in the history of the Soviet Union, this intervention began on a culinary note: the then president Hafizullah Amin was to be poisoned by the KGB. The operation was planned precisely: since Amin didn't trust his compatriots, he had a Russian chef. Several months before the planned attack, the Soviets replaced him with a secret agent.

The poisoning of Amin was to take place on December 27, 1979. Directly afterward, the Soviet special unit Alpha was to enter his palace and replace him with Babrak Karmal, Brezhnev's chosen man. Everything went according to plan, but for some reason the poison didn't have much of an effect on Amin—perhaps because he ate rather modestly. What's more, when he started to feel unwell, he asked for help from the Soviet doctors at the embassy near his palace. They were not aware of the KGB's plans, and they saved his life.

Nevertheless, several hours later the Alpha unit launched its raid on the palace. Having only just escaped death by poison, this time Amin was shot dead. Two hundred of his bodyguards also were killed, as was his five-year-old son.

Thus began the ten-year war that brought the Afghans massive destruction and a death toll of more than a million. On the Soviet side, tens of thousands of soldiers were killed.

XI

The Cook from the Afghan War

1.

One day my husband, Valentin Dmitrievich, came home from work, made a cup of tea, asked me to sit down, and said he had a question for me. At work he'd received an offer to fly to Afghanistan. He wasn't in the military but was a civilian employee of a factory where they repaired airplanes. But that's irrelevant, because at the time no one said there was a war in Afghanistan, just "peaceful intervention." We were helping the fraternal Afghan nation, which was in trouble. That was all.

I'll tell you something, Witold. At the time I was almost forty, and it's embarrassing to admit it, but until then I believed everything they said on television. Fraternal intervention? That meant fra-

Nina Karpovna

ternal intervention. If there was a war, Brezhnev would have told us, right? "We're helping"? That means we're helping—why on earth would we harm the poor Afghans in any way?

I took everything on TV at face value, every bit of nonsense. Whatever they said, I believed it was true. I had two sons, one of whom had just gone to a military academy while the other had recently graduated from high school, and I was always telling them: "A friend might cheat you; even I might at times. But the Party will never cheat you."

That's how I was. At my job I was a model worker. Head of the shoemakers' guild and chairwoman of the Party cell at the footwear plant in Kubinka. It was a large factory, and they chose me, although I was an ordinary shoemaker, to be Party chairwoman. By day I glued shoes together with the other cobblers, and in the afternoons I went to meetings with the managers. Always out ahead, always doing things for others. If I found a scrap of paper somewhere at the plant, I'd pick it up and dutifully put it in the trash bin; if any of my shoemakers had problems in their personal lives, they knew they could come to me for help at any time of the day or night. And always, whatever I was told to do, I did it.

It was only Afghanistan that changed things. For me it was a real school of life; everything I know about life I learned in Afghanistan. The good. And the bad too.

But one thing at a time.

My husband asked me what he should do. They were offering him good money: a salary, a bonus, and a supplement for working abroad. We'd never been rolling in it, but our sons had just finished school, and they were going to need support. But on the other hand—while it may have been fraternal intervention—there was some shooting. What if it was dangerous to go there?

If he didn't know what to do, he always asked me. All the strategic decisions in our house were on my shoulders, and they still are to this day. Perhaps he was hoping I'd knock the idea of Afghanistan out of his head, and then he'd be able to return to work and say: "I'd go, but my wife won't let me. You know, you understand, it's not possible."

And he was extremely surprised, because without a second thought I replied, "My dear Valentin Dmitrievich, I think that's a very good idea."

I don't know why, but I never take long to make decisions. I do what I believe to be right. And at that moment, plainly I thought it right to help our Afghan brothers, or to help the Party, or both—who knows what was going on in my head? I've already told you that I swallowed all the propaganda from the TV.

My husband was amazed. But I swiftly added: "You'll go, but with the solid backbone every man needs. In other words, his wife. With me."

2.

You'd like to know something about my life, Witold? Yes, of course.

The person who mattered most to me was my grandmother Olga Nikolayevna. Her father, my great-grandfather, was descended from the Don Cossacks and was an officer in the imperial army, so when the Bolsheviks came to power the whole family had to flee. From Odessa, where they lived, they went all the way to the city of Harbin in China, because that was the place of refuge for thousands of Whites—in other words, soldiers and officers who opposed the Red communists. They were going to organize an army there that would help them return to power. Nothing came of it, and on top of that both my grandmother's parents died in the course of their wandering. So at the age of twelve, my grandmother had to get a job. And the only work she could find as a child was to be a cook. She went from place to place until finally she was employed by one of the White generals. I only know his surname: Nechayev.*

Look at that, Witold—for years it never occurred to me that there were any cooks in my family, but now that I'm telling you this story, I can see that there was one. And it was the person who meant the most to me.

It was there, working for the general, that she was spotted by my grandfather Karp Alexandrovich. He was an officer who used to meet up with the general to conspire. Grandma brought them some food, and my grandfather fell for her—it was love at first sight. Soon after, he proposed and was accepted, and the general gave his consent for Grandpa to take Grandma away from him. Their first son, Sasha, was born in China, when Grandma was only seventeen.

They came back to the Soviet Union in the early 1930s when Stalin announced an amnesty for the Whites. But for the rest of his life my grandfather was blacklisted by the communists. The Whites weren't allowed to settle in large cities and had no

*This is probably Konstantin Petrovich Nechayev, who was born in 1883 in Łódź and died in 1946 in Chita.

chance of a career in the army, so first my grandparents ended up near Pskov, where my grandfather was a land surveyor and my grandmother took care of the four children they'd had in the meantime, and then later my grandfather was invited to Kubinka. He designed the railroad that runs around Moscow. Afterward the railroad workers moved on, but my grandparents stayed put. I still live in Kubinka today.

The only job my grandfather could get was in the forest. So he became a forester. They lived in peace; they had no complaints.

Grandma was tiny, thin as a rake, and loved to bits. Now, as we're talking, I'm remembering the delicious pierogi she made, the vareniki, pelmeni, and koulibiak. With tvorog [similar to curd cheese], blueberries, and everything else we could get there, near the forest. Later on, in Afghanistan, the boys were surprised that I knew how to whip up delicious pierogi or koulibiak for them out of nothing. And I knew it all from Grandma. You have to remove the bones from the fish and bake it separately, but be careful not to lose its juices. You fry an onion and some carrots, then wrap it all in French pastry and bake together.

Well, here I am telling you my entire family history—soon I'll be back to the Rurik dynasty. But you want to know about Afghanistan, not the card games my dear departed grandmother used to play.

So one thing at a time.

When I said I'd go with him, my husband wasn't entirely surprised. He knew that once I'd made a decision, there was no point in arguing. Though if he'd known what we were signing up for, I'm sure he'd have lain down in the doorway and not let us go, or, better yet, he wouldn't have brought up the subject in the first place.

But neither of us knew. So he just said in that case, the next day he'd give our answer to the collective. And that was that. We didn't discuss it any further.

Two months later, in January 1981, we boarded the plane. The boys, our sons, stayed at home on their own. I went to Afghanistan like a village granny moving to the city. I took an oil lamp, because we'd been told it was a poor country and there was no electricity. I took a small plastic tub, the kind you'd use to bathe a baby, and I planned to do the laundry in it. They warned us in advance that life there would be spartan. We'd be living in camping conditions, the only difference being that at a campsite there's no shooting. I even took a barrel of pickled gherkins, because no Russian should ever leave home without pickled gherkins. I also had twenty loaves of bread that we took as gifts, because there was no black bread there, and everyone was asking for good Moscow bread. Anyone with whom we wanted to be on good terms, including my husband's superiors, got a loaf from us.

I had cooking pots, frying pans, knives, and forks with me— because they don't use them in Afghanistan. We took everything that might come in handy.

For the first few weeks, my husband went to work every day from early in the morning to late at night, repairing airplanes. Meanwhile, I almost went out of my mind. I wasn't allowed to go outside, or to stand by the window, or to talk to anyone. Nothing was allowed. We were some of the last to arrive at the air base in Bagram, and there were no empty apartments left at the settlement where the Russians lived. So they put us up in a house that was still being built; we were the only people living there. It was a fifteen-minute walk to the nearest Russians, but we could only visit them under escort, with special permission.

All around our building lived Afghans: bearded, dirty, dressed in rags. While I was left at home, there were always several of them standing outside the block, staring into the windows. And I was afraid of them—I didn't know if they were just looking, or if they wanted to come back with their pals and throw a bomb at me.

Although to be honest, most of them were just looking. For them, seeing an uncovered female face, even that of a forty-year-old, was a major event. So most of the time I didn't sit just indoors but in semidarkness, with the curtains closed so they couldn't come up to the windows and stare.

We had two floors in the house, including a thirty-meter terrace on the first. A stone staircase led to the second floor, where there was a dining room, a bedroom, a kitchen, and a small room for a child—if anyone came with a child, that is. I see the suspicious look on your face, Witold. I'll say it again: no one thought they were going to a war zone—maybe the soldiers, especially the officers, knew what they were getting into, but none of the civilians knew. People really did think it was fraternal intervention; in fact, none of my acquaintances had brought a child, but several times children came to visit them. I think the strategists imagined it like this: "If you can take your wife there, if your children can visit, there's nothing to be afraid of, right?" On the same principle they told the children to walk in the May Day parade after the disaster at Chernobyl.

Bagram was a large base, the biggest airfield in Afghanistan.

Mainly airmen were stationed there, but there were tank crews too, and Katyushas were launched from there. Day and night we heard those Katyushas singing away, and when they started firing it was as bright as in the daytime. The earth shook. They'd do some firing at the Afghans, then move on.

So for the first few weeks I spent my time alone in the apartment with my baby bath and my oil lamp, and I thought I was going to lose my mind. All my life I've been very active—I've never sat still for a moment. At the age of fifteen I went to college, and ever since I've always been part of a collective, always with other people. And now I couldn't even buy a newspaper to have something to read.

To avoid going crazy, every day I washed the windows. The dust there is awful—there's sand blowing in all the time. But I'd spend a few minutes washing a window, then look down, and there the Afghans would be, staring at me. So I'd hide. And so it went, over and over again. Eventually the workday would end, my husband would come home, we'd talk awhile, and soon afterward the sun would set and we'd go to bed, because there was nothing to do.

Until one day our unit had a holiday celebration, and we were invited. The commanding officer noticed that several of the civilians, including my husband, had come with their wives. He came up and introduced himself. "I'm Andrei Yosifovich. What do you do, madam?"

"We all do whatever we can, Commander," I replied. "One sews, another knits, and I wash the windows five times a day while going crazy with boredom."

"What's your profession?" he asked.

"I'm a shoemaker."

"Then please come and see me," he said. "I have a job for you."

"But doing what?" I asked, very surprised. "Making shoes? What an idea! You'll have two new pairs each week."

The commander laughed and said: "I have standard-issue army boots—my adjutant takes care of them. You can be useful in the kitchen."

I was dumbstruck. I wasn't expecting that. I told him there was army technology in the kitchen—it was full of things I was clueless about. "I'm afraid," I said. "You'll give me a job, I'll end up doing something the wrong way, then they'll throw me out and shoot you."

To which the commander replied, quite seriously now, that currently the soldiers were doing the cooking. And that, as usual with men, they weren't putting their hearts into it. They kept adding too much salt or burning things.

"We need food like Mama makes," he said. "We need soup, then a main course, and compote for dessert—maybe some kissel too, or jelly with fruit—not just some garbage out of a can. Because if the food in the canteen isn't right for the soldiers, they don't come to it and they don't integrate. Morale drops. Food is very important in the army."

I made another wisecrack, while the other women didn't say a word. But the commander took me aside and said: "Nina Karpovna, I send people to their deaths every day here. Many of them don't come back. In this tough situation, I'd like them to have good food at least."

So how was I to answer that, Witold? The next day I put on an apron and went to the canteen.

3.

It was probably only during that conversation with the commander that it finally got through to me that perhaps this wasn't entirely fraternal intervention. So far, although I'd had to hide, I'd felt relatively safe. Bagram was within territory controlled by our troops. And my husband hadn't told me about the airmen who never came back from action. Maybe he didn't know? Or perhaps he didn't want to worry me? I don't know. But planes took off from our base to shell *dushmani* positions—we called the Afghans *dushmani*, which in their language means "enemies." They called us *mushaveri*, which in their language means "advisers." The helicopters that fired at them were from our base, as were the fighter planes. Several times the dushmani tried to capture the capital. If they had succeeded, they'd have cut off the entire Russian army from its supplies of weapons and food.

But I knew none of this yet. The day after my conversation with the commander I went to work, and right away—to stick with military terminology—I was at the front. I was rather nervous, first about how they'd receive me, because I'd never worked in a kitchen before, and second because there's a difference between cooking at home for a family and in a field kitchen for five hundred people. I had never made three hundred liters of soup or cooked a huge vat of potatoes, and I had no idea how much of what to provide, how much seasoning to add, nothing. Of course we had standard rules written down, and we had a large book of recipes for military cooking. But the commander had taken me on for the purpose of *not* cooking according to that book!

It was enough to drive you around the bend.

But never mind. I got there and shook hands with the head of the kitchen, Andrei Yevgenievich, and with the soldiers who'd been working there so far. In all there were five of us; on some days two of the wives of other civilian advisers came too, seven people altogether. They showed me where the various knives were, and the pots, the milk, the flour, the salt, tomatoes, and peppers. And we got to work. We made breakfast. And when the soldiers came along, I thought they should know who was cooking for them. So I went out and said: "Boys, I'm your new cook—my name's Nina. If anything's wrong, don't hit or shoot, just speak up. Everyone makes mistakes, but I'm going to try my best to make sure there are as few as possible." I looked around the room. I was twice as old as most of them. There was no one my age, and let me remind you, I was just coming up on forty.

When I went back into the kitchen, all the soldiers working there had eyes as large as saucers. They'd been doing the job for several months, but it hadn't occurred to any of them to show themselves to the guys they were cooking for. And here was an old gal from Kubinka ruling the roost. They didn't like that one bit, they most certainly did not.

But the soldiers we were feeding very quickly found their way into my heart. And I began to take care of them. We're to serve salad? Then let each man have a tomato with a smiley face made out of a radish. Let him feel like someone cares about him, like someone took the trouble, like someone's making an effort for him. That's what cooking is all about, isn't it? To make a person feel like someone cares about them.

The first time I mentioned those tomatoes to my colleagues

in the kitchen, they almost fell off their chairs. But Andrei Yevgenievich told them to do as I said. He knew I had the commander's support, and he didn't want to fall afoul of him. So there they sat, those great big lads, cutting smiles out of radishes.

When I think back today, Witold, I can hardly believe it. There was war all around us, and every so often someone was killed. The Afghans were scheming how to break into our base. And there we sat, cutting out radish smiles.

When they saw that there was a woman their mothers' age in the kitchen, the soldiers started getting attached to me. They'd come around as if for extra helpings or for more bread, but I could tell that they actually wanted to chat. The boys who had girlfriends would show me their photos, but in fact half of them didn't have a girlfriend. That was probably the saddest thing of all: the boys who had no one to miss.

One fine day along came Lyosha, for whom I would come to shed many a tear. He was eighteen, and he'd come to Afghanistan from a village near Baikal, straight out of school. He knew nothing about life yet, but just before flying out he'd kissed a girl at a village party, and he was counting on her to write to him. He was a textbook Russian, with a cloud of fair hair and blue eyes. He had a slight lisp, but that just added to his charm. He came to the kitchen one day with some silly excuse, and very soon he began to confide in me.

He reminded me of my younger son, who was the same age. My heart began to pound as soon as it occurred to me that my son could end up in this shit heap too, among these explosions, in this place where you could meet your death around every corner.

This boy Lyosha kept pouring his heart out. He talked about himself, but mainly about the girl. While doing so he'd help peel the potatoes and help the waitresses clear the tables—it was plain to see his parents had raised him for the world, not just for themselves. It was hard not to like him.

Our soldiers had a superstition that if anyone got a bay leaf in his soup, he'd get a letter. It meant a great deal to them, because the letters were often from their sweethearts. So the girls in the kitchen and I agreed that one day I'd toss two bay leaves in the soup, and they'd make sure Lyosha got one. If only you could have seen how happy he was, Witold! He was jumping for joy. He was as pleased as if he'd already received the letter, and not just one but a whole stack of them.

But later on, after lunch, something was bugging him, because he came to me in the kitchen and asked: "Nina Karpovna, you didn't put that leaf in my soup, did you?"

I tore into him. I said he must have no idea how hard we worked in the kitchen if he thought I had time to plant bay leaves in somebody's soup.

"Who do you think you are, Lyosha, for me to rope half the kitchen into making sure you get a bay leaf in your soup?"

It worked splendidly. Lyosha was on cloud nine, telling everyone that Nina Karpovna definitely hadn't put that bay leaf in his soup, that she'd slapped him down when he asked, and that soon he'd get a letter from the girl he'd kissed at the party. And when I saw how much it meant to him, I started asking about other soldiers who were feeling down. I did it discreetly. And as soon as I found out that someone had the blues, was refusing to leave his room or had some problems at home, then—*bang*! He'd get a bay leaf. It was very important for them, because they were all badly missing whomever they'd left at home: their wives or girlfriends, their children, their parents.

So I'd say to the waitresses, "If there's something wrong, if someone's sad, tell me, and I'll try to cheer them up." And sometimes I threw in two leaves, but only when I knew the person really needed it. You can't mess with destiny too much. And during lunch I'd go around the entire canteen asking: "Was there a leaf? You see! How lucky you are! Who would you most like to get a letter from?" And they'd start telling me about those first girlfriends of theirs, their schoolroom passions, or the female friends they had a crush on.

And then the mood in the canteen became jolly. People started talking to each other. And suddenly all the soldiers who hadn't shown up before started coming in for meals.

One day I heard the soldiers calling me "Mama." Mama Nina. Lyosha confirmed it. "Nina Karpovna," he said, "nobody in the unit calls you anything else. They all call you Mama."

Words can't express how moved I was by that, Witold. I've already told you I had sons the same age as those boys. If they were getting killed out there, far from home, I'd at least try to be a substitute mother for them.

So I'd do my best to talk to those children. Whenever time allowed, I'd come out during lunch and ask: "Well, kids, do you like the lunch? Is everything okay?"

And they'd shout back in unison, "Everything's okay, Mama Nina!"

And just like a mother, I'd give them second helpings. And nag my military cooks into cutting smiley faces out of radishes.

4.

All the products we used for cooking were brought to us twice a week from Russia by a large plane: flour, fresh and pickled vegetables, canned potatoes, cucumbers, cabbage, tomatoes, rusks, onions, carrots, and buckwheat. We were forbidden to buy anything from the Afghans—the commanders thought they might try to poison us.

One time, the dushmani shot down our supply plane. But for that sort of situation, we had storerooms where we kept food. In theory it should have been enough for a month of inter-rupted supplies. In practice I don't know if it would have lasted a week.

The work was divided into three shifts, with three people working each one. Those on the first shift had to work in the middle of the night, because they prepared breakfast and lunch simultaneously. It was impossible to do anything the day be-fore, because in the Afghan heat the food could go bad, and that was what we feared most: poisoning the soldiers, even un-intentionally, could land you in court.

Our group served three canteens: one for the pilots, one for technical workers—the engineers and advisers, such as my husband—and one for the ordinary soldiers.

We always made three appetizers. One was meant to be savory—fermented shchi [cabbage soup], for instance; one lighter—Hungarian *lángos* [fried flatbread], for example; and the third was something milk based.

The pilots ate at the same time as all the other soldiers, with one exception: if they were flying out before four in the morning, when the kitchen was still closed, they were given chocolate instead of breakfast, because flying on a full stomach is bad for you, since the g-force is so great.

Did any of them eat the chocolate? They usually kept it for later, and when they went back to Russia they'd take it to their girl, especially in the 1980s, when everything started to be in short supply there.

In fact, they had breakfast when they got back from their raids. Unless they didn't come back. Because that happened too.

The soldiers had special stores where they could buy everything not included in their rations: water, because there was always a problem with it in Afghanistan; fruit juice; pens; envelopes; candy; even watches. The staff were young women, so there were always lots of people there—the boys would come in and buy a single pen just for the opportunity to chat.

Not far from the base there was also a large mobile hospital. They saved the wounded there, but that wasn't all—they also had to treat infections spread by dirty hands, for instance. The doctors couldn't always cope. When the boys were brought in from the front, the medics didn't know where to start. Our kitchen also served the patients in the hospital, so I took food there for them several times, and that, Witold, was a real apocalypse. Boys without arms or legs, wrapped in bandages, suppurating wounds. Some had been under fire, some burned, some had had mines blow up in their hands.

I found it very hard to bear. They were just young boys. I felt extremely sorry for all of them—they died over and over again.

5.

So off I went to accompany my husband to the "peaceful inter-vention" in an allied country. And ended up as a cook at war. That's a completely different situation, you'll agree. To survive, you have to learn a few rules.

First, if they're firing, you must run away as far as you can. Don't stop to think or wonder whether it's our boys shooting or theirs. Just take cover—if there's nothing to hide underneath, you must at least protect your head, even with a metal cooking pot. I learned that relatively quickly.

Second, don't trust anyone. Not the locals, because they would always try to get close, but then we'd find out they'd re-ported to the dushmani who was who and what relationships at our base were like. Not your own people either, because there too were reasons for suspicion. One might be selling the dushmani weapons—one soldier actually stole our cans of supplies and sold them. It was hard to trust anyone there. Many of those young boys were addicted to drugs—the dush-mani handed out opium and heroin for free, near the base or at the bazaars. They were relying on as many of our men as pos-sible to start taking them. So the other thing I learned was that I could only trust my husband. But even with him I preferred not to talk about everything I saw happening.

Third and finally, don't make friends with anyone. Of course I'd listen if I could and try to help, but without getting involved. During war, a person might get killed at any moment. If you take every one of those deaths to heart, you'll go home a wreck. You have no alternative; you have to find a way to protect your-self.

This last lesson was the hardest for me. And all because of Lyosha. I'll get to that.

But first I'll tell you how one of the tank crew colonels tried to shoot me, shall I?

It was my day off. That morning I got up and heard a terrible racket. I looked out the window, and there below my house a whole column of tanks had stopped. Heat was pouring from the sky, and they were standing in full sunlight; it must have been at least 100 degrees.

I grabbed a pail of the water that had been brought to us from trusted sources and went up to the tanks with it, handing it out in a mug. "Would you like some water, boys?" I asked.

At which point the commander of those tanks pointed his pistol at me and started shouting "You" this and "You" that and "Fuck off." And he shouted to his men that none of them should talk to me or go near me or he'd shoot.

So I told him to put down his popgun or he'd do himself harm. And that I was a Russian, just like him—perhaps he knew there were military advisers living here in Bagram too? He wanted me to pour the water out, to which I said that every drop of water here was like gold. And why didn't he shoot me first, if he was so very stupid? If I didn't give his soldiers water, he'd lose them to heat and dehydration.

"Are you really a Russki?" the officer asked, showing me disrespect by using a familiar form of address.

"What do I have to do? Recite a poem? Sing the national anthem?" I said. "And actually, I don't remember us agreeing to be on familiar terms. Please tell me your full name and rank, because you pointed a gun at me, comrade, and I'm not leaving it at that."

When he finally realized I wasn't joking, he lowered his gun. He gave me his full name and let me offer his soldiers water. Those boys were terribly grateful to me. They were going into action against Massoud; it was a large column, and when they finally moved off they drove for about two hours. How many of those boys never came back? It's not worth asking.

That was the big problem in that war. The generals didn't respect the officers. The officers didn't respect the soldiers. And the soldiers didn't respect anyone, neither their superiors nor one another. I'm sure you've heard about dedovshchina, or hazing. The senior soldiers beat up the junior ones, make them polish their boots, tidy their beds, and wash their underwear. Lyosha once came to see me in the kitchen with a black eye and blood pouring from his eyebrow.

"What happened to you?" I asked.

"I ran into a door frame," he said.

But I knew perfectly well that wasn't true—someone had thumped him. Maybe someone didn't like him, or maybe they beat everyone up like that, I don't know. All I said was: "If anything were to happen, remember you've got your mama here."

He didn't answer.

There was no point in going to his superiors. Everyone knew what was going on.

As for the officer who aimed his pistol at me, of course I gave his superiors his name and took a lot of trouble to make sure it reached them. I could take that sort of liberty: just like I'd been high up in the Party at my shoe factory, here too they'd immediately roped me into joining the Party organization. Every month I was summoned to a meeting in Kabul, at the Soviet embassy. The commander was obliged to provide me with transport. So once a month I had a helicopter at my disposal. Evidently within the Party they had decided there should be some diversity; since there were only military people there, and I was a Party cook—after all, Lenin had said how important cooks were—they had to take advantage of my presence.

What were the Party meetings for? To protect the morality of the Soviet citizens during their peace mission in Afghanistan. Like, everywhere. To look out and see if anyone was behaving immorally, because there were lots of men and very few women. The citizens had to be trusted, but within the limits of reason—that's what they taught us. The girls who worked there used to come for a month or two, at most six, and one had to be very strict with them to make sure they didn't go home with a bun in the oven, or the result would be plenty of broken families. Quite apart from that, many of those girls had come for that very purpose. Today the young people meet via the internet, but in those days they met at war. Where else might a girl have a chance to meet an officer or a pilot?

Whenever an affair of this kind occurred, I'd go straight to the boy and explain.

"What do you want this for?"

If he was married, the conversation was easier. "Your wife writes you letters," I'd say. "How will you go back home afterward?"

One time the boy said: "My wife doesn't write to me."

"Because you don't write to her," I replied. "Sit down and we'll write to her together."

And I dictated the whole thing to him. "For lunch I had this and that. The sausage was good, the salad less so. I miss you, I love you, I can't wait to see you."

And then? When he received an answer, he stopped getting ideas about other girls.

It was harder if the boy didn't have a wife. How was I to explain to him that he should steer clear of my waitresses? I had a method. I'd say to the girls: "If he likes you, if it's true love, it's better to wait. War is not a good time for falling in love."

But how do you dissuade a young man who sees a young girl and is simply attracted to her? Then you had to roll out the heavy cannon, to use another military term. There was one proper Rasputin; he was having an affair with one of the waitresses, and then I saw him kissing another one. I told it to him straight: "Leave my waitresses alone or I'll rip your head off."

To which he said: "So I'm supposed to come to you for permission, am I?"

And I said: "It won't hurt to ask."

"Who are you to tell them what to do?"

"I'm the deputy head of the Party cell. That's enough. If you don't want to go to the front tomorrow, don't argue with me."

Of course I never would have tried to get anyone sent to the front—I wasn't that Party minded. But I was concerned about law and order. The Party didn't want them to have love affairs? The Party knew better than I did.

I tell you, Witold, I feel silly talking about all this nowadays. Those boys really were going to their deaths, and if they weren't killed, they'd watch their friends die. Many came back without legs, without arms, addicted to drugs. Many of them never started families; they were sick or disabled for the rest of their lives. Maybe whatever the Party thought, an affair of that kind was their last chance of having a beautiful experience?

Those waitresses of mine also had complicated histories. One was an orphan from a children's home. Another was a single mother. A third had run away to Afghanistan to escape an abusive husband. What right did I have to forbid them to fall in love?

But unfortunately, that's how my mind worked in those days. The Party above all. It was stupid—enough said.

Most of the people at the base regarded me as a chekist: a secret agent, there to report on what they were saying and what the atmosphere was like. I think the commanding officer thought of me like that too, so—although I was just a cook—he always spoke to me in a very friendly way and always listened to what I had to say.

In my defense I can say that I also used my little bit of power for good. For example, one day I was waiting at the airfield to collect a parcel. On the border they checked very carefully to make sure our people didn't take anything into Russia, because at the bazaar in Afghanistan you could buy a color TV, or a video player, or brand-name jeans—in other words, much better things than at the best store in Moscow. So our political instructors had decided that the soldiers weren't allowed to import anything, or people at home would realize communism was failing. The customs officers used to go through their suitcases with a fine-tooth comb. And what did they contain? Someone might have a pair of jeans, or a pretty scarf for his mom. Someone might have a dress for his girlfriend, or a box of perfume.

We hated the customs officers, because they were very nit-picky, and almost all of them were corrupt.

So one time we were waiting for clearance, and the customs officer in front of me latched on to a boy who had bought himself a small brown leather suitcase and a summer dress for his girlfriend. And the officer was bawling him out, saying he'd be fined or sent to a tribunal for attempted smuggling.

I couldn't bear it. I went straight up to him and said: "What on earth are you doing, comrade? Look at this boy! He's been serving the Fatherland. He could have been killed. It's obvious he wants to take something home for his loved ones."

The customs officer looked me up and down and then screamed, "And who exactly are you?"

"The wife of an adviser," I said.

There were various advisers; like my husband, they were civilians, but I could just as well have been the wife of a general. I knew that if I spoke with enough self-confidence, he wouldn't dare give me lip.

"And what are you doing in Afghanistan?" the customs officer asked me.

"What do you think I'm doing? I'm working." I didn't explain that I worked as a cook, because why should I? Better for him to think he was talking to someone important.

He looked at me, then at the boy, and it was plain to see from his face that he was a nasty man. Finally he said, "All right, off you go."

And he said to me: "I'll check who you are. And you might pay a high price for obstructing me in my work."

To which I replied: "Not higher than you'll pay, sonny. When they throw you out of here, the best job you'll get will be checking the cars at a parking lot."

And off I went.

I only got away with things like that because at the base they thought I was working for the secret services. For dressing down a customs officer in the course of his official duties, they could have put me on trial. But I did it so brazenly that I got away with it.

Afterward I told my husband about this incident. And he said: "Why did you risk it? Tomorrow he'll confiscate ten more boys' suitcases."

"Valentin Dmitrievich," I replied, "I came here to defend communism. But people like that are an even greater threat. They're worse than many a dushman."

That's how it was, Witold. Communism wasn't a bad system. Within the Party I met nothing but good people—it didn't collapse because of them.

Communism collapsed because of people like that customs officer with the face of a bulldog.

6.

We weren't allowed to socialize with the Afghans, except for the soldiers in the Afghan army and their wives. It was curious to look at them, because many of them had been to military school in Russia. And in our presence they knew how to behave like Russians. But as soon as one of the Afghan elders appeared, they changed in a flash. They spoke differently and treated women differently—even their facial expressions changed.

They had a separate kitchen, separate barracks, and separate commanders. But one of them had a yearning for Russian bread. One day he came to see me, smartly dressed, clean-shaven—which wasn't typical, not even for their soldiers, who had fashionably trimmed mustaches—and he asked if I'd like to do a swap with him: our bread for their flatbread, which was a kind of small round loaf that I liked very much.

Naturally I agreed, and we started talking. He had heard the soldiers calling me "Mama Nina," but he must have thought that was my first name. So he called me "Mamnin." I found that very funny and didn't correct him.

His name was Abdullah. He was very open with me, and he told me how the war looked from his perspective.

"Mamnin," he explained, "your people are doing a lot of harm to Afghanistan. In my family, two of us brothers are in your army, and two are in the partisans. The ones who are with the partisans have threatened to kill me and my wife if I don't join them. You were supposed to help and then leave. Why are you still here for yet another year?"

I didn't answer, because what could I say? I still believed that back at home, in the Kremlin, they had a plan I didn't know about. Meanwhile, Brezhnev had died and there was a new general secretary every few months—first Andropov, then Chernenko, then Gorbachev. And what about us? We learned to eat Afghan pilaf. It's incredible—you'll never eat anything like it. It's only the men who make it; they mix it with big sticks and eat it with their hands. We invited them to the base for every holiday—New Year's, Women's Day, the anniversary of the October Revolution, Victory Day—and they always brought several large pots of that pilaf. You couldn't tear yourself away, it was so good. They made one kind with meat, and another with fruit: pomegranates, apricots, peaches.

They also have extraordinary grapes there—they call them Kishmish, or sultanas. They're sweeter than sugar. Our men soon collected seedlings, and two years later we had vines growing up to the second floor—all the balconies were overgrown with them. We had some Ping-Pong tables, and when the vines produced a crop, the fruit was always piled up on them. Everyone ate their fill, and there was always plenty left over. Some people secretly made wine out of them, but I forbade my husband. It wasn't allowed. "You don't have a wife in the Party just to break the rules here," I'd say.

The soil there is very sandy, but in that climate everything grows anyway. At home carrots take a month to come up, but there it's a week. It's the same with other vegetables. The trees blossom and almost immediately they bear fruit. And in February you can see the most beautiful sight on earth: wild tulips on the steppes. They grow there by the million, very close together. As soon as they start to bloom the Afghans light small bonfires, pick the flowers, and toss the bulbs into the embers. They toast them on all sides and eat them. They're slightly bitter, but edible.

And then in March, migratory starlings fly over Afghanistan. Curiously they have their own domestic starlings that don't migrate, but they don't shoot them. They just wait for that migration. When they hear them flying past—and those migratory starlings can be heard from afar—they immediately race to the highest point nearby and kill them, at least a dozen each.

Abdullah asked me to let him shoot them from our roof. I was very annoyed. "You're not going to shoot at those poor little birds from my roof!" I said. But while I was out my husband let him do it several times, and then Abdullah brought us some starlings his wife had cooked to say thank you. I never ate them, but my husband did, and he said they were good.

7.

I soon learned to cook for an army. There was always one spicy, warming soup, such as rassolnik—you grate pickled cucumbers and add carrots, onions, and seasoning—or shchi, made with fresh or pickled cabbage, or borscht.

For sour shchi you need sauerkraut: you cut cabbage into very small pieces, add salt, you can add a little paprika, and you must add dill seeds. You salt the cabbage and squeeze it by hand to release its juice. You let it ferment for three days before you start making the soup. But they always brought us ready-made sauerkraut in jars from Moscow, because at war no one had time for the fermentation process. We just added the potatoes and seasoning. We did make our own zazharka, which is a mixture of stir-fried carrot and onion.

One time I sent one of the young soldiers to fetch some ready-made shchi. There was another soup waiting there too, rassolnik, and he brought me the wrong pot. So before I knew it I'd mixed two soups together. The result was cucumber shchi with added barley. So with my head bowed I went to see the canteen manager, Andrei Yosifovich, and I said: "Don't shoot me, but there's going to be a problem with the soup." And I explained that I knew it wasn't the right way to do things, but haste, the heat, too much work . . . Luckily our manager was a wonderful guy. He shrugged. "What's the problem?" he asked.

Together we went up to the noticeboard where our menu for the day was posted. He crossed out the words SOUR SHCHI and wrote SIBERIAN SHCHI.

Whether such a soup as Siberian shchi existed anywhere in the world, I'll admit to you, Witold, neither I nor Andrei Yosifovich had any idea. But we hoped none of our soldiers knew either. Or that they didn't read our menus anyway.

As luck would have it there was a boy from Siberia in our company, and to make matters worse, he read our noticeboard. After lunch he came into the kitchen and said: "Mama Nina, I'm from near Irkutsk, and at home we make Siberian shchi a different way."

"Really?" I replied, ready for him to argue. "How does it differ?"

"We don't add the cucumbers."

I went on playing the fool.

"And which is better?" I asked him.

He thought awhile.

"Yours," he said. "I'll tell Mom to make it with cucumbers."

The soldiers were full of praise for our cooking. Every day we did our best to have fresh salads and fresh vegetables on the table: tomatoes, radishes, cucumbers. They were very happy to eat them, and we were supposed to be making sure they had a healthy diet. Except that the planes from Russia brought us too few of those items; I quite often had to go to the market and buy things with my own money to make sure they had something fresh. They paid us well, so I could afford it, but I shouldn't have bought those things at the local bazaar because we weren't allowed to shop there. But I did. I never poisoned anyone.

8.

One morning one of our men came running in, shouting that someone was lying by the fence with bullet holes in his belly. And that he thought it was Lyosha. I ran there as fast as I could—and it was indeed Lyosha. I kneeled beside him and wept as if he were my own son. I couldn't get a grip so someone sent for my husband, and some people came from the kitchen too, but I just lay there on the asphalt next to Lyosha, crying my eyes out.

The tears still come to my eyes to this day. He had two months' service left, but the silly boy let an officer drag him into stealing and selling something to the Afghans. How exactly had he come to be shot? I don't know.

Afterward I went to see that officer, and I told him I knew all about it, I knew he was dragging young guys into his dirty business, but now things had gone a step too far. I brought up the topic at a Party meeting in Kabul. I said there was this officer, there was proof he was selling gas and other things to the dushmani, who knows, maybe even weapons, he was bartering for video players, lately he hadn't settled accounts with someone, and as a result a man had died . . . And suddenly I felt stonewalled. They all knew perfectly well who I was talking about, but the man had such strong support somewhere high up that there was no chance an ordinary cook could touch him. So they heard me out and then deftly changed the subject.

Although he was just an ordinary soldier, Lyosha had a ceremony like the military pilots.

Because whenever a pilot was killed, we had a custom that for three days the waitresses would serve all the dishes to the place where he had usually sat. They'd put out bread for him, then soup, then a main course and dessert. Then they'd take all of it back to the kitchen untouched, and we'd throw it all away—no one else got his food. The next day was the same. And then one more day. Only on the fourth day could someone take the dead pilot's place. What was the origin of this custom? It's curious, because we started it of our own accord. No one discussed it with anyone; no one stopped to think. The waitresses just brought the food, then took it away again. And then we found ourselves doing it for every person we cared about.

So that was how we said goodbye to my Lyosha. On the first day after his death, he got shchi soup. On the second, meat with potatoes and salad, then jelly. I can't remember what he was served on the third day. By then he was on the plane, in one of those metal coffins they used to transport the dead back to Russia.

Later on I found his parents. I called them—I didn't have the money to fly there—and I told them he was a wonderful boy and that he'd died a hero. I didn't go into the details—why would I do that?

I just told his mother we'd fed him the best we could. And that I personally couldn't have done more. We both wept.

And what about Abdullah? He finally joined his brothers and fought against us. He was killed during one of the first operations he took part in on the dushmani side. Those deaths were quite unnecessary, Witold. Just as that entire fraternal intervention of ours was of no use to anyone at all.

MENU

◇◇◇

Shchi

This recipe was given to the author by Nina Karpovna.

14 ounces (400 g) chicken
6 potatoes, diced
10½ ounces (300 g) cabbage, chopped
2 onions, diced
1 carrot, grated
6 tomatoes, chopped
1 bay leaf
Salt
5 garlic cloves, pressed

Place the chicken in a large pot and cover it with water. Bring it to a boil over medium heat, then add the potatoes. Once the potatoes are half-cooked, add the cabbage.

In a frying pan, sauté the onions until golden, then add the carrot and cook for 3 to 4 minutes.

In a second frying pan, sauté the tomatoes. Add the contents from both pans to the broth. Add the bay leaf, salt, and garlic, then cook it all together for another 10 minutes.

XII

The First Return of Viktor Belyaev

1.

Brezhnev died on us, Witold. I remember that day well and I'll never forget it, because his death was real madness at the Kremlin. Since Stalin's death in 1953, in other words in almost thirty years, no general secretary had died while in power, and no one could remember how to prepare the appropriate funeral.

The nature of the work was different than usual, because the place was full of international delegations, and most of the cooks were assigned to them. I worked with the French premier. I didn't have much to do—he flew in, took part in the formal events, and went straight back to Paris. So I had time to help my colleagues in the kitchen who were working on the menu for the funeral reception, but there wasn't much to do for that either. We made kutia with raisins, which is traditionally served at Russian funerals, and on separate tables there were blinis and compote. And a few hors d'oeuvres, but without the madness—no sturgeon or caviar.

The days of sturgeon and caviar were to pass into oblivion along with Brezhnev. But we didn't know that yet.

And just as for the past thirty years we hadn't had a single funeral, suddenly, with the death of Brezhnev, we had one a year. First his successor, Yuri Andropov, died; then *his* successor, Konstantin Chernenko. And every time it was the same: a funeral, kutia, blinis, compote, end of the solemnities.

Until someone finally decided against choosing yet another old man who would die within the year, and in 1985 the young Mikhail Gorbachev was appointed general secretary of the Central Committee of the CPSU. As you know, he brought us "perestroika," meaning reconstruction, and then the Soviet Union collapsed, to my great regret. But before that happened, we also had a perestroika in Kremlin cuisine.

Above all, we were given orders to drop the expensive banquets. The days of caviar dripping off the tables were over. Gorbachev himself was constantly on a diet—his wife, Raisa Maximovna, fought him about it. He mainly ate oatmeal and kept a close eye on his calorie intake, because he had the sort of physical build that meant he put on weight as soon as he let himself go a bit.

The whole Kremlin had to go on a diet with him.

I'll be frank with you, Witold, the cooks didn't have an easy time with Raisa Maximovna. She often replaced them, because they were always doing something wrong. Either it was the wrong sort of food, or the eggs were badly fried, or there was too little sausage, or too much. At that point I received yet another offer to become a lichnik, and once again I refused. My colleagues only had bad things to say about cooking for Gorbachev.

If he had a weakness, it was for champagne. The chefs used to make him lemonade according to his own recipe: ice, mint, lemon juice, a touch of raspberry—and a shot of champagne per glass.

His only extravagance that I remember from the receptions was beluga sturgeon, also cooked in champagne.

2.

In 1986 I was involved in the extraordinary final funeral at the Kremlin. The man who had died was Vyacheslav Molotov, a veteran of the regime, whom you are sure to remember in Poland—it was he who in 1939 signed the Soviet-German non-aggression pact with Hitler's minister of foreign affairs, von Ribbentrop. He lived to ninety-six and was the last of the Stalinist power elite—the only one to survive to the days of Gorbachev. I had met him, because now and then we brought him food from the Kremlin.

In his final years Molotov spent most of his time at the Leninsky sanatorium in Rublyovka, now a highly exclusive, nouveau riche suburb of Moscow. He had his own room there, and as it was a sanatorium for top Party members, we sometimes went there to cook. We always bowed low to him, because although he had no political significance by then, Molotov was a legend.

His private apartment was located right next to the Kremlin, on Granovsky Street, where before the war the entire Soviet elite had lived, including Rokossovsky, Budyonny, and Voroshilov.

When he died, as an important politician he was entitled to a state funeral. So I was sent to Granovsky Street to prepare the reception. At the apartment, two old ladies were waiting for me—his distant cousins—so I introduced myself, bowed politely, and they let me come inside.

The apartment was nothing special, a few hundred square meters right in the center of Moscow. Inside was a room with a fireplace, a dining room, a study, two bedrooms, and a large kitchen. I went into the kitchen and looked around to see what sort of plates I had at my disposal, what sort of pots, whether there were knives, how many, what sort, what equipment I'd be working with. I approached the table and tried picking up a plate, but it refused to come off the surface. Why not? Too much dirt! They were all the same. Molotov was very old and either didn't have the strength or didn't feel like washing the dishes. So he ate his food and just left the plates there.

I've never seen anything like it, not before or since.

The cousins saw me standing there looking alarmed. "Don't worry, Viktor Borisovich," they said. "We'll wash the dishes in the bathtub."

And they did. But there were still too few, so we had to bring some from the Kremlin.

I looked around that apartment—as I've told you, I'm interested in history, and an opportunity like that, to see how Molotov lived, comes only once in a lifetime. I thought I might see some notes, maybe a picture of him with von Ribbentrop. But no. There was nothing at all. Even if there had been something interesting there, the secret services were bound to have come and cleaned the place out before sending the chef.

The only things I saw were some figurines from various

countries and a portrait of him made out of rice—a gift from Uzbekistan.

That's all that was left of Molotov. Some dirty plates. And a portrait in rice.

3.

The man I call my mentor was someone I met in the days of Gorbachev.

It began with the approach of the XXVII Party Congress. As always for that occasion, many eminent individuals were coming to Moscow, from abroad too. For the special guests the Party had cottages built in Gorki Leninskiye, right next to where Lenin had lived. They were quite luxurious—each had a screening room, a billiard table, a study, and a dining room. And each was fully staffed and had bodyguards too. We called the houses *osobnyaki*, "little manors." And one day the boss told me that for the period of the congress he was sending me to an osobnyak, where I'd be cooking for Kaysone Phomvihane. Do you know who he was? I didn't know either. The premier of Laos, which was then a close ally of the USSR.

I was terrified. Remember that I was still young—I wasn't yet thirty—so I said to the boss: "How am I to go to an osobnyak? That's a big responsibility!"

And he replied: "Maybe you're right. Who should go with you?" He thought for a while and then said: "I know. You can go with Vitali Alexeyevich. Who's that? You'll find out when you get there."

All right, so be it. A few days later they put me in a car and took me there. Vitali Alexeyevich was already on-site—a tall, white-haired old gentleman, very polite and unassuming. We shook hands and started to work, but Vitali Alexeyevich didn't behave in the least like a better, more experienced chef. He asked me about everything, made sure we agreed about everything, and consulted me in every possible way: how much food should we order, what kind, and what could we do to make sure the guests from Laos liked it?

Eventually we got down to the cooking. I couldn't get over the man's culinary skills! He had such nimble hands, and he moved around the kitchen with such grace. I was surprised that someone so talented wasn't with us at the Kremlin on a daily basis. I asked him about it.

"So what's the custom at the Kremlin, Viktor?" He smiled. "Who's not allowed to cook there?"

"I don't know," I replied. "There are lots of rules—I can't possibly know them all."

"Think about it," he said. And smiled again.

I spent half the night racking my brain over who he might be, and whose toes he might have stepped on to prevent him from working with us. Until I remembered that the lichniki of the dead or those ousted from power couldn't cook at the Kremlin.

Had Vitali Alexeyevich cooked for one of the general secretaries? If so, then which one?

I spent the rest of that sleepless night wondering about it. And when I finally came up with the possible answer, I felt shivers down my spine.

The next day when we got up to make breakfast, I went up to him and said: "I've been thinking about it all night. Did you . . . did you work for Stalin?"

Once again, Vitali Alexeyevich just smiled.

4.

And so my good friend—later my mentor—had been Stalin's personal chef. He had lived next to Stalin's villa and had known all the legendary chefs, starting with Sasha Egnatashvili. We lived together at the osobnyak for two weeks; we cooked together, drank a daily drop of brandy together, and played dominoes together—it was the favorite game of the older Kremlin cooks. The premier from Laos was brought to the house late at night, after the congress sessions, so we weren't particularly interested in him or he in us. He didn't complain, and that was plenty.

Working with Vitali Alexeyevich was extremely good for my development. It was he who made me into a fully fledged chef, who opened my eyes to what our profession is all about. He taught me things no one else ever had, not at school or any other place.

For example, he taught me to fillet herring with a single stroke of the knife. Stalin loved herring—he would happily have eaten them every day of the week.

Vitali Alexeyevich taught me that a cook must go to work in a good mood. He can't be stressed, he can't get upset, and under no circumstance must he ever let himself be thrown off balance—though when you work for the government, it's not easy. "An upset chef means bad food," Vitali Alexeyevich would say, and he was right. He told me Stalin understood that perfectly, and could take his anger out on various people in his entourage and on his staff—but not on the cook. He knew that his own health and sense of well-being depended on the cook's mood.

I'll never forget the day we had to make dough, and I started to grumble.

"It never works for me," I said. "It won't come out right. I'll be wasting time again for no reason."

"Do you know how to sing?" asked Vitali out of the blue.

"How to sing? What's that got to do with it?" I asked, dismayed.

"Yeast is a living organism, and it can sense your mood perfectly. If you're nervous, it can feel that, and it'll sink. There's only one way to fool it. You have to sing to it."

"Are you being serious, Vitali Alexeyevich?" I asked.

He said he was being perfectly serious.

I tried it. And I really did succeed in fooling the yeast. My mom used to sing to me a lot when I was a child, so I knew plenty of traditional Russian songs. Ever since, I've always sung to my dough, and never once has it failed to work.

5.

Vitali Alexeyevich and I became close enough for him to start telling me a lot of stories about Stalin.

In moderation, naturally. Everyone who worked for the country's leaders, including me, was given a document to sign stating that we wouldn't talk to anyone about our work. This confidentiality agreement is permanently binding for the rest of your life.

On top of that, Vitali Alexeyevich had been a lichnik, a personal chef, and they had a whole lot of additional restrictions. As I've already told you, each of them was directly employed by the KGB. If you'd tried to contact one of them the way you reached me, you'd have run into trouble. The security service is responsible for the kitchen that feeds the leaders. The chefs are certified, they're vetted ten times more than I was, and each of them has a military rank. It's still like that today.

Eventually, Vitali Alexeyevich told me about the day Stalin died. On March the fifth, the date of Stalin's death, he was on shift in the kitchen. Like the rest of the staff, he and his wife and children lived on the grounds of the dacha, but that day he'd been to the city to take care of some business. He arrived before lunch, and Stalin's housekeeper, Istomina—the woman who was said to be Stalin's lover too—saw him through the window. Istomina was very fond of Vitali Alexeyevich. So she ran out into the courtyard to meet him and said tearfully: "The boss is dead. Beria has already started shooting his people."

"What am I to do?" replied Vitali Alexeyevich.

She showed him a car that was concealed at the back of the courtyard.

"Take it! Run and fetch your wife and children and get away before it's too late."

Istomina saved his life, because Beria really had given orders for many of the people in Stalin's entourage to be shot.

Fearing that Beria's men might be looking for him, Vitali Alexeyevich stayed with relatives in the countryside for months. And later, when he heard that Beria had been shot, he returned, went to the Kremlin, and asked if they'd take him back.

They did, but in keeping with the unwritten rule that former lichniki of general secretaries had no access to the Kremlin, he was given commissions in various other places. For instance, he worked at the dacha of Alexei Kosygin, the longtime USSR premier and one of the most important people in the country. Kosygin lived outside the city, in Sosny. It seems he was a total ascetic, which was typical of many communists of the older generation, and was happiest eating cheesecake, blancmange, and buckwheat. Vitali Alexeyevich told me that he could actually only cook him those three things.

Until one day Kosygin gave him a special task.

"Listen," said Kosygin, "tomorrow some congressmen from the USA are coming to see me. They must be well entertained, so come up with something interesting."

Vitali Alexeyevich thought and thought, and since he loved to play dominoes, as a snack he made them canapés shaped like dominoes. He sliced the bread, dried it a little in the oven so it wouldn't crumble, and cut it neatly to make each domino the perfect size. He buttered them thickly and made the dots out of black caviar.

It took an incredibly long time, but the result was fantastic. Imagine dominoes that you can eat. Very pleased with himself, he showed everyone those beautiful canapés and said he should get a prize for them.

But just before the party, Kosygin's chief of security came to find him.

"Come. He wants to see you," he said.

Kosygin was sitting in his study. When he was angry he spoke very quietly; he started talking to Vitali Alexeyevich in the softest voice imaginable. "What the hell is this? You such and such—if you ever dote over gourmet items like this again,

I won't answer for myself . . . The nation is standing in line for sausage. And you make dominoes out of caviar? Get out!"

Vitali didn't have to be told twice. He left the room immediately. And his story taught me one important thing: the Kremlin is not a place where you're appreciated. It's not a place where they praise you. If no one shouts at you, that's praise enough.

As for the dominoes, Kosygin was wrong. What Vitali had made were not sandwiches but works of art. It was like getting angry at Andrei Rublev for painting frescoes while the peasants starved.

But perhaps Kosygin was angry about something else, and took it out on the chef? That used to happen a lot. The cooks and bodyguards often served as whipping boys.

6.

For some reason people enjoyed my cooking. My bosses started sending me to serve important foreign delegations.

I can't remember all the VIPs I cooked for, but they included Fidel Castro, Nicolae Ceauşescu, Saddam Hussein, Erich Honecker, and of course the Polish leader Edward Gierek. But the real adventures began in Gorbachev's day, when the former US president Richard Nixon came to Moscow to pave the way for Gorbachev's meeting with Ronald Reagan. On the very first evening he came down to supper with his PA—and there was total silence. I'd made him some splendid food—blinis, fish, meat cooked several ways. All beautifully decorated and served. But there was this awful silence.

In the kitchen we were discussing what to do, because we couldn't understand. So we sent out the wine waiter. When he came back, we all leaped toward him. "You won't believe what's going on," he said. "Nixon and his PA are standing by the buffet with a camera. They're photographing every single dish."

I cooked for Nixon for several days and he was very satisfied, until one day he simply swung by the kitchen. From the doorway he asked, "Who's the chef here?" I was summoned. "Good morning," I stammered in English. He must have been expecting some big fat Ivan with a mustache. And here I was. A guy from Izmaylovo. He was so pleased to be able to talk to a young Russian that he started coming by every day. And he questioned me: What was life like for young people? How long did I wait for an apartment? How much did this or that cost? I felt awkward about him coming to see me like that, but the boss said it was all right, there was nothing wrong with it. And that I should talk to him if that was what he wanted.

One day I plucked up the courage to say I was pleased that he liked my food. But that in my view he was missing the best feature of Russian cooking.

"Oh?" he said, intrigued. "What is that?"

"The soups, Mr. President," I said, because he always left the soup. "Russia is famous for its delicious soups. We have borscht, we have solyanka, we have ukha. They're all very good for you. Especially for men," I said.

"It's too late for me now," he said, shrugging.

"Mr. President," I replied, "it's never too late. Soups are rejuvenating. Give them a try."

I knew he was a keen angler and loved fish, so the next day I made ukha for him. He ate it, asked for a second helping, and ate that too.

"It's really good," he told me. "I think I'll have to find myself a Russian cook in America." He smiled.

But the most extraordinary thing happened on the final day of Nixon's visit, when he asked me to show him Moscow. My boss agreed, so Nixon took just one bodyguard, and off we went. He didn't want to see the historical sights; he wanted to see how normal people lived. We went to the Cheryomushki District, because he'd been there before with Brezhnev several years earlier. When we got there Nixon asked where the local market was—he remembered it from that previous visit. He imagined that because he was without his entourage, with just a bodyguard and me, no one would recognize him and he'd get a look at ordinary life. So we went to the Cheryomushki market.

Of course everyone there recognized him, and a swarm of people came running up, giving him flowers, fruit, vegetables, and honey. I had to hold it all then lug it around, while Nixon just about wept with emotion.

At some point a very old woman emerged from the crowd, the kind of woman who sits at the market selling garlic and a few sunflower seeds to supplement her pension. She gave him the entire sunflower head that she had for sale. And this is what she said: "Mr. President, I have nothing else to give you. But I'd like to ask you for one thing in exchange. I lost two sons in the war.

Viktor Belyaev and Richard Nixon

War is the most terrible thing that can happen on earth. Please, please, do everything you can to make sure there are no more wars."

Nixon hugged her and gave her some sort of answer, but he was clearly very moved. We returned to the villa where he was staying, but he spent a long time walking around the park, turning it all over in his head.

Then I made him farewell ukha, and he suggested we have our photograph taken together and then left.

7.

I have overslept and been late for work only once in my life, but it was the worst possible occasion, because that day I was making breakfast for Margaret Thatcher. She was in Moscow with an entire delegation. They'd stayed up until late at night, and their flight home was at five a.m.

The boss had suggested I sleep over at the Kremlin, on a sofa. But I can't bear sleeping away from home, Witold. So I thanked him, and a Kremlin car took me home. I left work at one a.m., though I'd have to be back again at 3:30. I ordered a car from the Kremlin, set my alarm clock . . . and didn't hear it ring.

I woke up at 3:30—and started to panic. I alerted the entire family, my wife and children; my wife ironed my shirt, and my mom, who lived with us, helped me put on my pants. And I called the Kremlin housekeeper to explain what had happened and asked: Please open a can of peas, beat the eggs for the pancakes, and start boiling the water for me so it's simmering by the time I arrive.

But the worst was ahead of me—the car. This was Moscow in the 1980s—there were no taxis, and it was an hour on foot to the Kremlin. And the rule for the Kremlin chauffeurs who drove around the city collecting the staff was that they waited for a maximum of half an hour. If you didn't show up in that time, it was your problem. You'd do the explaining to your boss.

So I thought to myself, there's no chance the car is still there. With my heart in my throat, I called the Kremlin dispatcher, praying for my good friend Luba to be on duty.

It was Luba who picked up. Everything was all right now.

"Luba, I overslept!" I screamed. "And we've got Margaret Thatcher! Do something, help, I have to make her breakfast!"

"Ooh," said Luba, "that's bad."

And she sent me another car.

I put on my shirt and tie, ran downstairs, got into the car and . . . a second one drove up. It turned out the driver had made an exception and had waited for me.

So off we went, with me in one car and the other behind us. At the entrance to the Kremlin the soldiers saluted us, I saluted back—and began to laugh. Those guards gave me such a look.

"What the hell, Viktor, why scare us like that? We thought it was some bigwig coming in."

"You'll soon get used to it, boys," I replied. "From now on I'm always going to travel this way." That made them laugh.

Then I raced upstairs. Blinis, appetizers, cheese, sausage, ham—I quickly sliced it all.

I made it in time by a hair.

Thatcher came to thank me for the cooking, just as Nixon had. In fact, it was funny, because the first time she was due to come, the other chefs had told me there was no need to be concerned because she never ate what we cooked for her. They said she had no chef at home but did her own cooking, and she wasn't fond of food cooked by others.

So for her first breakfast in Moscow I made a little of everything, but I was ready for her either to eat nothing at all or to just jab her fork at her plate a bit. I gave her two salads, a little buckwheat, some cold meat, toast, jam, and pancakes—blinis—and got on with making the lunch.

Imagine my surprise ten minutes later when the waiter came in with an empty plate—the blinis were gone.

"She wants some more," he said.

What the heck—more? But I thought she wasn't going to eat anything!

In a panic I cracked some eggs, mixed them with water, milk, and flour, and fried two more blinis at top speed. The waiter served them, then came back in.

"And again."

I think she had eight of them. Even her colleagues were surprised she liked them so much.

The hardest thing was when delegations came from India or from Arab countries. The Arabs, like Saddam Hussein for instance, often brought their own chefs—they had to make dishes according to the rules of Islam, using meat from animals that had been slaughtered in the appropriate manner. We didn't know how to do that—how could we?

Whereas we did feed the Indians. One of them wouldn't eat meat, another wouldn't eat fish, a third would eat meat and fish but not eggs . . . What's more, none of them could be served beef, and you had to remember exactly what to serve to whom.

Even the vegetarian dishes were divided into various categories. The other cooks and I spent ages wondering how to deal with it all, until finally there was no option—we had to cook separately for each member of the Indian delegation.

I remember when they arrived, and the waiter who took water and fruit juice up to their rooms came back in a flap because he'd found them . . . standing on their heads. Later we were told that Gandhi practiced yoga every day, starting at five in the morning.

8.

When we had no foreign delegations, cooking at the Kremlin was prosaic and repetitive. For each lunch we prepared fifteen appetizers: fish, meat, and vegetable. We made stuffed pork tenderloin, chicken, and fish galantine.

But what was exceptional at the Kremlin was the way the dishes were decorated. Each of us took a special course in how to cut roses out of tomatoes, fences out of cucumbers, and flowers out of radishes—we all knew how to do it.

The appetizers couldn't be repeated more than once a week. Only caviar could, but if on one day there was red caviar, the next day it had to be black. Naturally it came from Astrakhan, the best, from beluga or other sturgeon. There's a special plant there for procuring caviar, and each plant of this kind had a special unit that worked for the Kremlin. Astrakhan made caviar for us, Murmansk provided smoked fish, and the Mikoyan Meat Processing Plant made sausages, wieners, and other cured meat products. When there were Party congresses, the delegations brought their own goodies: Ukraine brought sausages, the Baltic countries—Lithuania, Latvia, and Estonia—brought sprats and herring, and the Caucasian republics brought mutton, grapes, and other fruits. But the chefs at the Kremlin were only ever from Russia. I can't remember a single natsman, meaning a member of an ethnic minority. Why was that? I don't know. It must have been easier for them to vet us locals.

Naturally at work there were occasional conflicts, but we were all careful not to overdo it, because if anyone went too far, they'd be fired. And then try finding another job that after two years gave you an apartment and half-price vacations in Crimea, in luxury conditions too, because we had a special center there for Kremlin employees. Once every six months we could go to a special section at GUM, the large store in the center of Moscow, and use coupons to buy ourselves clothing. No other job offered anything of the kind. On top of all that, the Kremlin tailor could sew you an overcoat. He also made suits, and if you wanted, the cobbler would make you shoes. My wife and I had everything made by them. You only had to wait two years for a Zhiguli car, at a time when people who didn't work at the Kremlin waited ten. So I can't remember anyone arguing enough to lose their job.

But I do remember one incident when some of my colleagues got carried away. It was Women's Day, in the late 1980s. We gave our female colleagues some gifts and sat down at the Kremlin to have some snacks and drinks. We weren't meant to do that there, so the boss had told us: "Just have one drink each and get going." Those who were married, as I was, did have just a single shot and then left. But there were four young fellows with no wives or children who stayed put. As I was on my way out I said to them: "Boys, the commander will be doing his rounds in a few minutes. If he catches you, there'll be trouble." "Sure, Viktor," they said, "we're just about to leave too."

And they left the room. But not the Kremlin.

At seven in the evening the Kremlin was closed. And suddenly singing rang out from one of the towers. It could be heard all over Red Square—four male voices singing all the top Russian hits: "Katyusha," "Moscow Nights," then something from Alla Pugacheva's repertoire and things by other famous singers.

Unfortunately, it wasn't just the tourists who heard them but also the Kremlin commander. He summoned his men, who went all around the Kremlin but couldn't tell where the singing was coming from. The outer wall? No one. The tower? No one. The bell tower? No one!

They spent an hour looking. And do you know where they'd gone? Where the famous Tsar Bell is, the biggest bell in the world, which broke in the eighteenth century and has a large piece of metal missing. Those boys had crawled through the hole and sat inside the bell, with their sausages and vodka, and started singing. That's why the sound carried so far. And that's why they couldn't be found—they were inside the bell.

Unfortunately, they were fired. Afterward the commander told me that when he saw their little party he was extremely sorry, because he would have loved to join them—he'd gladly have had a drink too, and sung a few songs. Those boys were having a great time.

But it wasn't allowed. Not at the Kremlin.

OVERHEARD IN THE KITCHEN

Although Mikhail Gorbachev did what he could to save the USSR, fate definitely wasn't on his side.

The crisis that had started under Brezhnev simply worsened, and all the young general secretary's efforts got stuck in the quagmire of Soviet bureaucracy. Gorbachev plugged away, trying to force through reforms, but he wasn't just up against the hard-headed communists who had no interest in supporting his perestroika and glasnost; he was also hindered by the fact that many citizens of the USSR failed to understand or to support his activities.

On top of that, he had an adversary whom he himself had nurtured: Boris Yeltsin. This young, able apparatchik had made his name by having the house demolished where the Bolsheviks had shot the family of tsar Nicholas II. At first Gorbachev indulged Yeltsin, but later he tried to derail his career. Eventually the two men faced off in a deadly fight for power over the Soviet Union—or what would be left of it.

As if Gorbachev didn't have enough problems, on April 26, 1986, one of the reactors at the Chernobyl nuclear power plant exploded. Misled by his colleagues, Gorbachev first ignored and then tried to cover up the true extent of the disaster. The state's helplessness in the face of this tragedy was another brick in the wall of mistrust between Gorbachev and the Soviet public.

By now, the days of the world's largest country were numbered.

XIII

The Fairy-Tale Forest

Cooking at Chernobyl

In the marketplace beside the bus station in Varash, I feel as if I've stepped at least twenty years back in time. The asphalt covering the little square adjoining the station melted many years ago, but before that happened deep holes were worn in it. If you walk around the holes and keep going, you'll soon see some large plastic tubs containing catfish, carp, roach, and tench, all hauled out of the river Styr; a few of them even hold eels writhing like ribbons cut by Party officials. Some fish are still moving their gills, breathing their last gasp, smeared in the blood of other fish that were alive some ten minutes ago. If any of them catches a customer's eye, the fishmonger dexterously sticks a long knife into its head, guts it, scales it, and seconds later puts it in a plastic bag so the customer can carry on shopping: maybe a sausage from the store that belongs to the meat processing plant in nearby Trostianets? Or some vegetables from Torchyn? Perhaps a live goose, a chicken, or a pigeon?

It's all here.

You could also get your smartphone screen fixed, have a skirt or some pants sewn up, have your stockings darned, drink a cup of coffee, or dream of a better life as you eat a cheburek with meat filling or a roll stuffed with potatoes, sold—as in the entire post-Soviet landscape—by old women in headscarves.

Beside the rickety booth that serves as a bus station are several taxis. The first driver is wearing a trendy leather jacket and a cap with the logo of a ski resort. The second is in an old duster and a Soviet fake-fur hat. I'd rather ride with the second one, because he'll have more interesting stories to tell, but the one in the leather jacket is the first in line, and none of the people who got off the bus with me has gone up to the taxi stand.

I'll wait.

I look left and see Taras Shevchenko Avenue, one of the town's main arteries, lined with big, grand apartment blocks.

I look right and ... what the heck?! I look again. And again.

To the right of the bus station stands the Chernobyl Nuclear Power Plant.* I count the chimneys—one, two ... six.

No, it's not Chernobyl after all. Too many chimneys. It's the plant's twin sister, the Rivne Nuclear Power Plant, 180 miles to the west. And Varash is the town that has grown up beside the

---

*The Chernobyl Nuclear Power Plant is familiar as the site of the 1986 catastrophe, which is the topic of this chapter. As the reference here is to historical events from the days of the Soviet Union, the Russian form of the place name, Chernobyl, is used in this chapter. Nowadays this name has been replaced by its Ukrainian form, Chornobyl. The cooks whose accounts are given here often refer to other Ukrainian cities and towns, and in their speech the Ukrainian names are used.

power plant, just as the town that grew up beside the Chernobyl power plant is Pripyat, now featured in all the documentaries about the disaster as a ghost town. If you want to see what life next to a nuclear power plant is like, this is where you should come.

I'm not waiting any longer. I get into the first taxi with the driver who's dressed in a more European way. I'm going to see the women who cooked at Chernobyl just after the accident.

THE COOKS

They fetched Luba from the vegetable patch, where she was weeding the tomatoes.

And Raya—short for Raisa—from her apartment, where she was bringing up three children on her own.

Valentina was told at the store where she worked that she must go that same day. And she was immediately warned not to argue about it. What could she do? So she went.

Nastya found out while waiting in line to see the doctor, from a friend who worked in the personnel department. "But I'm on sick leave," she said in surprise. But her friend explained that didn't matter.

And Lidia was told by the head of the same personnel department, "Either you're going, or you can pack up and return to your village." So she went.

Olga spent two hours crying and wondering what to do— she had an eighteen-month-old child. She was afraid she'd infect the child with something.

Only Tatiana found out she was going to Chernobyl to cook for the people combatting the disaster the way a cook should— over her pots.

I managed to meet with all seven.

How they rounded up another eight girls to join the first group of cooks to go to Chernobyl straight after the disaster we shall never know: they're not alive. The first one died immediately after returning home, the second a few years later. Three died after the tenth anniversary of the disaster, one shortly before the twentieth anniversary, and two more a few years after that. In fact, of the seven who are still alive, six are in poor health and have undergone several operations—in some cases more than ten—of various degrees of complexity.

But let's start at the beginning. From the former village of Varash, of which only a few houses are left. And some memories.

Luba

Luba is now over sixty. She has a dark vest thrown over her shoulders, and she's wearing a hat made of some kind of animal fur, though I can't tell which. We're meeting at a small café by the Varash Palace of Culture. She can still remember when there were geese running around and cows grazing here.

It was a beautiful village, Varash. My father had pigs, cows, rabbits, and ducks. He and my mom worked at the collective farm, but by then the Soviets allowed you to keep your own animals at home.

Mom and Dad had eleven of us. I was the youngest, and I was as happy as a clam. Everyone loved me very much. And when I was in the third grade, a commission came to see my father to buy our house and small piece of land. They said a nuclear power plant was going to be built in Varash, and there'd be a reactor on the spot where our cottage stood. It made a huge impression on me. A reactor? A power plant? What on earth was that? Nowadays everyone has heard of nuclear power plants—Chernobyl made sure of that—but in those days the whole concept was completely new, and they were only just starting to build them.

My father didn't like the idea. Our family had lived in Varash for generations. We'd survived the war and collectivization, and now all of a sudden we had to sell our house and land and swap them for an apartment in a block? But the commission started persuading my father that if he wouldn't sell it voluntarily, in the future they'd take it away from him anyway, because since the secretary in Moscow had decided there was going to be a power plant in Varash, then pardon me, but a villager had no chance of blocking that decision.

So my father agreed that in exchange for our cottage he'd be given two apartments in the blocks they'd start to build here. About six months later some workmen came and built the apartment blocks, and we moved. Both my parents got jobs at the power plant, which was still under construction: Mom as a cleaner, Dad as a janitor. And suddenly my father became a great fan of nuclear power! He and Mom earned three times more than they had at the collective farm, and since they had a community garden, they went on raising geese, pigs, a few ducks, and some rabbits. They only had to give up the cows because there was nowhere to graze them.

Until one day my father, who was always very resourceful, said to me: "Luba, wouldn't you like to work at the power plant as a cook? You've always liked cooking. Maybe that's a good job for you?"

"All right, Dad," I replied. "What made you think of that?"

And it turned out his friend's daughter was working at the power plant as a cook. And every evening she tipped the uneaten leftovers into a bucket, her father drove his tractor up to the power plant, and they took it all home for their pigs. My father liked the idea of having free food for his pigs.

At first I was pretty annoyed that he hadn't been thinking about me at all, just his pigs! Then I found it funny. But finally it occurred to me that perhaps a job at the power plant wasn't such a bad idea. So I went along and applied. In those days the power plant was expanding very quickly, so they accepted me the very next day. That's how my whole life was shaped by the fact that Dad wanted swill for his pigs.

Things went on like that for several years: I cooked at the power plant, and each night my father drove up in his tractor to collect his swill. I remember that when he butchered the last pig, the first reactor was already in operation. He and the neighbor butchered it in our bathroom so they wouldn't have to carry the carcass. Sausage, headcheese, ham—Mom and I made it all ourselves.

Right outside they were building a reactor. They were going to split the atom, and you could see it all through the window. And here in the bathroom, my father and the neighbor were slaughtering a pig.

In fact, the reactor ended up in a different spot, not on our land. And they changed the name of our village from Varash to Kuznetsovsk, in honor of a communist who was a spy among the Germans during the war. Only when Ukraine became independent did they change it back to Varash.

Olga

"All my life I've been a terribly poor eater," says Olga.

We're sitting at her home, not far from the church in Varash, and Olga is emptying the contents of her fridge onto the table. And just as you'd expect of a professional cook, she has a great deal in her fridge: homemade sausages and headcheese, vegetable salad, smoked fish, eggplant roulade, pickled gherkins, pickled carrots, and to go with it all, a bottle of homemade horseradish-root vodka that I brought.

Mom says I ate nothing but marzipan, which isn't true. But it is true that I was picky. If in those days I'd have said that I wanted to be a cook when I grew up, I think they'd have fallen off their chairs laughing.

In my town in the 1960s they built a large chemical plant. After school, I wanted to get a job there. But my brother-in-law was already working there, and he said: "Olga, it means working with chemicals. You don't know what's in them, but you're young and pretty, you're going to have children. Better not go there."

I decided he was right, so I went to cooking school instead. And look how stupid life is. Instead of the chemical plant, I ended up at Chernobyl.

But to start at the beginning, I come from the Ivano-Frankivsk region, and there, in a place called Burshtyn, we had a very good cooking school. That was where I went. They threw us into the deep end—a month of theory, how a grater works, this and that, how to use a meat grinder, and then we did practical work at a restaurant, a bar, or a canteen. Before a year was up they had put us on a bus and taken us away for practical work out of town; with my best friend, Nadya, who came from a village near mine, I went to the nuclear power plant in Varash. It wasn't just me and Nadya—there was a whole bus full of us, but Nadya was my closest friend. Why Varash? I didn't know it yet, but my school had signed an agreement with the management of all the Ukrainian nuclear power plants, which meant that cooks from our school served every one of them. And not just cooks, because waiters, bakers, confectioners, and store assistants also went from Burshtyn to our Rivne Nuclear Power Plant—because that's its official name—and also to the Khmelnytskyi, South Ukraine, and Zaporizhzhia nuclear power plants.

And to Chernobyl. I knew lots of girls who cooked at Chernobyl. I knew waitresses and confectioners too. Most of them were either there at the time of the disaster or not long after. And most of them are not alive anymore.

If you did well in the practical work, they gave you a job and you could stay. That was before the Chernobyl explosion—no one knew that radiation could be dangerous.

The beginning was tough. They brought a whole group of us here on June 1, 1980. The beds in the dorm where they put us up were crooked, just boards nailed together. There were still farmhouses and cottages all around. None of the reactors were in operation—they were just gearing up to turn them on. But there was still an immense amount of work to do: two thousand people to feed, and five of us cooking. Slice the bread and cold meat, make scrambled eggs, clean up, then start again, slice the bread for lunch, make the soup, fry the chops, clean up, and then the same thing for supper. If we were just five minutes late people were dissatisfied, because they were having a tough time too, and they didn't want us to be late with their meals.

Our canteen kitchen was at the site where one of the reactors now stands. Nadya and I lived together at the dorm, and every day we went to work together. We had to get up before five, because breakfast began at seven on the dot. We worked in canteen number seven. Numbers one, seven, eight, nine, and thirteen are on the power station grounds, and the rest are in town.

One time I couldn't keep up with the pace, so I went out for a while and fell asleep in the stoker's room—there wasn't any central heating yet, and they heated those rooms of ours with coal. I woke up in the middle of the night. The girls didn't know where I was, and they'd left without me. I got out through a window—it's a miracle I didn't fall into a pit.

Later I was transferred to the Forest Song restaurant, in Ukrainian that's Lisova Pisnya. There was even more work to do there, because apart from the normal daily job we served weddings, funerals, and delegations from Moscow, from Kyiv, and from other power plants. And since they were going to activate the reactor any day now, there were an awful lot of those visits. Never mind if it was Saturday, or if your child was crying. Go and work.

I remember how in 1981 they finally started up the first reactor. I'd never seen a party like the one that was held at the restaurant that day. They must have gone through a whole tank truck of vodka. And a good thing too. Our management and engineers deserved it. They'd worked hard, and they finally had their success. That day the girls and I worked until four in the morning.

The next day we were visited by a commission, because ten kilos of meat had gone missing from the kitchen.

Those were the days of Brezhnev, the crisis, so everyone

stole whatever they could. Cooks were always under suspicion, because there was a saying that anyone who had a cook in the family wouldn't live in poverty, and somehow there was a wide-spread belief that we stole.

I can say with my hand on my heart that I never took anything. Even if I'd wanted to, I'd never have dared—you could go to prison for that. Every day they counted how much meat, how much cheese, charcuterie, and vegetables had come in; it was quite enough for me to be able to eat at work.

But food went missing, that's the truth. Especially during the weddings. The bride and groom, who knew what went on, always posted someone in the kitchen to keep watch. If not, a large piece of meat for the soup would go missing, for example. Now try making borscht with no meat. Who took it? No one knew. Who was to blame? The cook!

In fact, we all knew perfectly well who took it. But we couldn't talk about it, because those people were far more highly placed than we were.

But I liked Varash very much from the start. It was a town under construction, full of young people, and there was a great energy here. We worked hard, but we had a youth club where once or twice a week there were dances. There were new people arriving all the time, there was always something going on, and everyone was friendly. I had female friends who lived in Pripyat, next to the Chernobyl power plant, and they told me it was the same there. We had opportunities of a kind that didn't exist in other towns in the Soviet Union: well-supplied stores selling meat, fish, and fruit. Everyone earned a good salary, certainly higher than the Soviet average.

A particular type of person used to come to those places. Those with the most get-up-and-go. The boldest.

Raya

People started saying something was wrong at Chernobyl on the day of the accident. We had strong ties with Chernobyl: the cooks from there used to come to us for training. There were often engineers from Chernobyl at our place too. They were sister power plants, close to each other, so they were bound to be in contact.

But at the start it was just tittle-tattle: someone couldn't get through on the phone to her daughter who lived in Chernobyl, someone else couldn't reach a friend, somebody had heard something but didn't know what.

Though I remember Olga coming to work and saying she'd had a call from Ivano-Frankivsk to ask if everything was all right at our power plant. Her brother-in-law was involved in politics; he'd been listening to Radio Liberty, and they'd reported that there'd been a terrible accident at a nuclear power plant in Ukraine. We looked at our gherkin barrels—that's what we call our power plant chimneys—and we could see there was nothing wrong with them. So we went back to work. It never occurred to me that it could be something so serious.

A few days later there was a May Day parade, and everyone attended it as if nothing had happened. It would be years before people started to admit that somebody knew something at that point. But they didn't tell anyone else for fear of being accused of spreading disinformation—you could be prosecuted for that. Varash was a closed town, of special significance. Just admitting that there was a leak could get you put in jail.

But after May Day, it all happened very fast. There was no one to do the cooking, so they had to bring in cooks. There's nothing odd about that. If an army's on the march, the cook is one of the first to go too.

At the time I had three children: my daughter Zoyka was in sixth grade, my son, Ivan, was in fourth, and little Alonka was in first. Like most of the girls, I worked at the Lisova Pisnya restaurant, but the personnel manager called to say I was to go to the power plant—our restaurant was subordinate to the power plant.

So I went. And the personnel manager said I must pack, because tomorrow I was going to help clean up near the damaged reactor. I said what could I, a cook, do about a damaged reactor? Should I lie down on it? Cover it with a blanket? Or maybe with a pot? That was the first thing. Second, I had three children I was raising on my own, because my husband had left me, and there was no one to take care of them.

The personnel manager shrugged. She said Zoyka was already twelve, so she could look after the younger ones.

At first, Witold, I found it absurd. My Zoyka, so little, was to take care of the house? But that's what happened. And Zoyka coped with everything. She cooked, and did the laundry, and sent the other two off to school.

Much later on I learned from friends who worked at the other power plants—because there were five of them in Ukraine, and we all knew one another—that only from us, for the first expedition, did they take women who had small children. I think I was the only one who was raising her children alone. The personnel manager had never liked me—evidently this was her little gift to me.

They gathered fifteen of us into that first group, some from Lisova Pisnya, some from the canteen, some from the power plant or somewhere else in town. We all knew one another—Varash isn't a large town, and one cook is sure to know another.

As we drove there in the bus, we sang the whole way. Someone had a bottle of brandy, so we drank it for Dutch courage. And we tried very hard not to look out the window, because outside there was an apocalypse. The forest had burned down. There were cows standing in the charred forest, mooing pitifully, because the people had been taken away and there was no one to milk them. Several were lying on the ground, probably dead.

We passed deserted villages with gardens full of vegetables, jars full of birch sap, beehives, bees, honey. They were just begging you to stop and gather it all up.

But we weren't allowed to stop. We were forbidden.

Imagine a world with no people in it. It was a strange sensation: just a few days earlier you had plans, aspirations, a job to do, and three children. Ordinary problems, like those of millions of people throughout the country. And suddenly, three or four days later, you're driving across weird terrain to a place where you don't know what lies ahead. And you don't know if you'll ever return.

These days, whenever I pass a vehicle on the road that's taking cows to be slaughtered, I think about us driving there that day in exactly the same way. At those moments I always think to myself: you poor creatures, you have no idea where they're taking you.

Luba

They put us on board a bus outside our restaurant, and it took us to Rafalivka, a place four kilometers from here where there are railroad tracks. They introduced us to our brigade leader, Valentina Timofeyevna Savitskaya. "Good day, good day"—we all recognized her because she was the manager of a store not far from the power plant. Right from the start she made a good impression on us. She'd have done anything for others. If you said that something didn't suit you, Vala would come running to arrange something better for you. You had a problem? Vala would spend half the night awake thinking of a way to help.

In Rafalivka we boarded the night train to Kyiv, where they gave us breakfast and drove us to a boat on which we sailed toward Chernobyl. We disembarked, walked a short way to the final bus, and were there.

That was when I saw the reactor, just that one single time. It was still burning and belching out smoke. After that we spent a month in the middle of the forest, and the trees shielded the reactor from view.

They took us to a former pioneer camp located in the middle of the forest. It was called Fairy-Tale Forest. Doesn't that sound nice? Vala told us to go to bed early, because we'd have a wake-up call at six in the morning. But for ages we couldn't get to sleep. Then the soldiers woke us at four. Why so early? Because of some of our colleagues. For the first two days some cooks from another power plant had been there. They were supposed to make breakfast; show us the kitchens, the cold stores, and the water intake; and familiarize us with the equipment, and then at noon they were due to be taken home. But instead of waiting to do that, they'd run off through the forest in the middle of the night.

At the time I was furious with them, because we had to do everything in their place. I couldn't understand how anyone could behave that way.

Now I just feel sorry for them. The forest was where the worst radiation was. They were trying to save their lives, but they must all be dead by now.

Valentina

I'll never forget that buzzing for as long as I live. I sometimes dream I'm back in the Fairy-Tale Forest and I can hear it again.

But one thing at a time. ORS, the acronym for the Workers' Supply Division, to which the kitchens and stores at the power plant were subordinate, decided that I should be the brigade leader, in charge of a group of cooks. I didn't want to be, because I'd never worked in a kitchen before, only in a store, and I knew it would be hellish work, but the woman who ran the Party cell to which I belonged sweet-talked me into it. "Vala," she said, "if not us, the Party members, then who?"

She knew that if she mentioned the Party I'd agree, because I was a genuine communist believer, and I was always running to and fro to sort something out for someone. In those days the Party was my entire life. I still can't come to terms with the fact that they've done away with it.

On the other hand, the Party cell boss didn't go herself. Even my beloved Party was already full of people who had plenty of fine words but no intention of putting any of what they said into practice through their own efforts. And one of the reasons why the Party eventually fell apart so easily was people like her.

When we arrived, everything was in place, as my colleagues have already said. There were cows and hens wandering around the forest, the whole place was full of troops, and the girls from the Zaporizhzhia Nuclear Power Plant who were there before us had run away into the forest. We were given a dosimeter to measure the radiation, and we tested our surroundings—in some spots it showed up, in others it didn't. All right, we thought, it's not too bad, let's go to bed. I'd settled down and was trying to get to sleep when suddenly one of our girls, Anna Dimitrovna, started screaming her head off. "What's the matter?" I asked. It turned out the girls had been fooling around with the dosimeter, checking the objects around them. And the bedclothes we were supposed to sleep under had sent it off the scale. So had the bed. And it was only a little better in the bathroom, under the showers. I took the dosimeter, held it against my quilt, and it went *bzzzzzzzzzzzz*. Same with the pillow, the towels, and the bed frame and mattress too. And that girl Anna said to me: "Valentina, I'm not going to sleep here—it could be dangerous."

At that point I made what must have been the stupidest decision in my life. I said they could do as they wished, but I was going to get some rest. I lay down on my radioactive mattress, pulled my radioactive quilt over my head, and went to sleep. I remember thinking badly of Anna Dimitrovna: imagine such a young girl throwing her weight around!

When the girls saw me lying down, they went to bed too.

Anna hesitated the longest, but what could she do when we'd all gone to bed? Finally she lay down too.

Now I know I shouldn't have let them sleep in that bedding. I should have gone and made a scene, fought for those girls' health, battled for them—Anna Dimitrovna was only eighteen!

And now Anna Dimitrovna is dead. She died around fifteen years after Chernobyl. I don't know if she bore a grudge against me, because we never talked about that night or that dosimeter again. I can only curse myself for my stupidity, and say in my defense that although I was the brigade leader, I was young and stupid, and I'm paying for that mistake with my own health too.

The next day we started work at four in the morning, and at full steam right away, because the girls who'd run off had left a dreadful mess behind. The sink was cluttered with unwashed dishes, the pots were dirty too; we had to sweep and wash the floor and then set about making breakfast. I knew that as brigade leader I must set the pace, so I toiled away the fastest of all. And I kept on smiling at them or winking. In that sort of situation, if the brigade leader starts complaining or sits down, it's the end. Everyone sits down beside her, and work is out of the question.

At a quarter to six we were all ready. I sent Olga and Nadya, who were good friends, to serve the meals. They put on such lovely chef's hats. We hung a noticeboard next to them with the name of our Varash ORS and the message A WARM WELCOME TO ALL, BON APPETIT! And Olga, who had some artistic talent, painted some flowers and little roosters on it.

At seven minutes to six, as I remember well, the first members of the clean-up crew arrived. Or as we tried to say at the time: the first guests.

And suddenly, out of the blue, before they'd fully entered the room, I heard that dreadful *bzzzzzzzz* again.

It turned out that we had dosimeters—like Geiger counters—in the canteen too, by the entrance. And those counters started to buzz just like when we'd held them to our bedding: *bzzzzzzz, bzzzzzzz, bzzzzzzz, bzzzzzzz, bzzzzzzz.*

More and more people came in, walked up to us, and took the food from Olga and Nadya, and that sound merged into one great, never-ending *bzzzzzzzzzzzzzzzzzzzzzzzzzzzzzzzzzzzzzzzzzzzzzzzz zzzzzzzzzzz.*

Those people who had driven out to us from Chernobyl were radioactive, just like our bedding and our towels. They had come straight from the power plant; they were the ones who worked right next to the reactor and were in closest contact with the radiation.

It was a dreadful sound.

We heard it from morning to evening, with two-hour breaks while we were cleaning the canteens.

But after three days, the dosimeters disappeared. I don't know when or how, but one day we arrived at the canteen and they were gone. At first I thought someone had stolen them—it's shameful to admit it, but I saw it with my own eyes: by then some people were already trying to make extra money. But then the soldiers who were stationed not far from us told us to give back our dosimeters too. They'd received orders. Radiation seems completely safe: you can't see it, there's no smell, and it won't do you any harm at first. Why scare people by reminding them they're being exposed to it?

Someone must have applied that sort of thinking.

Olga

Valentina Timofeyevna put me and Nadya, my friend from the school in Burshtyn, *na vydachy*—in other words, in charge of serving the meals. She advised us that everyone there was working hard, everyone was in a difficult situation, and for most of these people the meal was the only pleasant moment in their day. We had to do everything we could to help them gather strength in our canteen so they could continue their work.

Vala gave me the job of serving because I was always laughing more than anyone else. Whether there's a reason or not, it's my nature to avoid being sad. Young, blond, and smiling, that'll be nice for everyone—that's what our Vala was thinking. And she gave me Nadya for company because she knew we got on well, and if we were together we'd make lots of jokes.

The soldiers who supervised everything gave us work clothes, protective masks, and dosimeters. They told us to change our clothing twice every twenty-four hours—the things we took off went straight into recycling—and we weren't allowed to remove our masks.

For the first half hour we dutifully worked in those masks. But it was impossible to wear them any longer—we couldn't breathe. I never put on a mask again.

That first day I baked bread, then sliced it, decorated the tables with flowers, and folded the napkins to make them look nice. Then, at a quarter to six, I put on a kokoshnik, which is a lovely chef's hat, thought about something pleasant to spread my good mood to the people I'd interact with that day, and Nadya and I stood by the hatch to serve the meals.

And I'll tell you something, Witold. To be a good cook, you must have sensitivity. A person without sensitivity isn't empathetic and will never cook anything well. A good cook senses other people's moods, and that's why cooks see many things that other people don't notice. And on that first day I knew things were very bad. Much worse than we were being told, because they were still telling us it was just a minor accident, the sort of thing that's always happening at a nuclear power plant. But when I saw those soldiers who came to us from the site of the reactor, I knew it wasn't true. That it was tragic.

The food there was very good. It was our first day, and we did our best. And if they didn't like scrambled eggs or oatmeal, there was always plenty of chocolate, and lots of fruit on the tables. Not many people saw those things at home, but they didn't even glance at it. They just wanted to drink. Nothing else.

They were burning up, Witold. Burning up from the inside.

They'd take three or four glasses of compote each and ask for more. They didn't want anything to eat, they didn't even glance at the chocolate, they just drank and drank and drank. I won't mention the fact that no one took any notice of me or my kokoshnik.

Valentina

I have never worked harder in my life than at Chernobyl.

I started my day at three a.m., because that was when we drove off to gather our supplies. I went to get them myself, because my signature was on all the forms, so if a single packet of butter went missing I could be accused of theft. What's more, I was a good choice for the job because I am a bit sassy, and the supplies officer needs to be like that. You might have to push your way into line, you might have to talk firmly to someone or sweet-talk someone to get something sorted out. I'd done the same sort of work before at the store in Varash, so it came naturally to me. One time, shortly before Victory Day was to be celebrated on May 9, I was sent to get beer for our workers, but the manager of the warehouse in Lutsk said the factory had a stoppage so there wasn't going to be any beer. I told him that was his choice, but without the electricity we produced, the factory wouldn't make beer, and he wouldn't be opening his warehouses either. And I hated to think what might happen if the people in our town didn't get their beer.

So I talked him around by bullshitting away like that about how we were the only ones in the region who had beer for our veterans.

My bosses were counting on skills of this kind when they put me in charge of the cooks—and the supplies—for the Fairy-Tale Forest. Everyone knew it wouldn't be easy. And that if anyone could cope with it, it was me.

So every day I went to fetch the food from the distribution base near Pripyat—I drove there in a big truck for the vegetables, fruit, cheese, milk, and bread. There my bullshitting skills were of no use at all: at that time there were three canteens like mine, so there were only three vehicles to be loaded. And since the state gave Chernobyl priority, the distribution base was very well stocked, so we didn't have to wait for anything— everything proceeded at lightning speed.

But once a week I was given an extra truck, and I went to Kyiv to get fresh meat, processed meats, flour, and pasta. And that was where the problems began, because although I was coming from badly irradiated terrain, and had myself been exposed to radiation, I was sent to the same supply base as the supplies officers from all the city's canteens and restaurants. Everything went smoothly, so I never made a fuss—I just had to wait with all the others. Until in the third week a strange thing happened. When I appeared, the other drivers blocked our way and refused to let us enter the base. So I got out of the truck to find out what was going on, and in response I heard a torrent of abuse—"You" this and "You" that, "Go back to your Chernobyl instead of infecting us."

My Chernobyl?

"People," I said, "I'm not even from there! I'm helping put out the fire, because otherwise we'll all die, both me and you."

But they refused to listen.

I went to see the accountants and explained that the other drivers wouldn't let me in. They replied that they'd sort it out, but to that I said: "Listen, people have a right to feel afraid. There was a van in front of me that takes milk to a preschool. How can they know I'm not going to make that milk radioactive?"

"So what are we to do?" they asked.

"Let me in through a separate entrance, away from the line."

And from then on that's what they did. I never had to wait again. And I never met anyone at that entrance. Was I sorry? Witold, I've always had a task-driven rather than an emotional attitude to my work. I was actually pleased I wouldn't have to wait in line.

Olga

We had a medical station at Fairy-Tale Forest, where there was an ancient doctor from Russia who was supposed to help us if anyone felt weak or had any other health issue, and on the very first day I was affected by dreadful allergies: my throat was sore and my nose and eyes were streaming. That was how my body reacted to the radiation. So I went to see him to get some eye drops.

This doctor, Alexander Iosipovich, was already retired and had worked as a doctor during World War II. He'd volunteered for Chernobyl because apparently he had taken part in some secret Soviet experiments related to the atom bomb, so he knew something about radiation. He regarded it as his duty to help us, but the commanders didn't really know what to do with him, so they'd assigned him to the cooks. He watched everything that was going on there and shook his head. He didn't talk to anyone; he just made endless phone calls. We all found it rather odd, but we thought old people often behave strangely and there was no reason to worry about it.

But one day, when I went to see him for eye drops again, I questioned him.

"Alexander Iosipovich," I said, "you seem sad. You never come to our canteen—I don't see you at meals. Has something happened to you? Maybe we can help?"

And he looked at me as if he'd seen a ghost. Then he said: "Ten years. Ten. And none of you will be left."

I felt shivers down my spine. But I went on with my questions: "Why do you think that, Alexander Iosipovich?"

And he said: "No one here understands how powerful the atom is. You've heard of Hiroshima? I went there, and I saw people who were dying in agony. I saw children who were born deformed. And this is far worse than Hiroshima."

I ran out of there in tears and was afraid to go see him again. I spent two days suffering with my eyes before I went back for more drops.

And a week later Dr. Alexander Iosipovich wasn't with us anymore. Instead of him they sent a jolly young nurse, who had no idea about radiation and who responded to all our doubts by telling us to wash our hands and take a shower twice a day.

Some people said the old doctor had committed suicide—they said he was the only one of us who knew where all this was heading, and how it would end, and he simply couldn't bear it. But I think it was even worse than that. The army had taken the doctor away and sent him back to Russia because he'd started saying what he shouldn't. Considering he told me, he probably told others too. They preferred us to be in the dark.

But none of us knew that yet. I remember that around the same time the doctor vanished, people I knew from Varash started appearing at the canteen. They started bringing in not just our cooks but also our engineers, firefighters, and ordinary builders. One young man named Kola, who was a builder, saw me and said: "Oh, Olenka, so they've sent you here to die too?"

I told him off for talking like that, because no one was going to die here.

"I've got a husband, I've got a small child, I have someone to live for."

He smiled gently and apologized. Then he said: "Olga, here you are, out in the forest, and you don't know a thing."

And off he went to drink his compote.

Valentina

I only got upset once.

Now and then concerts were held for the people who worked at Chernobyl. Many artists refused—we didn't know that at the time—but several very famous and well-loved performers did come to sing for the people working there.

For one of the first of those concerts they brought in a singer from Moscow whom I adored. When I met my husband, his songs were playing; that man meant a lot to me in those days, but I don't want to name him, Witold, because this isn't about blaming anyone. Those singers showed courage by entering the zone. I just want to tell you how I felt.

The day before the concert I arranged for some of the other girls to fill in for me at work, because for me it was like Christmas or Easter—the only day when, for three hours, I allowed myself to leave work. On the day of the concert I borrowed some lipstick from one of the girls and put on my Sunday best. Two days earlier, when we were in Kyiv, I'd bought a lovely bouquet of flowers, the prettiest I could afford.

Four of us went to the concert, but the rest had to stay behind, because we were serving meals nonstop. I sat in the front row with those flowers, and I was excited and happy like never before.

And after the concert, without asking anyone's permission, I climbed onto the stage with my bouquet and headed toward my beloved singer. As I approached him I started talking from a distance—I've always been good at schmoozing. I said that I knew we were meeting in rather unusual circumstances, but otherwise we wouldn't have had the chance, and his songs had been with me at all the most significant moments in my life. I was getting close, and he could see me, but something was wrong, Witold. My favorite performer, instead of being pleased, instead of thanking me or exchanging a few words, if only out of politeness, if only to fob me off, started backing away from me. He ran off as if I were a leper.

And suddenly it dawned on me that I really was a leper. That I was dangerous, radioactive. That it was true—anyone who touched me, or accepted flowers from me, or embraced me could fall sick or even die.

How had it happened? When? Why?

Then some guy ran up to me and tried to smooth things over. He said I should put the flowers on the floor, that the performer was very pleased but unfortunately he was forbidden to accept anything from people, "orders from above, I'm sure you understand, Madam." But I wasn't listening anymore, Witold.

I wept like never before. But don't get me wrong—I have no grudge against that man. Later on I read in the newspaper that they were forced to make those trips, and they were afraid too. And they had a right to be—I'm not judging them. Apparently Alla Pugacheva, the famous singer, socialized with the men doing the clean-up, signed autographs, accepted gifts, but she never gave birth again afterward and has thyroid disease to this day—I'm repeating what I've read in the Russian newspapers.

But that day something snapped inside me. It took me ages

to get over it. The girls tried to comfort me, but I didn't know how to explain to them what exactly had happened to me.

The next day my professionalism won out, and I pulled myself together and went to get the supplies. But to this day I can't listen to that singer. Whenever they show him on television, I have to change the channel, though he used to mean so much to me.

Chernobyl didn't only ruin my health. It ruined my memories too.

Luba

All right, perhaps it's time to tell you something about the food?

I'll tell you one thing, Witold. Although I was a cook, and although I'd worked at a power plant and also at a good restaurant before, never in my life had I seen such an abundance of good food as at Chernobyl. As if the state wanted to reward people for sending them to such a dreadful place. Go and die, but eat well first.

There was a whole sea of produce there. Little cubes of butter, full-fat cream—it sounds funny, but in those days, under Gorbachev, that was a real delicacy—strawberry, blackcurrant, and cranberry compote, on top of which there was a Soviet drink called mors [made of lingonberries and cranberries], and to eat there was aspic, meat, ham, sausage, saltwater and freshwater fish, smoked, roasted, any way you liked. And all sorts of fruit: watermelons, melons, oranges, pomegranates from Azerbaijan. A fellow from Italy sent us a gift of two railcars full of lemons, so every day we made lemonade.

The menu was drawn up for us by food technologists to

provide the right number of calories. And there was plenty of cooking. Goulash, salads, pizzas, cheesecakes, meat rolls. Various soups, including pea, buckwheat, Ukrainian borscht, Russian borscht, all required to include meat, of course, for strength. And if we had the time and energy, we made pancakes or baked buns.

Each person was given a glass of cream too—we were told calcium helped against radiation, so there was also a lot of tvorog [similar to curd cheese] and other cheeses. In spite of which, everyone believed vodka helped the most. I was convinced it helped against radiation, and although I'm not a drinker, every day before work I forced myself to drink a shot of it.

There were also fruit juices, whatever kind you liked, and I have never seen so much chocolate in all my life.

But, as Olga has already told you, the workers weren't particularly interested in food. Not even the chocolate. "If you won't eat it, take it with you," I'd say to one of them, "give it to a child." He'd give me a look that immediately made it clear that you couldn't take chocolate away from this place, and you certainly couldn't give it to a child. So they used to hand it back to us, and we'd give it to the militiamen who had a checkpoint on the road nearby. We preferred not to take it home either. Later on I heard that some people bought it up and sold it at the markets in Kyiv—without saying where they got it from, of course.

Gradually other canteens began to open near ours, at similar pioneer camps, and Valentina thought up the idea of doing better than them. We all sat down together and discussed what we could do, what these people needed. And we devised a plan to set up a table the length of the room laden with all the healthiest foods, so they could help themselves to dessert and enjoy the sight of it all at once. We wanted to give them some comfort. We knew it wasn't easy for anyone, but even in the most dreadful times, if you eat well you'll feel better for a while at least.

So we did it—we set up three tables end to end the length of the dining room. We called this the Vitamin Table, and every day it was a point of honor for us to make it look as beautiful as possible. What wasn't there? Raya made lovely looking little roses out of pearl onions dipped in sugar. I carved carrots into flowers. There were also little hedgehogs with pickled apples on their backs. And large thermos flasks filled with digestive teas made with Siberian herbs. Everything was pure, fresh, and delicious.

We worked so hard that our hands were sore and our eyes stung. One time I was so sleepy that I went to work without any shoes. But everyone who came to our canteen left satisfied.

Raya

After a while we stopped getting it all done on time, and so several other cooks and assistants joined our brigade. Some of them were great, hardworking girls, but there were also some tricksters who just wanted to get rich. For Chernobyl our salaries were 50 percent higher than normal; they paid well at the nuclear power plants anyway, so for a cook from Kyiv or from out in the countryside, that was very good money—but at the same time they didn't want to work hard. "I have to make the soup? I don't know how." Valentina would transfer them to serving the meals—if you can't cook, you can pour—but once again we'd hear, "I don't know how. Best if someone comes and pours the soup for me."

Valentina dealt with those women splendidly. "So you don't know how to pour soup? Then go and give the mop some exercise."

Anyway, here I am saying nasty things about that girl, but she died soon after our time at Chernobyl—she's gone to heaven, may she rest in peace. It turned out she took some sausages to her village. She and her husband ate them, and apparently everyone there died because of those sausages. Is it true? I don't know. We ate those things too, but we're alive. Though we were only there for a month; she was determined to get her house renovated and buy a TV and video player for it—expensive items in those days—so she spent almost a year at the Fairy-Tale Forest. She'd work for two weeks, then for a week go home, somewhere outside Kyiv. Then two weeks on again. And apparently she took home a sack full of food every time.

Though how she got it out of the place I can't imagine. The militia were there every step of the way, and they were extremely careful to make sure no one took anything. They searched each of us in case we had something in a handbag or were carrying something under our jackets. At Chernobyl, just like everywhere in the Soviet Union, it wasn't the little people like us who did the stealing—it was far bigger people. They'd search us, but meanwhile whole trucks full of produce stolen from the canteens were being driven away.

But I only found out about that many years later.

People said that girl was let through with the sausage and other food because she was sleeping with the chief of the militiamen. But I'm not telling you that to disparage anyone, Witold—I'm deliberately not telling you her name. I just want to give you the opportunity to find out what sort of a place we were working in.

All the produce came from outside the contaminated zone. We were forbidden to cook anything that had been picked in the neighborhood, but we were in the middle of the forest, and at some point blueberries appeared, and mushrooms; the soldiers stationed nearby started picking the mushrooms and asking us to fry them in butter and cream. We did that, sure, but I never ate what I fried for them. And I told them over and over again that it might be radioactive.

But whenever I said those mushrooms could make them sick, the soldiers just laughed at me.

Valentina

At some point there were five canteens around Chernobyl. And suddenly someone from management called me.

"Congratulations to your comrades," he said, "and to you. You've come first in the competition. You have the best food, served in the most attractive way and by the nicest staff."

"Great," I replied, "thank you, but what the hell is this about a competition? Who ran this competition, and how? What's it based on? What's going on around here?"

So it was explained to me that during a particularly hectic time, they'd come up with the idea at headquarters of evaluating who was managing the best. They disguised two people, a man and a woman, in the white costumes worn by the clean-up crews and sent them off to all the canteens around Chernobyl. They tried the food, made notes, and then came back a second time—obviously anyone might have something go wrong now and then, and they wanted the competition to be as objective as possible.

Apparently our girls won unanimously: best food, nicest service, most attractive decor. The commission had particularly high praise for our Vitamin Table and recommended that the other canteens should have one too.

The girls and I were pleased—it's always nice when someone appreciates your work. But the greatest recognition is the kind that comes from the people you're cooking for. We had a notebook by the exit in which people could write their comments, but for ages none of us had the time to look at it.

Until Olga noticed that people were writing in it. So after work we went to get it, opened it, and saw that it was almost full. And people were praising us to the skies, saying our food was as tasty as Mama makes. That they liked it here, and that we were great. "Thanks to you, I've had a home far from home," someone had written, and those are the words that really stayed with me.

Raya

Returning to Varash was tough. No one here was waiting for us with open arms. Everyone knew we'd been exposed to the worst radiation. At one point former friends were afraid to invite me in for a cup of tea. "Raya," they'd say, "we miss you, but you understand . . . we have small children."

I had small children too, but I did understand.

It took several years, but somehow everyone forgot about Chernobyl. The Soviet Union collapsed, and even more serious problems began.

Valentina

I went to Chernobyl twice more, every time as a brigade leader. And I got so close to my cooks, and they grew so fond of me, that back in Varash I didn't want to return to the store, but to the kitchen with them. I worked at the canteens and at Lisova Pisnya, like all of us. I was a brigade leader and a supplies officer, but also a cook.

There was a girl named Lesia working with us at the Rivne Nuclear Power Plant who had worked at the Chernobyl plant earlier on and lived in Pripyat. And when the reactor exploded, she left everything there in Pripyat. She told us that when the officials came to fetch them, they forbade them to take anything at all, just documents. "You must walk out of here just as you are—it's an evacuation." No one told them they were leaving for good. So she left everything behind: money, jewelry, family photos. She and her husband had a dacha, and they had money put aside, but it was all lost.

God, how she cried. She'd come to work with dark rings around her eyes, so I could see she hadn't slept all night for weeping. And at work it was the same.

Her husband had worked at Chernobyl as a technician. He came to Varash with her, but he didn't stay for long; he went off to work on a building site, and that was the last we heard of him. Then she started crying even more. I never once saw her smile. One time I told her: "Lesia, you can't turn back time. You'll rebuild it all. There are plenty of other guys in the world, aren't there? You'll get an apartment too, and you'll earn some money. You can't spend your whole life in a state of anxiety."

But she just looked at me as if I'd murdered her closest relatives. And then she hissed: "You're the lucky ones. You've got somewhere to go home to."

Well, between you and me, I don't regard myself as lucky. My health fell apart very badly after Chernobyl. But never mind; I'm not going to argue over whose suffering is greater.

It was impossible to console her. Although she was rather nasty to me, I went to the personnel department to ask them to give her an apartment as soon as possible. "She deserves it," I said, "she left everything behind in Pripyat." And she did get an apartment ahead of the line, largely thanks to me. But as soon as she stopped working, she also stopped acknowledging me in the street. No "Good morning," no "Hello, how are you?" I knew from other people that she was saying awful things about me, so I tried calling her. "Perhaps we should clear the air?" I asked.

She hung up.

But I don't bear her a grudge. Chernobyl didn't just rip our health apart. It crippled our souls too.

Olga

The competition for the best canteen that they unexpectedly organized when we were at Fairy-Tale Forest was such a hit at the headquarters of all the nuclear power plants that they decided to go on doing it. They put out the fire at Chernobyl, built the sarcophagus, and announced another competition. Each power plant was to choose a cook and an assistant to help her, they'd all gather in one place, and they'd cook. And for some reason our Workers' Supply Division boss chose me to represent our power plant. And as my assistant I chose my close friend Nadya. The competition was to be held in Enerhodar, the city where the Zaporizhzhia Nuclear Power Plant is located.

We started getting ready for the competition, and we met up several times as we tried to decide what to cook. But Nadya wasn't feeling well at all. Two days before the competition, she went to the hospital in Kyiv.

It turned out she had leukemia. The doctor who examined her immediately told her to stay there, at the hospital. I had to go to the competition in Enerhodar alone.

I went as if in a trance, Witold. I can't remember anything about it—I don't know who I met, or what anyone said to me, and I've forgotten what the prizes were. All I can remember is that there were representatives from all the Ukrainian nuclear power plants, including Chernobyl, because it went on officially operating for many years after the disaster. I knew their cooks from courses we'd taken together. And I remember changing my plans at the last moment—instead of the fish Nadya and I had intended to cook, I used a different kind. I cooked some herring, put them through a meat grinder, and shaped the resulting mince into several little fish, which I decorated with lettuce and carrots. It was a recipe Nadya and I had thought up together when we were still at school. Since I was thinking about Nadya the whole time, I wanted to make something that I associated with her.

I made a second appetizer that was very simple too: tongue with horseradish sauce and honey. Again, it was a recipe Nadya and I had made for the Vitamin Table outside Chernobyl. I also made Scotch eggs in aspic and sausages in dough, served with baked apples.

I have no idea how or why, but I got the top prize, Witold. They applauded me, gave me a diploma and some money as well, I think, but as soon as the competition was over I boarded the train to Kyiv and raced off to the hospital.

Five days had gone by since I'd last seen Nadya, but she'd changed as if several years had passed. The doctors took great care of her; at that time they still had patience for those of us who became sick after Chernobyl. Later on things changed, but they gave Nadya the best possible care. They could see she was young and that it wasn't time for her to die yet. They planned to give her chemotherapy, explaining that her hair would probably fall out, but no one said this might be the end.

But Nadya knew it already. "Olga," she said, "I can tell I'm dying." To which I replied: "Nadya, why say such a silly thing? In a year I'll need you for the competition, because this time I won it by a fluke, but that won't work a second time."

It so happened that a year later the cooking competition for all the nuclear power plants was held at our plant in Varash. I made ordinary borscht, with ordinary Pozharsky rissoles. I came in last. Everyone was surprised that a year earlier I'd won but now I did so badly.

Then I went to visit Nadya at the cemetery and I took her to task: "You see? I told you so."

I go to visit her every two or three days. I believe she's my angel who persuades God to provide various things for me. My health, for example. I'm the only cook from Chernobyl who has never had problems with it. I haven't had a single operation or—so far—suffered in any way, though I was there just as long as all the other girls.

I believe my best friend has had a word with the right person up there in heaven.

★

All the cooks from Chernobyl feel forgotten.

"The clean-up crews have extra money for their pensions. But what about us? We have nothing," they say. "When we were needed, then of course everyone was kissing the ground we walked on. But now, when we don't have enough pension money to last the month, they just ask, what's so important about a cook?"

So even in their retirement, most of the women have to earn extra money somehow. They cook for weddings, christenings, and sometimes, at the busiest times of the year, for restaurants.

Valentina Savitskaya, who was a brigade leader at Chernobyl, is now trying to fight for their pensions. She has been in court several times and has managed to scrape up a few thousand hryvnias more for some of the girls. But it's all a drop in the bucket.

"What causes me the most grief is that I know how many people are getting Chernobyl supplements illegally," she says. "Around fifteen years ago an acquaintance offered to get me a supplement for my pension as a special favor. It was a lot—it would be about ten thousand hryvnias now. She wanted a thousand dollars in exchange for her help. So I said: 'My dear woman, why should I have to pay for that? I really was at Chernobyl— I'm entitled to that money.' To which she replied that she knew

I was entitled to it—that was why she was only asking for a thousand. She charged those who hadn't been in Chernobyl several thousand.

"At the time I was extremely offended. But the truth is that the people who paid her that money now have far better pensions than I do. I can put my principles in my pipe and smoke it."

Sometimes Valentina wakes up in the morning to find her legs covered in festering wounds. Or else they're entirely black and blue.

"The whole time there's radiation coming out of me," she says. "I used to go and see doctors and tried to do something about it. Now I know it'll be like that for the rest of my life."

★

Raya is allergic even to her own sweat. And to sunlight.

"I was so thin when we got back that the girls thought I was going to die. They started coming to see me, bringing me food. Why do they keep dropping in on me? I thought. And they were coming to say goodbye. Just a few more days, maybe weeks, they thought, and I'd be gone. They'd even agreed on who'd look after my children so they wouldn't be taken to orphanages."

Because of Chernobyl and her allergies, even in summer she has to go around in gloves. But that's not all. To date she has had eleven operations: a hernia, a lump on her thyroid gland, another lump on her thyroid gland, the removal of part of her intestine—typical problems for people who've been exposed to radiation.

"I've lost count of all the gliomas and lymphomas I've had," she says. "And my thyroid gland's shot to bits. And now that I'm older I have problems concentrating, and cataracts."

★

Luba gets lost in thought.

"The first to die was that girl who was with us, Anna Dimitrovna—the one who was afraid to sleep the first night in the radioactive bedclothes. She and her parents had gone to their community garden, and she fell over and didn't get up again. But she'd never been sick before. They did an autopsy, because when someone dies so young, they have to make sure no one poisoned them. Afterward the doctor told my husband that she was entirely eaten away inside. Entirely."

Luba can't carry anything heavier than a bar of soap. For years she has suffered from a hernia; she has been through a very difficult operation, for which she had to go all the way to Moscow.

Cooks making meals for the clean-up crews after the Chernobyl disaster

"Am I sorry I went to help after the disaster?" Luba is making sure she has fully understood my question. "If I knew then what I know now, I'd have run away from there as fast as my legs could carry me. I'd have run across the border into Poland, into Germany, into Switzerland—anywhere, but as far away as possible. It has done me no good at all in life. I don't believe that suffering ennobles us. I've suffered a great deal, but I don't feel any nobler for it at all."

MENU
◇◇◇

Parisian Salad

This recipe was given to the author by the Chernobyl cooks.

As a substitute for the watercress, you can use lettuce, sorrel, or any lettuce mixture—though, nota bene, watercress is thought to be better for the health than any other vegetable.

2 pounds (900 g) asparagus
¾ bunch watercress
7 tablespoons (100 g) mayonnaise
2 tablespoons milk
1 tablespoon freshly squeezed lemon juice
Lemon slices, for decoration

Bring a large pot of water to a boil. Add the asparagus and parboil it for 2 to 3 minutes. Reduce the heat to medium and continue cooking for 5 to 10 minutes, until soft. Drain the asparagus, place it in a covered dish, and refrigerate it for 2 hours.

Chop the watercress. In a bowl, combine the watercress, mayonnaise, milk, and lemon juice. Place the chilled asparagus on a serving platter and arrange the watercress mixture on top.

Decorate with the lemon slices and serve.

XIV

The Second Return of Viktor Belyaev

In 1989, three years after the Chernobyl disaster, Viktor Belyaev gave himself a break from his job at the Kremlin.

"I went on contract to Syria," he tells me. "A friend of mine knew the Soviet ambassador in Damascus well, and the ambassador happened to be looking for a chef. I went to earn a bit of extra cash, and to have a change of scenery. My interest in history had returned, and I'd volunteered on several archaeological digs at ancient Roman sites. It was fabulous: we dug up the villa of a rich patrician. There were amphorae, frescoes on the walls, all very well preserved; it looked as if the owners had just gone out for a while and were about to return, while we rummaged around in their things."

When Belyaev went away, Mikhail Gorbachev was still running the country, and there was nothing to suggest that anything would change.

Belyaev came back two years later. And found himself in the middle of political turmoil.

"Quite literally," he says. "Because I'd been told to come to the Kremlin on August 18, 1991. And that morning I was woken by the phone—it was my officer friend from the Kremlin. 'Viktor, switch on the TV, quick.' So I did, and I saw tanks on the move. The Yanayev putsch had started, when the old communists tried to save the USSR. My wife said I shouldn't go, because anything could happen. But if you've worked at the Kremlin for all those years, there's one thing you do know: there might be some reshuffling high up, one man will lose power, another will gain it, but that's not your concern. You're there to cook. And as long as you do that, you won't come to any harm."

He reassured his wife, got dressed, and went to the Kremlin. As in the past, the administration had sent a car for him.

"I went in, and it was a madhouse," he says. "Someone running, someone shouting, someone being led away in handcuffs. I went to see the personnel officer as usual, as if nothing was up, to find out what job they had for me. On the way I passed Yanayev himself, who smiled broadly at the sight of me and asked why he hadn't seen me there for such a long time—we knew each other from various Kremlin banquets—and I passed Boris Pugo, who also took part in the putsch. There was something absurd about the fact that while the country's fate was hanging in the balance, there I sat, having a cup of tea with the personnel officer while she explained where she'd like to send me."

The place where Belyaev was sent was even more extraordinary.

"I ended up at Stalin's private dacha in Kuntsevo," he says. "The place where Alexander Egnatashvili and Vitali Alexeyevich used to work, and where Stalin lived and died."

How did that come about?

"It was one of the most unusual experiences I ever had. The Kremlin management wanted to do something with Kuntsevo. Gorbachev had built a modern villa for himself there, but he didn't make much use of it, and someone thought it was a pity for such a large estate close to the center of Moscow to go to waste. The idea was to hire out Kuntsevo for congresses and conferences, or even privately, so someone could have a luxurious stay in this historic place.

"And I was offered the job of manager at Kuntsevo.

"I didn't give it a second thought. As I've told you, I've always loved history. What's more, I had befriended Stalin's personal chef, who had told me a lot about the dacha. So I agreed. And immediately they called for a car to take me there for a tour.

"The dacha was built in the Finnish style, and next to it there was a small lake, from which at one time they had procured fish. Two hundred yards away was the building Gorbachev had put up, in which, as in all similar buildings for high-ranking Party members, there was a pool, a library, a sauna, and even a small cinema.

"The putsch ended, Yeltsin won, Boris Pugo shot himself, and I employed cooks and waiters; we bought tableware and ordered seedlings, because I wanted to revive the old greenhouses, which no one had used since Stalin's day.

"The dacha looked exactly the same as on the day Stalin died. There hadn't been any renovation, and I think hardly anyone had been in there at all since his death. The couch he died on was still there, and by the entrance to the room there was a brown stain on the floor, which didn't look very enticing.

The tables, chairs, rugs, desk, and the tableware we found in the kitchen were all original, all items that Stalin had used himself.

"I remember that he had some very curious mirrors in the dining room. They were crooked in such a way that when he turned around he could see the whole room. His colleagues would think he was adjusting his uniform, but really he was watching to see what they were doing when they thought he wasn't looking.

"And in the hall he had mirrors that gave him extra height.

"The news that it would be possible to rent out Stalin's former dacha spread throughout Moscow, and a famous movie director approached me with a request to make a documentary about his life there. As the manager I had nothing against it, nor did my bosses, so several weeks later a film crew arrived—as it turned out, the first and last. They brought an extraordinary fellow with them: an ancient man who'd been Stalin's bodyguard and who recounted before the camera everything he knew about the place. I went along with them, because you can imagine how very interesting it all was.

"The way the place is designed, there's one building—the dacha—with a long, carpeted corridor that leads to a second building where the kitchens were located, as well as rooms for the bodyguards, a Georgian stove for baking bread, and even a large fish tank in which fresh fish were kept. The old bodyguard guided us very precisely around the servant's quarters, and then we walked along the rugs carpeting the corridor—all original—into Stalin's dacha. We opened the door and went inside. And the old man turned as white as chalk.

"The director and I exchanged glances. We asked the old man if anything was wrong, was he feeling unwell, would he like us to call a nurse? But he just stared into space. Until finally he looked at us, shook his head in terror, and said: 'He was here.'

"Shivers went down my spine, Witold. That was all he said. And then he insisted on being taken home as quickly as possible; he refused to do any more of the interview and wouldn't accept any money from the film crew. He just wanted to get away as fast as he could.

"Later I talked to my colleagues who worked there, and we came to the conclusion that perhaps the place still smelled of Stalin. Since his death the dacha had been locked up, it hadn't been aired out, and the old man smelled an odor he remembered from his youth. That was all.

"Though I must tell you that whenever I spent the night there, I felt very uneasy. I was afraid. It was as if there were a strange presence in the place.

"I worked there for two years. Meanwhile, the Soviet Union collapsed, and Boris Yeltsin replaced Gorbachev at the Kremlin. As for the collapse, to be honest, at first no one fully understood what was going on. Yeltsin and Kravchuk, chairman of the Ukrainian Supreme Soviet, went to Belarus to see Shushkevich, the top man there, and they signed an agreement, but no one had much of an idea what it all meant. Today I think they did it deliberately so that no one would understand."

XV

Wild Boar Goulash, or the Soviet Union's Last Supper

"I should have poisoned them, one after the other. Put arsenic in their wild boar. Or poison in the sausages or anything at all. No one should have come out of there alive."

Polina Ivanovna is a rather stout woman of around sixty. We're talking at a time when the Belarusians are protesting against their president—whom they refer to as "passing-himself-off-as-president" Alexander Lukashenko, because he plainly fixed the 2020 elections—so she asks me to change her name. She doesn't want trouble; as it is she has had quite enough of it in her life.

So I change her name. And go on listening.

"All the evil that has happened in my life, and in the world as a whole, began on that day, December 8, 1991," she says. "It started with that drunk Yeltsin. And those other two rogues who signed that disgraceful agreement. How could they butcher the Soviet Union, our mother, our Fatherland, our provider? Every country yokel knows you don't slaughter a pregnant sow. But they didn't know, so they butchered the country that defeated fascism, that sent a man into space, the world's greatest superpower! Tell me, Witold, how did they manage to do so much evil in just two days? What sort of devil got into them?"

Well, I don't know. I grew up in the shadow of the Soviet Union, and somehow I don't miss it all that much. But for now I'll keep quiet.

1.

It was a strange acquaintance—between Vyacheslav Kebich, a Party apparatchik from Belarus and its first premier after the collapse of the USSR, and me, a writer from Poland less than half his age. I found my way to him because I wanted to re-create the recipes from the supper at which the Soviet Union was brought down, and he was the man who organized it. He must have been feeling bored in his retirement, as for more than a year he played cat and mouse with me, answering some of my questions and promising to answer others if I went to see him.

We couldn't have had less in common. In 1994 Kebich had lost the presidential election to Alexander Lukashenko and been put out to pasture, but he remained friends with Boris Yeltsin to the day Yeltsin died. In his phone he had the private numbers of Nursultan Nazarbayev, the president of Kazakhstan, and of Vladimir Putin's bodyguards—supposedly Putin himself doesn't carry a cell phone, so the surest way to get in touch with him is via his bodyguards. (I asked him to call Putin on my behalf to ask about his grandfather Spiridon, who was a cook, but Kebich just smiled: "It's a number for truly special occasions. Otherwise they'll block me.")

Did he ever have such occasions? He refused to say.

He was born in 1936 in the village of Koniuszewszczyna in what was then Polish Belarus. His father served in World War I on the Russian side and later fought for the Polish army during the war against the Bolsheviks in 1920. The family carefully concealed this fact when their village, along with the rest of Belarus, was annexed to the USSR at the start of World War II— for serving in the Polish army, Frantz Kebich might have gone to feed the bears in Siberia.

Bent over by old age and illness, Kebich settled into a comfortable fake leather chair and gave me a colorful and engaging account of his life. After the war, the Kebich family was not doing well at all. Although young Vyacheslav was a very good student, graduating in the town of Pershai with distinction and a gold medal, his education nearly came to an end after high school.

"Just as I finished high school our cow died," he said. "My father said, 'Son, forgive me, but you're not going to college. We can't afford it.' Luckily my mother stepped in. She knew how important it was for me, and somehow she brought my father around. But the first years of college in Minsk were miserable. My diet consisted mainly of potatoes and *salo*—pork fat."

Kebich graduated from the polytechnic and for several years worked illegally in West Germany—another blot on his CV that he had to cover up when he went into politics, in addition to his father having fought against the Bolsheviks—and when he came home he rapidly built a career in industry. At the age of forty he was put in charge of Minsk's Kirov Machine Tool Plant.

"There I turned out to have managerial skills," he said. "I was soon flying high."

Within the collapsing Soviet Union, the factory that Kebich ran not only brought in a profit but also exported to more than forty countries.

"We employed several thousand people. And each year, on top of their salary, everyone received a large bonus," he boasted. "I used to talk to the workers at every level, asking what they needed, and then we tried our best to deliver. It's not like how people in the capitalist world think, that workers only want as much money as possible. In those days we built saunas on the factory grounds. Our employees wanted that, because it was a way for them to become better assimilated. We also opened a small botanical garden where they could spend their breaks. All this was inconceivable, not just in Belarus but also in the entire USSR."

Kebich's innovations were so unusual that although the factory made a steady profit, now and then he got into trouble with the various monitoring bodies.

"A sauna? Profligacy! A botanical garden? Whoever saw such a thing!" he recalled. "Those were the people who destroyed the Soviet Union: vacuous, hardheaded officials who weren't capable of thinking outside the box. They'd probably have fired me from my job—I was ready for that. But luckily my efforts were noticed in Moscow. And so began my career in the Party."

I visited Kebich several times, and I think the old apparatchik enjoyed our meetings. He repaid me with some extraordinary stories. "You can publish them when I'm dead," he'd say whenever he got ahead of himself and said a little too much.

And he'd smile roguishly.

In 2020 he did die, of COVID. And thanks to him I had a unique perspective on the collapse of the Soviet Union and its aftermath. As viewed from the kitchen, of course.

2.

We're in the Białowieża Forest (its Polish name). Apparently Khrushchev shot someone here (in another version of this legend, someone took a shot at Khrushchev), and it's also where Raúl Castro fell out of a speeding car. Apparently the Romanian dictator Nicolae Ceaușescu didn't hit a single wild boar here, even though the gamekeeper drove the animals right toward his barrel. Apparently, in an act of desperation, a drunken soldier whose girlfriend had dumped him tried to shoot Leonid Brezhnev here.

All "apparently," because everything having to do with the hunting trips enjoyed by Party bigwigs in the Białowieża Forest has always been top secret. The old hunter I was taken to see, who guided Brezhnev, Castro, Ceaușescu, and other dignitaries on their hunting trips and could certainly have told me a lot on the subject, is now over ninety and has advanced dementia. Most of the unusual stories about this place will pass away with him.

The Białowieża Forest has always attracted great leaders. Centuries ago, the Polish king Władysław Jagiełło spent the whole winter here with his troops, gearing up for the Battle of

Grunwald. Then all the subsequent Polish kings hunted here, and after the partitions of Poland by the neighboring empires, almost all the emperors did too. The remains of a hunting lodge that Alexander III commissioned are still in evidence in the Białowieża Forest.

Poland very nearly ended up with none of the forest within its present borders. The first Polish overlords following World War II—the communist president Bolesław Bierut and the prime minister Edward Osóbka-Morawski—fought hard for it. They showed rare courage in standing up to Stalin, and when the border was established they insisted the Białowieża Forest remain in Poland. Stalin took a different view, but Bierut and Osóbka-Morawski stuck to their guns. Amazingly, Stalin gave way. Importuned yet again, he apparently waved a hand and said, "Let it be half-and-half." But then he drew the new border with a red pencil in such a way that the Soviet Union got the larger half—and about 60 percent of the forest was assigned to Soviet Belarus.

In the mid-1950s, Stalin's successor, Nikita Khrushchev, visited Marshal Josip Broz Tito in Yugoslavia. Tito took him on a hunting trip to a state-owned hunting lodge built on Tito's orders and exclusively for his personal use.

"Khrushchev went crazy for it," says Anna Dengubenko, a retired employee of the national park in the Belarusian part of the forest. "He saw how well one could discuss politics while hunting. And he said he immediately wanted to have the same sort of place in the Soviet Union. Kirill Trofimovich Mazurov, then head of the Belarusian Communist Party, suggested hunting in the Białowieża Forest. Khrushchev happily agreed."

A few months later the squalid town of Kamieniuki, capital

of the Belarusian part of the forest, began to expand at an unprecedented rate. Preschools, schools, restaurants, and also the embryo of a future natural history museum and zoo came into being.

At the same time, at the edge of the village of Viskuli within the forest, the construction of a hunting lodge began. It was designed by an architect named Mikhail Baklanov in a style that made reference to the communist architecture common in Moscow.

"Granite was imported from Ukraine, and marble from the Caucasus," says Dengubenko. "Every day some five hundred people worked at the building site, and it was finished in record time, just six months. The locals, who still had access to the site, were amazed when they saw bidets being installed; in those days they were a novelty in the capital city, let alone in the middle of the forest."

Khrushchev came to the forest for the first time in January 1958, by train from Moscow.

"One cannot say he fell passionately in love with his hunting lodge," says Dengubenko. "The walls hadn't had time to dry, and after his restless first night in the damp interior, he decided to spend the next few nights on the train. But when he went hunting, he saw how much game was there, and he started to like it."

A few years later the natural history museum and zoo opened in Kamieniuki. It was an unusual place.

"The gentler animals were let loose, and tourists were allowed to feed them," says Dengubenko. "So the wild boars leaned against the barriers, waiting for the tour buses to arrive; one time a deer walked into the manager's office and refused to be chased out at any price. Forty mouflons were brought in, and five hundred pheasants, a decision that many people criticized, because they weren't local species. But as soon as they were released, the local wolves dealt with them very quickly. You could say the problem solved itself."

<h1 style="text-align:center">3.</h1>

There's a big white monster coming straight at a little girl, wanting to eat her up. That's Polina Ivanovna's earliest childhood memory. She remembers that in those days her parents were working at a collective farm, picking beets, and they'd left her, about three years old, on a blanket at the edge of the field.

Luckily the story ends well. The monster turned out to be a stork that was catching frogs nearby.

Polina was born in a medium-sized village in southern Belarus. Her grandmother supplemented her pension by cooking for weddings and wakes, and as soon as her granddaughter was big enough she started taking her with her. Polina liked cooking.

"Everything I made was very tasty," she says. "One time Granny showed me how to make the batter for *draniki*, our traditional potato pancakes stuffed with meat, and I was soon making it myself. I earned money helping Granny. It was just pocket money, but I was only twelve or thirteen, and that was my first income. When the local Party boss married off his daughter, I cooked three hundred rissoles for the wedding party all by myself. I thought my hands would fall off. But they paid me double."

Polina found cooking so appealing that she couldn't imagine doing anything else.

"I went to cooking school in Minsk. I studied there for two years and did very well. Various restaurants and canteens all over the city gave our students internships. The teacher liked me very much; she kept saying I had a real knack for cooking, and one day she said: 'Polina, I have a special place for you to gain your work experience.' 'Where's that, Anna Valentinovna?' I asked. 'Polina,' she said, 'it's the canteen at the Council of Ministers of the Soviet Republic of Belarus.'"

And so Polina Ivanovna ended up at the headquarters of the Belarusian premier.

"Once they'd gotten me there for the internship, they wouldn't let me go." She still smiles about it. "I remained there for good. The money wasn't great, and there was a lot of work, but I bonded with the collective and I felt good there. And there's one thing I can tell you, Witold. I started work in the days of Tikhon Yakovlevich Kiselyov, who was the chairman of the Council of Ministers until the 1980s. Then I worked for eight successive chairmen of the Council of Ministers. And as long as communism lasted, they all ate very modestly. No one ordered delicacies—they all ate the same as the ordinary workers. The only privilege the chairman had was a waiter to take food to his office. But just as often he came downstairs and stood in line like an ordinary worker. It never occurred to anyone to let him go ahead."

4.

Soon after becoming chairman of the Council of Ministers, Vyacheslav Kebich met Boris Yeltsin. He had to go see him in Moscow to secure a large line of credit for Belarus.

"Yeltsin ate modestly," Kebich told me. "Of course 'modestly' doesn't mean bread and margarine—'modestly' compared with what he could have eaten as the president of Russia, which was then part of the USSR. One heard stories of how in Brezhnev's day there had been buckets full of black and red caviar at the Kremlin. I myself, as director of the Kirov factory, ate caviar by the spoonful at various meetings in Russia, dished out of large bowls. Meanwhile, at Boris's, there was indeed caviar, but spread thinly on small canapés. Those were different times. He understood that well."

The conversation about a line of credit soon became a drinking party.

"There was vodka, obviously—you couldn't do business with Yeltsin without it," said Kebich. "He never ate with it, so neither did I. Boris had a strong head, and after the thirteenth or fourteenth toast I forgot what on earth I was there for, but luckily he remembered. 'So how much credit do you need?' he finally asked. 'One million rubles,' I replied.

"He agreed at once, signed the documents, and out of joy and intoxication, I forgot to sign. We had to send out the documents again by courier."

In September 1991 Kebich's post as chairman was replaced by that of premier (or prime minister). Shortly before, a physicist named Stanislav Shushkevich became the head of the Belarusian parliament—in Soviet times, that was something like the head of the republic. When we spoke he was living in a modest flat in central Minsk. He died in May 2022 at the age of eighty-seven.

"There was perestroika, chaos, and we were afraid we wouldn't have enough gas for the winter," he recalls. "It was forecast to be exceptionally cold. We couldn't come to terms with Gorbachev.

So we wanted to devise a joint plan that would guarantee gas for Belarus. I went to Kebich and said: 'Let's invite Yeltsin. Let's take him to the Forest and host him in style, with hunting and vodka, like in the old days. Under those circumstances it'll be easier to come to terms.' Kebich agreed. At the first opportunity I suggested it to Yeltsin, and he eagerly consented. Then we thought of having Kravchuk join us from Ukraine, because a meeting involving three leaders of Slavic republics was on a completely different scale. Was anyone thinking of bringing down the USSR? I certainly wasn't. For me it was meant to be a meeting about gas: for us and for the Ukrainians."

The year 1991 marked a fierce fight between Yeltsin and Gorbachev for control of the country. Power was increasingly slipping from Gorbachev's hands as he tried to reform the collapsing Soviet Union. Early that year he had organized a referendum, in which more than 70 percent of citizens had voted to retain the USSR. But throughout the year, the parliaments of successive republics had ratified declarations of independence. In April it was Georgia. In August, Belarus, Lithuania, Latvia, Estonia, Moldova, Ukraine, Uzbekistan, and Kyrgyzstan. In September, Armenia and Tajikistan declared independence, and in October, Azerbaijan and Turkmenistan followed suit. The holdout, still hesitating over what to do, was Kazakhstan. Meanwhile, Russia already had a president for its new, independent form—Boris Yeltsin.

"It was a strange situation," recalled Kebich. "One after another each republic had declared independence, but Gorbachev was still sitting in the Kremlin as president of the USSR. No one knew who was responsible for what, or how much power Gorbachev had and how much the individual countries. No one knew how to say it, and it wasn't easy to talk to Gorbachev because he was annoyed with everyone. In August it came to Gennady Yanayev's putsch, when the old communists tried to put a stop to it all. To be frank, in my heart I was on their side. But it was all done too softly and too late. By then the Soviet Union only existed on paper. The corpse was already in the morgue. All that was needed was a coroner to sign the death certificate."

5.

Stepan Martysiuk was one of the hunters who led the hunting trips for Party dignitaries from Moscow and other communist capitals. We're meeting at his house in one of the picturesque Forest villages. Just as you'd expect in the home of a hunter, the empty eye sockets of hunting trophies gaze out at us from the walls. Martysiuk's old hunting uniform is also on display.

"The work was pleasant, in the open air, and one could earn a good salary," he recalls. "Though the hunting was rather bogus," he adds after a moment's thought.

"How so?" I wonder.

"If Brezhnev came specially from Moscow to hunt, we knew he had to catch something. But in nature it's not like that: the wild boars are in a certain part of the forest one time, and in a different part another time. So we had a small herd of boars prepared just for the dignitaries' visits . . ."

"What do you mean, 'prepared'?"

"We fed them potatoes and other treats, which we scattered close to the hunting pulpits where the hunters gathered. The wild boars got used to the sound of human voices or car engines—that meant there'd be something to eat. And they instantly came trotting under the pulpits. So we kept them in a special enclosure, and whenever one of the VIPs came around, we'd let them out. They ran straight toward people. It was impossible not to hit them."

"So the hunting was faked . . ."

"They went hunting to de-stress or to sort out political matters. Brezhnev often brought some of his generals whom he wanted to promote. They expected us to take them to a spot where there were sure to be wild boars. I can only say that no other animals, such as roe deer, red deer, hares, or even pheasants, were kept like that, and if someone shot one of those, it was down to his genuine hunting skills."

"Did they often shoot them?"

"Most often Khrushchev, but I don't remember him—I never went hunting with him. Apart from him, Raúl Castro's wife was good with a gun; but despite being the minister of defense, her husband was a terrible shot."

When Martysiuk had barely two years left until retirement, the director of the national park offered him a job as administrator of the hunting lodge at Viskuli.

"He told me it was the perfect job," recalls Martysiuk. "Gorbachev never came there at all, and that was the truth. None of the Belarusian Party heads—neither Kebich nor Shushkevich—was keen on hunting either. 'There's not much to do,' the director told me, 'no responsibility, and the money's good. And you'll have a bigger retirement pension.'"

"And so?"

"I agreed," says Martysiuk, spreading his hands. "If I could go back in time, I'd beat myself about the head. And refuse. Not for love or money. You should keep as far away from politics as possible, especially big-time politics. But as it is, the shame dogs you for the rest of your life."

"What shame?"

"They brought down the Soviet Union at my hunting lodge. And I got it all ready for them: I heated the rooms and changed the bedding. I even fetched them the typewriter on which they typed out their shameful agreement. Of course, it wasn't me who did it, but my staff—the forty people who worked at Viskuli did all that on my orders. But it dogs me, not them. People think we knew what they were debating there."

"So you didn't know what they were writing, Mr. Martysiuk?"

"If I had known, no one would have gotten out of there alive," says the former manager, flaring up. "I had a gun—all my life I was a hunter. I repeat: if I had known what they were up to, I'd have shot them."

6.

"We found out when exactly Yeltsin would arrive roughly a month before his visit," recalled Vyacheslav Kebich. "Everyone remembers that Shushkevich welcomed him and hosted him. But I had to do all the dirty work. All the logistics of the visit were up to me: the transport, coordinating the planes, providing limousines for everyone, the accommodations, and finally the food. The lodge at Viskuli was also under my supervision. To make it as pleasant as possible, I took the best cooks from the Council of Ministers."

"Including Polina Ivanovna?"

"Yes. That's why I introduced you to her. She was the one who prepared the Soviet Union's last supper. She knows everything. I took other staff members too; I made sure there were pretty girls to present flowers to the delegations, and the right amount of Forest vodka—but other drinks too, including Western alcohol. I even took three masseurs from Minsk; there was a traditional Russian bathhouse on the grounds at Viskuli. One of them was a sauna master—he knew how to control the steam and how to conduct an entire special ceremony. In fact, the first time I heard the call for us to bring down the Soviet Union was during the ceremony at the sauna."

"From Yeltsin?"

"From Gennady Burbulis, his right-hand man. But let me tell it in order, one thing at a time."

★

"No one knew what sort of a meeting it was going to be," says Polina Ivanovna. "The chief of staff simply told me that some important guests were coming. And that there'd be a lot of work, but he'd pay me a bonus for it. I didn't think about it— what was there to think about? It'd be a nice change. I'd only been to the Białowieża Forest twice before, including on a school trip. To get everything ready, I went there two days in advance with two of my colleagues from the kitchen. We were told there'd be around a hundred Russians, some Ukrainians, and our people, and for a while they said Nazarbayev might be coming from Kazakhstan. So we even got some mutton to make him feel at home, because they eat a lot of it there—and in the Forest, out in the provinces, there was no chance of buying it. We brought most of the other produce with us too.

"When we arrived, Yeltsin's limousine was already there, kept specially in a heated garage. There was a chauffeur who always went around in a jacket and tie, even though his boss would be flying in only several days later. There were bodyguards too; they were more of a problem. At first they threw their weight around, saying they'd be monitoring us, watching to see what we cooked, and checking whether Yeltsin got sick afterward. And when they'd had a few glasses of the local hooch, they started trying to grope us.

"I was already divorced by then. I won't tell you about my husband, Witold, because there isn't much to say, but I was very short with guys who drank and had wandering hands. I let one of them have it with a dishcloth—because we really did work from dawn to dusk there—but he just started to laugh and said he'd come and find me in the middle of the night. We three girls all slept together, because who knew what crazy ideas a man like that might have? They were some sort of commandos, judo or karate experts, and who the hell knows what else, but they were behaving like kids at summer camp.

"Kravchuk's bodyguards arrived only the day before the meeting. And luckily Yeltsin's bodyguards immediately got busy with Kravchuk's and left us in peace. Some strange friction was starting up between Russia and Ukraine at the time. Ukraine had only just elected a president, but the Russians didn't much like that, so they spent the whole time talking about them behind their backs, 'the khokhly' this and 'the khokhly' that.

"'Khokhol' was a rude name for a Ukrainian in the Soviet Union. Kravchuk's men wanted to buy hooch, but Yeltsin's crew refused to tell them where they'd bought theirs. Kravchuk's men wanted to find out what route the delegations would be taking and who would sleep in which cottage, but again Yeltsin's guys went, 'Why do you want to know that, you khokhly?' And they laughed. Once the presidents and premiers had arrived, Yeltsin's and Kravchuk's bodyguards punched each other in the face. While the leaders brought down the Soviet Union, their bodyguards smashed one another up.

"But let's get back to the cooking. My colleagues and I divided the food into the things we could make in advance, such as the batter for draniki or hard-boiled eggs for the salad, and things that had to be done just before serving. It soon became clear that we wouldn't be able to manage to cook for everyone. Luckily there was a pretty good restaurant in Kamieniuki, fully staffed with waiters and chefs, so my boss rushed off to make a deal with them. Two of their cooks and several of their waiters came to help us. The rest fed the less important members of the delegations at their restaurant. It was a twenty-minute drive from us, and many of them were staying there anyway.

"As for the actual food, there were no special delicacies there. Perhaps Yeltsin's cooks made him some unusual dishes in Moscow, but not here. There were cold meats, there was cheese, and for breakfast oatmeal and blinis.

"The only curious thing was the wild boar. On-site, there was a whole fridge full of wild game: venison (roe and red deer) and wild boar, because whoever heard of coming to a hunting lodge and not giving it a try? But officially they'd invited Yeltsin to hunt, and on the first day everyone was ready for some hunting. There was a gamekeeper, there were rifles, there would be a battue. But it soon became apparent that Yeltsin wasn't going to do any hunting; none of his people were either. By the time he flew in, he had a hard time finding his way to the airplane door, and then he almost fell off the steps."

7.

"It was a fiasco, not hunting," says Stepan Martysiuk. "We all got ready, expecting it to be like in Brezhnev's time: a wonderful hunt, then they'd have a meal of wild game in the forest, or *kulish*, and after that they'd get drunk and see to their business. I organized it all, including a cauldron standing ready in the forest to make soup, and a portable minibar. Then it turned out only two of the Ukrainians were going to hunt: President Kravchuk and the premier, Fokin.

"I can't tell you how disappointed I was. But there was no reason to take offense—it all went according to plan: Kravchuk and Fokin walked toward the pulpits, my people released the wild boars from their pen, and the animals raced in the direction of the hunters, expecting to get some food. But Kravchuk had gone with five bodyguards, and those guys made lots of noise—one moment they were smoking a cigarette, another they were swearing, another they were cracking jokes. They scared off all the wild boars. Instead of running under the line of fire, as they'd been taught, the boars sat in the forest and refused to move.

"Kravchuk waved a hand, claiming it was a waste of his time. But Fokin went deeper into the forest with my most experienced hunter, Yevgeny Luksha. As soon as things quieted down, Fokin shot a boar."

★

"I remember it well," says Polina Ivanovna. "We were cooking up a storm, because making food for that many people is no simple matter. Then in came the hunters, who said the Ukrainian premier had shot a boar. And with a laugh they tossed it, dripping blood, bristles and all, onto the floor by the larder, as if to say, 'Cook it.'

"I thought I was going to lose it. 'People,' I said, 'if you want it cooked, then skin it, butcher it, remove the shoulder or the saddle, and we'll think of something, but what am I supposed to do with a wild boar that's still bleeding?' But I'll tell you something, Witold. It was hard to find anyone sober there. The locals distilled their own hooch, using spring water and nothing but natural ingredients. Brezhnev had given them special concessions so they could do it legally. In the courtyard at the lodge, there was a barrel full of that local hooch. Anyone who wanted could go up and pour himself some.

"So that boar just lay there; to get anything out of the larder, we had to step over it. Until finally someone took pity, dragged it away, then skinned and butchered it."

8.

"As I've already said, the first to bring up the idea of sidestepping Gorbachev was Gennady Burbulis," recalled Vyacheslav Kebich. "But of course he didn't say, 'Let's bring down the Soviet Union.' It was put far more subtly, in order to sound us out. He said something like, 'So what if we were to try bypassing

Gorbachev and coming to terms behind his back?' That's what we were there for, so of course everyone applauded it. And then Burbulis asked, 'And what if we were to form a new structure for the union, without Gorbachev?' Then everyone waited to hear what Kravchuk would say, and what Shushkevich would say.

"By now it was clear the stakes were high. Form a structure without Gorbachev? What exactly did that mean?! But we were already so tired of Gorbachev, and of the impossibility of coming to terms with him on anything at all, that we all applauded. All right, we don't know how, but let's do it.

"We left the sauna and went to have supper. And the next day the negotiations began. Point by point, the entire agreement had to be thought up and written. Problems arose too. We weren't equipped to sign any important documents—we didn't have a typewriter, or a typist, or a fax machine. My people found a typewriter and then brought in a typist from the nearby collective farm, but she was so terrified by the sight of all those famous people that she was incapable of typing. And no wonder—she was an ordinary girl from the village; she probably didn't even know some of the words that would have to be in the agreement. Then Burbulis sat down at the typewriter. Or dictated the agreement, letter by letter.

"But to get a fax machine, we had to send a plane all the way to Minsk. When it came back, it turned out several journalists were on board. Somehow they had gotten wind of the fact that something important was happening.

"Today, in retrospect, I can see the Russians were well prepared for that meeting. Because at some point Burbulis said:

'Gentlemen, there's an important point missing! To form a new organization, we'll have to do away with the old one!' And he started explaining to us that the Soviet Union had originally been called into being by four republics: the Russian, Belarusian, Ukrainian, and Transcaucasian. Transcaucasus no longer existed, because it had split into smaller republics. So by a strange coincidence the successors of all three extant republics were here, in Białowieża Forest. And we merely had to write that the original agreement, made seventy years ago, was no longer valid.

"I'll tell you something, Witold. If anyone had told me what the consequences would be—that the country would cease to exist, that it would fall apart, and that we'd have wars, in Yugoslavia and in Donbas—I'd never have signed it. But at the time I was sure we were doing away with the Soviet Union and creating the Commonwealth of Independent States in its place. We were changing the name, but everything—the currency, army, and borders—would remain the same.

"Well. Now I can say it—we were swindled."

★

"The head of the Belarusian KGB was among the people there," says Stepan Martysiuk. "I knew him, because he used to come with us to hunt. And he told me, 'I must inform Moscow what's happening here.' I didn't even protest. I suspected that Gorbachev would send a platoon of commandos, shoot us all, and that would be the end of it. And I'll tell you something, Witold. Any other general secretary would have done that. There would have been no stone left standing. But not Gorbachev. All he could do was weep."

"I regarded Boris Yeltsin as my friend," said Vyacheslav Kebich. "I wept at his funeral for the loss of a really close pal. But since you ask, I must say that in the matter of the Białowieża agreements, Boris cheated us. He was playing a completely different game, for an entirely different stake. It was all meant to look spontaneous: someone asked in the sauna, 'What would happen if we removed Gorbachev from power?' Then someone suggested we write a memorandum, which proved to be not a memorandum but an agreement abolishing the USSR. In fact, there was nothing spontaneous about it. Boris knew perfectly well what he was coming to us with. He took advantage of our naïveté, Shushkevich's and mine; we two had only just started our journey in politics. In my defense I can say this: it was the tail end of 1991. All the Soviet republics apart from Kazakhstan had signed declarations of independence. I've already told you the USSR was a corpse waiting for the coroner to sign its death certificate. We were the coroner. And the Białowieża agreements were the certificate."

9.

"I conferred with my colleagues about what we could do with the wild boar that would be quick but also tasty," recalls Polina Ivanovna. "And we agreed to make goulash. It's a dish everyone likes; we'd add herbs, marjoram and garlic, to bring out the taste of the wild game and to reflect the climate of the place we were in.

"The boar was served for supper on the day before they signed the agreements. You asked what was presented at the

Soviet Union's last supper. So there were sausages, salads, cheeses, a little caviar, a little fish, and some rissoles. But the pièce de résistance was the boar shot by the premier of Ukraine. Wild boar goulash.

"The next day they dismembered our country, just like that boar.

"And that was that."

MENU
◇◇◇

Wild Boar Goulash

This recipe was given to the author by Polina Ivanovna, who cooked it as the last dish ever served in the Soviet Union.

1½ pounds (700 g) boar meat from the haunch
4 shallots with shoots
2½ cups (250 g) button mushrooms
3½ tablespoons (50 ml) olive oil
2 tablespoons (50 g) butter
7 ounces (200 ml) dry white wine
7 ounces (200 ml) single cream
Salt and black pepper, to taste
5 tablespoons mustard

Cut the boar meat into strips. Cut the shoots from the shallots and slice them lengthwise, then cut the shallots on the diagonal to a length of 3 to 4 inches (8 to 10 cm) each. Cut the mushrooms into thick slices.

Heat a frying pan. Pour in the olive oil, then add the butter and fry the boar meat until browned.

Add the mushrooms, shallots, and shoots to the pan and stir. Lower the heat to medium, pour in the wine, and cook for 4 to 5 minutes. Add the cream and salt and pepper, stir it all together, and remove the pan from the heat. Add the mustard and mix again.

The shallots can be replaced with leeks if desired. Dijon mustard—or a milder kind—is best.

XVI

The Sanatorium Cook

A cook, apart from anything, is a cook.

VLADIMIR PUTIN

1.

If things didn't go his way, he threw his apron to the floor and walked out. At the Astoria, which before World War I was one of the most expensive restaurants in Saint Petersburg, the staff would start to panic—because it was he, senior chef Spiridon Putin, who had the key to the cupboard where the pricier alcoholic drinks were kept. If there was no Putin, there was no Armenian brandy or French wine.

Or so the family legend goes.

He would retain this impetuosity until the end of his life, though in retirement he would live in a small apartment and would relax by going fishing and smoking innumerable cigarettes.

His grandson Vladimir met his grandfather only a few times, but he hasn't forgotten that Spiridon was a master of his profession. Another family legend has it that once, in the days of the tsar, Rasputin came to lunch at the Astoria. What did Putin cook for Rasputin? Maybe one of the dishes for which the Astoria was famous—chicken julienne? Lamb cutlets? Or maybe zander "Orly" in tartar sauce, garnished with caviar?

That no one remembers.

According to the family story, the court charlatan liked the food so much that after the meal he summoned the chef, and when he arrived Rasputin handed him a gold coin. The older members of the Putin family swear that it was among the family keepsakes until recently; someone still remembers it, but then came two wars, Stalinism, the thaw, perestroika, and somewhere along the way the coin went missing.

Apparently no one remembers how Spiridon Putin ended up at one of the best restaurants in imperial Saint Petersburg. Some say he was a pauper from Pominovo, a small village outside Tver. He was looking for any sort of job, and at the age of twelve he started working in restaurants. He soon appeared to have golden hands, so the chefs began to teach him the profession. By the age of thirty he had become a respected head chef.

But others say the Putins were a clan of cooks, and Spiridon learned his trade from his cousins.

The golden days of the tsar ended with the start of World War I. From the kitchen, Spiridon went straight to the front. Many years later his grandson Vladimir would tell the movie director Oliver Stone, who recorded an informal documentary interview with him, how first his grandfather fired at an

Austrian soldier from a trench—but when he hit the man, he instantly ran up with a first aid kit to dress his wound and thus saved his life. "If he hadn't fired, the Austrian would have killed him," said Putin.

So Spiridon had to defend himself. But he didn't want to kill.

This grandfather is surprisingly similar to Vladimir Putin's Russia, which also—if you believe the propaganda—only ever uses weapons in its own defense.

2.

The Russians first learned about Putin the cook from a different free-flowing interview. A little earlier Boris Yeltsin, who had started to annoy the Russians with his alcoholic excesses, had unexpectedly anointed the chef's grandson Vladimir as his successor. There was preelection fever in the air, and soon it would become clear whether the energetic young judo practitioner with a KGB past was going to replace Yeltsin in the post of president. The election he had to win was coming closer.

Putin's conversation with three Russian journalists, published under the title *First Person*, was designed to acquaint Russians—and the world—with this little-known politician.[*] In it Putin talks about his family, his career in the KGB, the years he spent in the German Democratic Republic, his wife, and even about the grandmother who secretly had him baptized.

*An American edition appeared under the title *First Person: An Astonishingly Frank Self-Portrait by Russia's President Vladimir Putin* (New York: PublicAffairs, 2000).

And about his grandfather.

"Apparently my grandfather cooked rather well, because after World War I he was offered a job in The Hills district, on the outskirts of Moscow, where Lenin and the whole Ulyanov family lived. When Lenin died, my grandfather was transferred to one of Stalin's dachas. He worked there a long time," said Putin, then still a candidate for president of Russia.

"He wasn't a victim of the purges?" asked the journalists.

"No, for some reason they let him be. Few people who spent much time around Stalin came through unscathed, but my grandfather was one of them. He outlived Stalin, by the way, and in his later, retirement years, he was a cook at the Moscow City Party Committee sanatorium in Ilinskoye."

Since then, just about every biography of the Russian president has stated that his grandfather was Lenin's and Stalin's cook.

3.

Spiridon Putin's family was decimated by the blockade of Leningrad and the war against the Germans. Of his four sons, only two survived: Vladimir and Alexander. Vladimir, for whom the president is named, was then a citizen of Leningrad, and he volunteered for the army. He was assigned to an NKVD unit that carried out acts of sabotage behind enemy lines, near the town of Kingisepp. When their food ran out, they went to a nearby village to ask the peasants for help. The peasants informed on them to the Germans. Vladimir Putin Senior's unit fell into an ambush.

Of twenty-eight men, only Vladimir and three of his fellow

soldiers managed to survive. Putin-the-father was wounded, and while escaping pursuit he spent a whole night in a lake, breathing through a hollow reed. Miraculously he managed to get back to Leningrad, but he was exhausted and his wound was severe. If someone hadn't helped him across the river Neva, he'd have had no chance of survival.

Luckily there turned out to be a neighbor serving in the same unit. He swam across the Neva with the wounded Putin.

"Go and live—I'm going back to die," he said in farewell, and returned to his unit.

News traveled fast in besieged Leningrad, and, with their two-year-old son Viktor in tow, his wife, Maria, managed to find the wounded Vladimir. Like every citizen of Leningrad at the time, little Viktor was constantly hungry. So his father gave him his entire food ration—the hospitals, like the schools and preschools, had their own canteens.

When the nurses saw what was going on, they refused to let Maria and the child enter the hospital. The hospital food was for the wounded, not for those who were dying of hunger in the city. They were treated like they were already corpses.

Little Viktor Putin didn't survive the siege. He died of diphtheria. Once Vladimir Putin Junior was president, in a moving article written for the magazine *Russian Pioneer* he described how his emaciated mother was carried out of a collapsing building on a stretcher. She escaped death at the last minute.

4.

In all his interviews, the late Alexander Putin, the future president's uncle and one of the only two Putin brothers to have survived the blockade of Leningrad, stressed what a modest person his father, Spiridon, was, and also what a good cook. "He learned his trade in the days of the tsar, when the art of cooking was flourishing. He especially liked cooking meat and fish, but he didn't have a trademark dish," he said in an interview for *Komsomolskaya Pravda*. "Everyone was always satisfied. Until he reached the age of seventy-two, they asked him [to cook] for banquets. My father got very angry when limitations on produce were introduced. How can there be limitations on a cook? He should know for himself when to add something and how much!"

He continued: "He was a man of principle, and even in times when food was in short supply he never brought anything home from work. Not even canapés. He lived modestly, in two tiny little rooms. He received a monthly pension of 120 rubles and never asked for more. He was inimitable. There are few people like that nowadays."

Apparently Spiridon Putin had no esteem for his job as a cook. He regarded it as thankless and regretted not becoming an engineer or an architect. He didn't want his children or grandchildren to follow in his footsteps.

That's roughly all we know about him. But I wanted to find out more.

When I visited Gorki Leninskiye, where Lenin lived out his last days, I asked the guides and the manager about Spiridon Putin. They all went quiet.

"We're still looking for the documents," said the manager diplomatically.

"But I thought Shura Vorobyova cooked for Lenin," I said, pressing the point.

"If the president said his grandfather worked here, he worked here," replied the manager. "I'm sure the documents will turn up soon."

In Saint Petersburg I talked to a longtime, legendary manager of the Astoria restaurant. He told me straight-out that he had never heard of the president's grandfather. But later on, just in case, he asked me not to give his name. The longer I tried to find information on Spiridon Putin, the more he eluded me. The more I tried to confirm his life story in any of the archives or documents, or at least to talk to someone who knew him personally, the higher the stone wall I came up against.

Until finally I realized that I wasn't going to find any proof that Spiridon Putin cooked at the Astoria or that Rasputin gave him a gold coin.

Why not?

Because there isn't any. Just as there is no proof that he cooked for Lenin or Stalin. All his life Spiridon Putin cooked at sanatoriums, including one for Party members—and that was it. Indeed, perhaps Stalin's successor, Nikita Khrushchev, could have been among them, and Vyacheslav Molotov too, because Vladimir Putin's uncle Alexander said so in an interview. And maybe once or twice he was asked to cook something for a banquet at which Stalin was a guest. Maybe he did actually work at one of Stalin's dachas for a while. Maybe he was one of the cooks whom the Kremlin invited to work at large banquets, or he filled in for someone there?

We shall never know. But I'm sure of one thing: half of his life story is fabricated; it's a combination of facts and pure fiction.

The story of Spiridon Putin is probably the best example of

how—from the kitchen onward—Russian propaganda works. It doesn't matter if a story is true. What matters is that people believe it. The grandfather who delighted Rasputin, and who then cooked for Lenin and Stalin, was for Vladimir Putin a superb advertising gimmick before the election, because in his biography he combined the eras for which the Russians—despite all the evil of those days—feel most nostalgic.

"Since the leaders of the USSR trusted my grandfather, you can trust me," Vladimir Putin seemed to be saying.

And so they did.

5.

Since gaining power, Vladimir Putin has never surrendered it. He has reigned supreme at the Kremlin for more than twenty years. What does he eat? Occasionally the Kremlin publishes the menu from one of his meetings with the leader of another country. For instance, in December 2019 Putin met at Yalta with Alexander Lukashenko, the president of Belarus. On that occasion the appetizers included a pumpkin salad with tomatoes and cheese, squid with pureed carrots, green pea soup, and red mullet with artichokes and quinoa; the entrée was veal steak with roasted leeks; and for dessert there was mandarin sorbet and a strawberry tart.

But I know from Viktor Belyaev that leaders rarely eat what's on the table: they have a proper meal only once the official meetings are over. What does Putin eat when no one's looking? The only fact Belyaev betrayed to me is that he's obsessively fond of ice cream—any dessert that makes its way onto his table is served with at least one scoop of it.

During the meeting at Yalta, Putin gave Lukashenko a samovar and a supply of tea. In exchange, Lukashenko brought him a basket of victuals: ham, horseradish and mustard, candied cranberries, cheese, *basturma* (cured beef) from Grodno, and sirloin steak. Russian journalists sneeringly commented that the Belarusian was bringing better and better gifts—on a previous visit he had come with several sacks of potatoes grown on Belarusian collective farms. A few months later, mass protests began in Belarus. Hundreds of thousands demonstrated against Lukashenko, who has been in power for more than twenty-five years. But Putin must have liked the Belarusian treats—during the protests he came out in support of the mustachioed, comb-over-coiffed dictator. Because although the Russian president once said that anyone who doesn't regret the collapse of the USSR has no heart, but anyone who wishes for its return has no brain, under his control Russia is trying to reconstruct the Soviet empire. Putin may be a modest eater, but he has a vast appetite for power in the region and in the world at large. Russia has attacked Georgia, interferes in conflicts in the Middle East, and tries (sometimes successfully) to influence elections in the United States and the European Union.

But the most glaring example of this is the invasion of Ukraine that began in 2014. That was when Putin showed that he won't stop at anything.

Maybe thanks to his grandfather, Putin does have a soft spot for chefs; one such cook is Yevgeny Prigozhin, who for many years was a restaurateur in Saint Petersburg before being put in charge of Putin's special operations and earning a place on the FBI's most-wanted list for interfering in the 2016 American presidential election. His private army, known as the Wagner Group, is famous for extracting the most hardened criminals from prison to fight in the war against Ukraine, on the promise of reduced sentences—if they survive. Prigozhin sent them to the worst sections of the front, including the fighting for Bakhmut, the city that has taken the longest time to capture—and is the most blood-soaked site on the entire front since World War II. The Ukrainians calculated that, on average, in some places on the front one member of the Wagner Group was killed every seven minutes.

The survivors got their promised freedom, including Anatoly Salmin from Pikalevo, who before being enlisted for the group was serving a sentence for the brutal murder of a friend. But he was lucky—he survived, returned to Pikalevo, and now the whole town lives in fear of him.

The Wagner Group shed a great deal of blood capturing Bakhmut, after which—to everyone's astonishment—Prigozhin rebelled against the Russian elite (especially the Ministry of Defense, which he accused outright of a fatal attack on his men) and began a desperate march toward Moscow. Mistakenly called by many a putsch, the march ended in less than twenty-four hours, but before that Prigozhin and his men succeeded in putting the Kremlin leaders' noses out of joint and amazing many Western experts when, without firing a single shot, they captured the southern army command center in Rostov-on-Don and later in Voronezh and reached a point less than 125 miles from Moscow, before suddenly abandoning their advance. Of course, all this was possible only because the Russian army was unsure how to react to Prigozhin's raid and did not know if it was the unplanned action of a single man (or a small number of people) or—as has been known to happen before in Russia—the result of a more extensive power grab.

Prigozhin called off his troops and surrendered in less than a day. Apparently it was Lukashenko who negotiated between him and the Kremlin.

What exactly was negotiated—and what exactly this rebellion was—we will probably never know. Nonetheless, readers of this book should no longer be surprised that in Russia the grandson of one cook clashed with another cook in the fight for power.

XVII

Crimean Tatar Cuisine

1.

"Would you like some chebureki?" Erfan Kudusov is looking at me with all the magic power of his gently slanting dark eyes, those of a boy who may have grown up but who hasn't lost his charm or sense of fun. "Mine are the best in all of Kyiv, no joking."

I like chebureki, which are Tatar pierogi made of flour, salt, and water. And I believe him when he says they're delicious. But if we start partying, we won't be in the mood for work. So first I ask for a cup of Tatar coffee, as thick and black as asphalt melted by the sun on the Black Sea in summer; I settle upon the rug on which guests are received here and switch on my Dictaphone. Crimea. Exile. Crimea again. Exile again. On top of that, cooking, love, and war. There's a story to be heard.

Erfan doesn't have childhood memories of Crimea, because he wasn't there. He was born a quarter of a century after the deportation that was meant to snap the spine of his ancestors, the Crimean Tatars. The only thing he can remember is the food his grandmother used to make: chebureki, *köbete* (a pie filled with meat and rice or vegetables), *yantiq* (chebureki that are grilled rather than fried), *sarma* (meat wrapped in vine leaves), and shorba (a meat soup). Whenever his grandmother, a superb cook, put a pot on the fire, the eyes of the older people—those who remembered Crimea—would glaze over as they began to reminisce about the steppes, their fields, houses, and vineyards. Their neighbors. And their life on the beautiful peninsula where the Tatars lived for hundreds of years, and which in these stories sounded like paradise.

Erfan's father was only two years old in 1944 when his parents—Erfan's grandfather and grandmother—were deported to Uzbekistan, but he always claimed he had a perfect memory of his family home near Simferopol and every room in it.

"We regarded his stories as harmless whimsy," says Erfan. "After all, we knew my father had been too young to remember anything. His memories of the house were thought of as fairy tales, like the kind we let old people tell to indulge them."

In his childhood, Erfan heard so much about Crimea that sometimes he saw it in his dreams.

"I felt as if I'd been there; in my dreams it seemed real. But now I know those memories were passed down through my genes," he says. "In fact, all my forebears, right up to my father, were born there and died there. It was only my mom who was born in Uzbekistan, two years after the deportation. I was in the first generation that had no connection with Crimea apart from our ancestors' memories. Stalin came up with the idea of cutting the Tatars off from their land and transferring them to an entirely new place. In Uzbekistan, we were supposed to mingle with the Uzbeks and cease to exist. Stalin came close to succeeding—I am the best example of that. But one thing at a time."

2.

Dilyara Seitvelyeva—or Dilyara-khanum to the Tatars, because "khanum" is their honorary title for a highly respected woman—is a serene lady with a friendly smile, whose face doesn't betray that she's over seventy. We're meeting in the garden adjoining her children's house in Kyiv, where Dilyara is staying.

"But I'm going back to Crimea soon," she warns. "I shall never move away from there. It has cost my family too much for us to be able to live there."

So I reach a hand toward the generously filled bowl of Crimean dried fruit and nuts—it would be insulting not to eat what's set out on the table—sip my coffee that's as thick as tar, and listen. Dilyara-khanum is certain that the Russians had been planning for many years to deport the Tatars.

"In the days of Catherine the Great we were displaced," she says. "But the worst times came with the Bolsheviks. When they took over, first of all, like other ethnicities that they found inconvenient, we suffered famine. In 1921 more than a hundred thousand people died of starvation in Crimea. Another fifty thousand left the peninsula in search of a better place to live. That's one in five."

Later on the Tatars faced equally difficult times. In an effort to subordinate them entirely, the Soviets applied their favorite methods: terror and assassination. In April 1938 the NKVD executed their elite: writers, thinkers, scholars, clerics, and members of the Mejlis—the Tatars' governing body.

During World War II the Germans took advantage of the Tatars' hatred of the Russians and used them to help fight the Soviet partisans in Crimea.

"When the Soviet Union recaptured Crimea from the Germans in 1944, they took their revenge by deporting us. Every last one of us," says Dilyara. "Officially it was a punishment for collaborating with the Germans. But we all know that was just a pretext to get rid of us. The deportation was an extremely complicated operation. The war was still on, and millions of soldiers were away at the front. But in just two and a half days the NKVD deported almost two hundred thousand people from Crimea to Uzbekistan. No one was left."

Today the Tatars regard the deportation carried out on Stalin's orders as genocide.

In fact, following the deportation there were still two Tatar villages in Crimea, located on the Arabat Spit, a long way from anywhere else. The inhabitants spent their time catching fish and lived far enough from civilization that the NKVD machine passed them by. Bogdan Kobulov, the general known as "the Samovar," who was in charge of the resettlement operation, first heard about the two remaining villages at a point when both he and his men had already been awarded medals for the operation. Embarrassed that the operation hadn't been quite so effective after all, he had the inhabitants of both villages herded onto a barge, tied up, and thrown into the sea.

They all perished.

In Crimea, which had been in Tatar hands since the days of Genghis Khan, not a single Tatar was left.

3.

"It only recently became clear to me how our parents and grandparents lived after the deportation," says Erfan. "I was talking to my mom about something, and she used the phrase, 'When we still lived in a dugout.' I had heard that they lived in tough conditions at first, but I thought it had lasted around a year or eighteen months, and then they'd built houses. But now that I'm living in exile myself, I've finally started to ask questions. And it turns out my mom lived in a sort of cave until she was twelve! In a pit dug out of the ground and covered in tarpaulin. What's more, there were many times when my friends and I went to play in the spot where she had lived; we called it 'the pits,' and we thought some archaeologists or engineers had been excavating there, but it never occurred to me that I was running around in the place where my family used to live, my closest relatives too—my mom, my grandma, my grandpa, my uncles and aunts."

"The first year after deportation was dreadful," adds Dilyara-khanum. "People were hungry and got sick. They started to die."

Almost half of the Tatars who were deported in 1944 died of hunger or illness during that first year.

Many years later Dilyara's brother, Mustafa Jemilev—or Mustafa-khan to the Tatars—was one of the most famous activists for the Tatar minority in the Soviet Union. Altogether he served fifteen years in prisons and labor camps, all because he fought for the return of the Tatars to Crimea.

"Mustafa-khan said that when Stalin died, the whole school was hysterical," Dilyara tells me, referring to her brother's school days. "Everyone was crying, including the headmistress and the teachers. Everyone except for the Tatar children. They knew very well what Stalin had done to our nation. Mustafa-khan mentioned that one boy, age twelve or thirteen, had quickly run home for an onion and told the younger kids to rub it on their eyes. 'We have to cry,' he said, 'otherwise they'll take our parents away to prison.' And so it was for years. We adapted. If necessary, we even wept. But everyone knew the truth."

Those who survived were subjected to very strong indoctrination. "My father was very pro-Tatar," says Erfan Kudusov. "Our activists used to meet at his photographic studio. They'd sign joint letters that they sent to Moscow, to the general secretaries, because they were strangely convinced that if Stalin, Khrushchev, or Brezhnev knew about the fate of the unfortunate Tatars, they'd be sure to stand up for them. Of course the only thing those letters prompted was the anger of the KGB. My father's studio was searched many times over."

While his father was an ardent Tatar patriot, Erfan describes himself as a child as an equally ardent product of Soviet propaganda: "If I'd lived with my father, I'd probably have grown up to be a dissident. But my parents divorced, and I only saw him a few times each month. And Mom was so terrified that something might happen to me that she started sending me to meetings of the Komsomol, the communist youth organization. As a kid and into my teens I believed deeply in communism, convinced that we were living under the best possible system. It's silly to admit it, but I was completely brainwashed. Sure, I couldn't entirely get my head around why it was that in this best

of all systems—where, as Lenin said, all nations were equal—
ours seemed rather less equal. But Lenin also said that on the
road to communism, mistakes can occur. I simply regarded it
as a mistake made during the fever of war. And one that could
be fixed."

Except that the years went by, and no one fixed the mistake.
Moreover, after several decades in exile, the Tatars who tried to
return to Crimea under their own steam were met with a very
firm reaction from the authorities. In the 1960s the Soviet
Union sought people to come and work in Crimea, and at first
the officials failed to spot the several hundred Tatar families
who had managed to return.

"My wife's family was among them," says Erfan. "What
those people went through is unimaginable. At the time I was
happily singing Komsomol songs. But my future parents-in-law
were going through a terrible time solely because they wanted
to live on the land of their forebears."

That was when Dilyara-khanum's brother, Mustafa Jemilev,
went to prison for the first time.

4.

In 1975, Dilyara was pregnant with her first child when her husband made an important decision.

"He left the army, and instead of coming to join us in Uzbekistan, he went to Crimea to look for a house for us," she says.
"My brother was in prison at the time. My husband went into
the unknown, and I didn't know how it would end either. But
the die was cast. From then on, our life was going to be completely different."

A few months later Dilyara-khanum joined her husband, who had found a house in a small village cut off from the world, not far from Bakhchysarai, the former capital of the Tatar khans.

"The house was abandoned, rotten, and decaying; it was hard to live there. We had no running water or electricity. The nearest bus stop was two kilometers away, and once a day we could travel to a bigger town. My oldest son was born in those conditions. Soon afterward, my parents came to join us. They both wept with joy. My father was born before the end of the nineteenth century; by then he was over seventy and had never expected to see Crimea again. But they also cried with sorrow, because Crimea had been badly neglected under the Soviet regimes."

The Seitvelyev family's presence in Crimea was, from the authorities' point of view, illegal.

"They put every possible stumbling block in our way," says Dilyara-khanum. "Above all, they wouldn't register us. That meant we couldn't work, although the manager of the run-down local collective farm was very keen to employ us and kept asking for our advice about all sorts of things, because my husband and I were both qualified engineers."

In fact, the authorities were consistently targeting all the Tatars who had managed to slip through the net and settle in Crimea. They applied all sorts of repressive measures. Usually the militia arrived in the middle of the night; the families, often with small children, were packed into a vehicle, driven far out into the steppe, and left with no food or water.

"I know a man whom they deported that way eight times," says Dilyara-khanum. "Each time they also emptied a large crate of garbage into his house, or poured sewage into it, so he'd have nowhere to return to. But every time he came back, cleaned the house with his neighbors' help, and started over from scratch. If there's something we Tatars are good at, it's definitely starting over from scratch. The Soviets taught us that very well."

So Dilyara-khanum and her husband lived in Crimea but were officially registered in another part of the Soviet Union, in Krasnodar Krai. They couldn't work, and they lived purely on what grew around their home.

"We couldn't even plant things in the garden," she recalls. "Not a single watermelon or pumpkin. What did we do? We picked everything that grew wild along the road, various medicinal plants, including wild rose and dogwood. Our friends brought us food too, or planted vegetables for us—not by the house, but by the road, for instance, or somewhere on the fringes of the collective farm. Thanks to that, we got by."

After two or three years the local KGB realized that their repressive measures were ineffective.

"They had wasted a lot of time and energy, because we kept coming back anyway, and giving birth to children. There weren't meant to be any Tatars in Crimea, but there were more and more of us," says Dilyara-khanum. "They had to do something. From then on, whenever they took Tatars into the steppe, a bulldozer came and demolished their houses. Then they really had nowhere to return to."

"So what did they do? Did they leave?" I ask.

"No way." Dilyara shrugs as if I know nothing about the Tatars or their strength in the silent battle against the Soviet Union. "Anyone who went to Crimea in that period knew it wouldn't be easy. We were ready for anything."

The repression of the Tatars reached its peak in 1978. That was also when the first serious tragedy occurred: in utter desperation, a man named Musa Mamut, whom the authorities were planning to deport with his family into the steppe for the umpteenth time, doused himself in gasoline and set himself on fire.

"They wouldn't even let us go to his funeral," says Dilyara-khanum. "My husband and the other men in the neighborhood went there by car. But all the roads to his village had been cut off, and the militia and the police turned away anyone who tried to take part in the ceremony. My husband got there by walking a very long way across the fields."

Since no one from the Seitvelyev family was living in Crimea legally, they regularly had to travel to the place where they had last been registered.

"By now the authorities knew that we weren't leaving Crimea voluntarily," says Dilyara-khanum. "So they took advantage of our departure, and on April 12, 1979, they came for my mom, who'd been left at home alone. This was after the death of Musa Mamut, and they were afraid of our desperation. So ten cars came to get Mom, an old woman all on her own, including a fire truck, just in case. Meanwhile, they wouldn't let us back into Crimea; instead, Mom came to join us in Krasnodar Krai, and we were forced to stay there for the next ten years."

In Krasnodar Krai, Dilyara's family lived through the death of Brezhnev, and also the death of their father, whom Mustafa-khan tried unsuccessfully to bury in his beloved Crimea.

"We watched in horror as the Soviet Union not only removed us and our friends from Crimea—they also got rid of every scrap of evidence that the Tatars had ever lived there.

They destroyed our old cemeteries; collective farm combines drove over those sites instead. They changed the names of almost all the places that came from our language. They changed our madrasa, Zincirli, founded in the sixteenth century—where in the days of the khanate, philosophers, poets, and astronomers had studied—into . . . a mental hospital. Please don't think I have anything against the mentally ill. But the Soviets didn't do such things by chance."

"Meaning?"

"They were very good at exploiting symbols, and if they made a place that for centuries had been the fountain of Tatar science and art into a hospital for the mentally ill, then believe me, they knew perfectly well what they were doing. But this obliteration of the evidence of Tatar culture was also expressed in much more trivial ways. In the town in Krasnodar Krai where we had lived, there was a bus station. In Gorbachev's day small private enterprises were allowed, and a Tatar woman opened a little bar there, where she sold chebureki. So she had a sign above the bar saying CHEBUREKI in large block letters, because what else should it say? But you have to know that chebureki were the primary Crimean Tatar export; the entire Soviet Union ate them, from Brest to Vladivostok, and everyone knew they belonged to Tatar cuisine. But we were living too close to Crimea; even the cooking, even our chebureki were a political issue. So one day the militia came to see the woman. And the next day the sign saying CHEBUREKI was gone, and a new sign saying SOUTHERN PIEROGI was in its place. It didn't matter that the woman who made them was a Crimean Tatar, or that she made them exactly the same way as the Tatars on the Crimean peninsula had made their chebureki for centuries."

5.

While the Seitvelyev family was battling with the authorities, Erfan the young Komsomol member finished school in Uzbekistan and then left for college in Russia.

"I studied law," he says. "I didn't realize it then, but I was the only student among the Crimean Tatars who was allowed to. There was a whole list of professions to which we were not admitted, including law and journalism. But the authorities must have thought the Komsomol had brainwashed me enough for me to be harmless. They agreed to let me study law, though not in Moscow; I studied in Ivanovo, two hundred kilometers from the capital."

Meanwhile, Gorbachev came to power in the Soviet Union. He was the first Soviet leader to try to come to grips with some thorny issues. Apart from his introducing those standard bywords, "perestroika" and "glasnost," there was a spirit of freedom in the air for the first time in many decades. Wanting to take advantage of the moment, the Crimean Tatars organized a major demonstration in Moscow's Red Square to insist on their right to return to their homeland.

"Although I'd never lived in Crimea, I felt a surge of Tatar sentiment," says Erfan. "And I longed to return to the land of my forebears too. While I was still in college I did an internship at the prosecution service in Simferopol, where I got very good testimonials. I wrote my master's dissertation on especially horrific murders, graduating summa cum laude, and I wanted to go back and work there. I submitted an application and waited. There was no answer, so I boarded a plane and went to see what was going on. I arrived at the prosecution service, and it was all very nice—a cup of coffee and a friendly chat—until the secretary said that the chief prosecutor wanted to speak to me. 'Great, let's talk!' He greeted me very warmly and asked about my journey, but then he said, 'It's my lunch break, so let's head outside.' And once we were outside he asked me directly, 'Tell me, son, is it true you were born in Uzbekistan?' 'Yes, that's right.' 'Crimean Tatar, are you?' 'Yes, I am.' 'Son,' he said, 'I'll be frank with you. You've got all the qualifications to work here. But I have orders from Moscow not to give any of you a job.'"

"And how did you react?"

"I was crushed. In the first place, until then I had genuinely believed in communism and in the fact that the Tatar resettlement was some sort of wartime mistake that could be fixed. And here I had proof in black and white that it wasn't a mistake but a deliberate policy. And second, Gorbachev was telling us on TV that from now on the Soviet Union would try to change and would correct its errors. But in private, outside the office, the chief prosecutor of Crimea was telling me he had orders from Moscow not to employ Tatars. So what was the truth? Who was lying? I didn't know. But that day in Simferopol, my transformation process began."

Political changes may have been slow to happen, but under Gorbachev the Tatars did start leaving Uzbekistan en masse for Crimea. Their exodus was so great that Aeroflot, the Soviet airline, started up a direct flight from Tashkent to Simferopol. At the time it was one of the most overbooked flights in the entire Soviet Union; sometimes as many as three planes flew in a day.

"My sister was living in Tashkent then," says Dilyarakhanum. "And as absolutely all the Crimean Tatars knew our family because of my brother, her house became a stop-off point on the journey. There was always a key under the doormat, and anyone who needed to stay the night or freshen up could drop in, make a cup of tea, have something to eat, and rest before continuing their trip."

"I settled in Yalta," says Erfan, "at the home of a distant cousin. Every day there were more and more of us in Crimea. The atmosphere was one of a joyful picnic. You'd go outside, and every few minutes you'd bump into a relative or a friend. 'When did you fly in? Where are you living? Is there anything you need? Come on, let's have a quick drink.' That's what my life was like in those days. I sorted out my work too: Gorbachev agreed that people could open private businesses, so some Jews in Simferopol opened a bank. They went to Moscow, got all the necessary permissions and licenses, and returned to Crimea. But then it turned out they couldn't find anyone willing to work for them: people thought working for a state-owned firm was far more stable than a job at a private bank. So those Jews had a tough nut to crack, until suddenly along came thousands of Tatars, including accountants, cashiers, and economists. They took me in at that bank too, and I must tell you, it was the most unusual job I've ever had. Imagine a bank whose owners were Jews but all of whose staff were Muslims. And what's more, there was never any conflict at all."

Erfan soon realized he had a flair not just for prosecuting horrific murders but also for the world of business. He worked in banking for several years and then started up a real estate firm. He eventually leased several urban squares from the city and established markets on them.

"Two of them sold flowers, one sold construction materials,

and one was a sort of flea market selling antiques, pictures, and assorted junk. I made a very good living. But there was one thing I was always sure about: I could sell real estate, I could work in a bank, I could run my own markets, but I never, ever wanted to do anything connected with food. No restaurant, no bar, nothing to do with gastronomy. Quite simply, no. Several of my friends had gotten involved in that business, and I could see how tough the work was and how much dedication and time it demanded. I decided to keep far away from the restaurant business for the rest of my life."

6.

So Erfan ran his flower markets, and Dilyara-khanum, who had returned to Crimea for the second time in the late 1980s, got back to basics by working to develop Tatar education. Her brother, Mustafa Jemilev, became chairman of the Crimean governing body, the Mejlis.

"More of us had arrived from Uzbekistan than Stalin had deported," Dilyara-khanum says. "We opened schools, and the young people who had been unfamiliar with the Tatar language of their grandparents suddenly started speaking it. It seemed things could only get better. A few years later my children went off around the world to be educated. We couldn't afford to support them financially, so they had to earn for themselves as best they could. My younger son, who was in Turkey, got himself a summer job as a waiter at a Turkish holiday resort. And one day he came home to Bakhchysarai, looked around the district, and asked me about a house that belonged to one of my cousins.

"'Is Auntie planning to use that house? Why is it empty?' he asked. I replied that I didn't know if they were going to make use of it, because they had a second house, and this one was in a rather pitiful state. 'Mom,' said my son, 'that house is the ideal place to set up a restaurant.'

"I'll be honest with you, Witold, I had no idea what he was talking about. What did he mean, 'set up a restaurant'? Those of us who were raised in the Soviet Union never had such ideas. We'd grown up within a system that reviled expressions of private initiative. Everything had to be state-owned. Back in Uzbekistan, to support us, my mom had taken milk and cheese to the market, which I found highly embarrassing, because my teachers at school referred to people who did that sort of thing as 'profiteers' and 'relics of the previous system.' As a child I didn't want my mom to be one of those 'relics,' and this mindset was deeply rooted in me. But I tried to see it all through my son's eyes. There were more and more tourists coming to Crimea. It was mainly those who had property by the sea who earned money from them; although Bakhchysarai is a historic city, the former capital of the khanate, hardly anyone was profiting from tourism there. My cousin's house was beautifully situated close to the khans' palace, on a hillside that was pleasantly cool. There was also a spring beside it, and our ancestors had discovered that the spring water produces the best coffee. It occurred to me that perhaps he was right . . ."

The whole family got down to work. They had no money to hire a construction crew, so with their own hands they renovated the cousin's house and built small platforms on the hillside for the restaurant's tables.

"We did it all ourselves," says Dilyara-khanum. "And our family recipes ended up on the menu. Most of them were

Crimean Tatar dishes, but there's something you need to know. We spent several decades living alongside the Uzbeks, and they have one of the world's best cooking traditions. We could hardly fail to be influenced by it, so nowadays all Tatars cook Uzbek pilaf—rice with meat—and *manti*, which are meat dumplings. Now they're part of our tradition too, just as our exile to Uzbekistan has become a part of our history.

"We named the restaurant Musafir. My son calculated that it should start to bring in a profit after three years or, being optimistic, two. But we were making money within six months. It was a crazy moment. I was involved in politics, and at the same time my chebureki were what the guests liked most. So I'd be sitting at the Mejlis, in a meeting about education, when my son would call and say, 'Mom, help, we have a large group.' So I'd apologize to everyone, leave the debate, run off and make chebureki, dish them up, and an hour later I'd go back to the Mejlis. Many of the fruits and vegetables we served were from our garden; the meat was either ours or from our neighbors; we also cooked the way my mom taught me, just as her mom had taught her. On the menu were chebureki, yantiq, sarma [meat wrapped in vine leaves], dolmas [peppers stuffed with meat], *imam bayildi* [eggplant stuffed with meat and vegetables], and *nohutlu et* [lamb with chickpeas]."

7.

Everything in Crimea changed in November 2013, when Ukraine's president, Viktor Yanukovych, refused to sign his country's association agreement with the European Union. For several days, tens and later hundreds of thousands of people gathered on the streets of Kyiv. The police dealt with them extremely brutally, and several hundred people were killed. But the number of protestors didn't drop. Under pressure, Yanukovych was forced to flee to Russia.

Ukraine's moving closer to the European Union could have meant it would slip from Russia's sphere of influence, so Russia did not ease up. In late February 2014, Crimea, until then part of Ukraine, was captured by Russian troops. A month later a referendum was called, and a majority of the citizens of the peninsula declared themselves in favor of becoming part of Russia.

"It's nonsense," says Erfan. "The pro-Russian party in Crimea had so little support that it never got into the local parliament. Yes, most of the people in Crimea speak Russian, but they didn't want to be part of Russia at all. They printed out those results for themselves at the Kremlin before the pseudo-referendum had even taken place.

"As for me," he continues, "when the Euromaidan protests took place in Maidan Nezalezhnosti [Independence Square] in Kyiv, I went along day after day with a large Crimean Tatar flag. I wanted the Ukrainians to know that we Crimean Tatars were on their side. But when the 'little green men' appeared at Yalta—in other words, Putin's soldiers in disguise—I raced there as fast as I could, because I'd left my wife on her own in Crimea with our four children. When I saw that the seat of power was already in Russian hands, I didn't wait. We packed up, and we all left for Kyiv with two suitcases. We thought the war might last a month or two, but that Ukraine would prevail. It never occurred to me that I was in yet another generation that would have to leave the land of our ancestors, perhaps forever."

"During the Russian invasion, Musafir became the natural place for meetings of those who were opposed to joining Russia," says Dilyara-khanum. "The Tatars are inoculated against Russia and its love of us and our land. But we're also taught that for now, Russia is much stronger than we are. We can't risk being destroyed yet again. People won't want to grab stones or weapons. They'll wait. My husband and I have stayed on in Bakhchysarai. Our middle son and his family have too. We're hanging on. It's not easy. On the one hand the Russians put out signals that they'd like to win the Tatars over, but on the other they kidnap our activists—some of them are in prison. But several guys were found horribly tortured and murdered. It's a clear sign to the others that no one should dare stick their necks out. We can see the danger."

When the Russians came to power, Musafir, which in 2013 won an award for the best restaurant in Bakhchysarai, suddenly started to be levied financial penalties. According to the new authorities, the restaurant was operating without the required license.

"We had to close it," says Dilyara-khanum, sighing. "But my children took a risk and found a new site in the very center of Kyiv. Yet again we've had to start from scratch. Now you can try our Crimean Tatar food, our family recipes passed down the generations, in Kyiv."

"Beginning in 2014 my wife, our four children, and I spent two years wandering among various friends and activists," says Erfan. "It was an awful life. A month here, two weeks there, a week at a hotel that someone else paid for. Since we've been in Kyiv my children have changed schools five times. We finally had to face the fact that there's no option, that for now we have no chance of returning to Crimea. We sold our apartment in Yalta, and with the money I decided to open a business in Kyiv. I started wondering what it should be. Do you remember me telling you that all my life I'd kept as far away as I could from gastronomy? I meant it. But here in Kyiv, one of my Tatar friends told me that the only thing the Crimean Tatars could do in the Ukrainian capital was make chebureki. That's the way they see us, period—we won't change that in a year. They don't associate the Tatars with art, or marketing, or banking. The Tatars exist to make food. So I've rented a site for ten years, and I've hired two cooks. Both are very religious—right now you're sitting next to the prayer rugs on which they pray five times a day. And I've opened a chebureki bar not far from Kyiv's main street."

"And how's it going?"

"Until the pandemic it did very well. I created a sort of mini-Crimea for the people of Kyiv: in addition to the food, we have a gallery with Tatar art, books, pictures, and ceramics. We're not doing so well now. But I'll tell you something odd. My father was two years old when Stalin deported him from Crimea, but he claimed he remembered his home perfectly. I never believed him. But I have two sons, twins, and when my wife and family left Yalta, they were two years old as well. Now they're ten. And they can describe exactly what our house looked like, where the kitchen was, where the stairs were, and where their bedroom was. Now I know that we Tatars have a far deeper relationship to Crimea than Putin and the other politicians imagine. We survived deportation, and we're surviving it now as well. Thanks to our friends. And thanks to our cuisine—because whenever they deport us we don't have time to pack, but we always take two things with us: the Quran and our food."

◇◇◇

Chebureki

This recipe was given to the author by Dilyara Seitvelyeva.

FOR THE FILLING:
*1 pound 5 ounces (600 g) lamb, minced or very finely
   chopped*
1 cup (150 g) diced onion
Salt and black pepper, to taste

FOR THE DOUGH:
8¼ cups (1 kg) flour
About 3 cups (750 ml) water with 1½ teaspoons (10 g) salt
Vegetable oil, for frying

MAKE THE FILLING:

In a bowl, combine the lamb, onion, and salt and pepper.
Place in the refrigerator until ready to use.

MAKE THE DOUGH:

Make the pastry using flour and salted water. Wrap the
dough in plastic and refrigerate it for 30 minutes.

Divide the dough into pieces, each weighing roughly 1
ounce (20 to 30 g). Roll each piece into two circles of two
sizes, one roughly 4 inches (10 cm) in diameter and the

other 6 inches (15 cm) in diameter. Place a spoonful of the filling on the smaller circle and cover it with a larger one. Trim and crimp the edges. The Tatars have a special tool for this named a *chygyryk*, a crimping wheel that often has a finely decorated handle and is used purely to trim pastry. But if you don't have a crimper, you can use an ordinary knife to trim the pastry and crimp it with a fork.

Once the chebureki are ready, heat the oil in a saucepan or deep frying pan. Immerse a cheburek in the oil and fry it for several minutes, flipping once, until it is golden in color.

Traditionally chebureki are made with mutton, but nowadays beef, potato, mushroom, and even sweet cheese fillings are equally popular.

XVIII

The Third Return of Viktor Belyaev

One day while I was still working at Kuntsevo, Yeltsin, who by then was president of Russia, came to see what Stalin's former dacha was like. I gave him a tour, showing him every corner of the place, including the vestibule where Stalin's jacket was still hanging and his boots were still standing—every last detail. Then we walked over to the more modern part, and Yeltsin's bodyguards brought out a bottle and they drank a shot of vodka each, and finally Yeltsin said, "What do you intend to do with all this?"

So I told him our plans were ambitious, but for some reason we had no visitors.

Yeltsin looked at me. "Viktor Borisovich," he said, "come back to where you belong."

And so after five years of absence, I returned to the Kremlin.

1.

Under Yeltsin, my career reached its peak—I became the Kremlin's head chef. Everything having to do with food was my responsibility, meaning that on a daily basis I fed the three hundred to four hundred people who worked there, as well as all the guests. I planned the menus for two Kremlin canteens— because they have canteens there, like at any workplace—and for all the official receptions. Only the lichniki didn't answer to me but directly to the KGB.

2.

Then President Yeltsin was replaced by President Putin, and I went on running the kitchen. I took part in organizing many splendid receptions, and I also traveled with the president to promote Russian cuisine around the world. Often without enough sleep, often under stress. Many times I slept at the Kremlin, on a couch or even on the floor. Tons of produce; hundreds, sometimes more than a thousand guests. I'd sleep two hours of every twenty-four, and then would come the next meeting, the next reception, the next day of work. I had more than two hundred people under me: cooks, waiters, and dining room staff. And I knew that if anything got screwed up, I'd be the first to get it in the neck. If a single one of those thousand people were poisoned, I'd be the first one they'd drag over the coals. If the food was no good, the same thing would happen.

But if everything was all right, no one would praise me either. At the Kremlin, as I've already told you, merely not being berated was a compliment.

But, Witold, there's a price for everything in life. A young man has no idea—he thinks he's unstoppable, he thinks he can work twelve, fifteen, eighteen hours a day and he's going to live forever. By the time he realizes the truth, it's too late. After a few years of working at that pace, I had such a massive heart attack that I had one foot in the grave.

I can't remember anything about it. In the middle of my work, I simply sank to the kitchen floor.

I woke several days later in the hospital, hooked up to various machines. There was my wife, in tears, and my children. I realized that I had almost paid with my life. So as soon as I felt better, I went to the personnel department and handed in my notice. I had no idea what I was going to do next, but I knew that if I wanted to go on living, I had to stop working at the Kremlin. The stress was too much.

But to this day, most of the chefs who work at the Kremlin are people I hired and trained.

3.

You ask me what makes a good chef. Above all, he should be dedicated to his work. If he finds it punishing, or if he doesn't want to learn new things, he should change his profession. Our energy, our mood really do have an effect on the food people are going to eat. Stalin's chef taught me that.

At the schools nowadays, they teach nothing but techniques: cut it like this, then cook it in the oven at such and such degrees, job done. But technique is just the first step in cooking. Will anyone tell you to sing to your dough? Only I will.

4.

After resigning from my job at the Kremlin, I founded a catering firm. I also travel all over Russia, and like I used to in the army, I train cooks. Recently, at a food technology school in Chelyabinsk, I told the students about the time when Brezhnev and French president Valéry Giscard d'Estaing went fishing together and my colleagues and I set up a portable stove, which we used to make ukha, soup made from the fish they caught right there. After I told the story, I asked if anyone had any questions and saw a hand go up. It was a young woman, a student, and she asked where I had learned to be so good at fish processing.

My God, fish processing? Cutting off the tail and fins, scaling and gutting? Really? My grandmother taught me how to do it, because she needed help in the kitchen. At school we had separate classes to teach us about saltwater fish and freshwater fish, as well as special lessons on fish from the sturgeon family. At the Kremlin, every chef knew how to dress a carcass. And even though sausages and cold meats came to us already prepared, if the need arose, every one of us could prepare them.

And here's a future food technologist asking me about fish processing?

I started asking them about what they were learning at their school. Meat processing? A single lesson to cover everything— from poultry to lamb. What about fish, or game? Forget it. And then someone like that goes off to a restaurant with their diploma in food technology. It's like giving a pilot a diploma for being able to press the start button.

5.

So I'm being very industrious in my retirement.

Where my professional life is concerned, I'd like to be like Maria Alexandrovna, who was a cook at one of the canteens when I worked at the Kremlin. Maria Alexandrovna started working as a kitchen helper when she was fourteen. She specialized in soups. She stopped working at the age of eighty-two. I was in charge at the time, and I organized her send-off into retirement. And you know what? Once she had left, people stopped liking the soups. People called me or came to see me and said, "Have a word with the cooks, because those soups are inedible."

I went to the canteen. I observed the staff, and they were doing everything just right. It was simply that people were so used to Maria Alexandrovna's soups that they didn't want any others.

I'd like to be that sort of chef. So good that when you leave, people immediately sense the difference. And one day they'll say: no one roasted meat, or made ukha or blinis, like our Viktor.

6.

Sorry? What became of Stalin's dacha after I left? It was locked and bolted again, but I suspect nothing there has changed since then. The jacket is still hanging there, those boots are still there, and I bet the odor of Stalin still lingers.

Afterword

Three months after this book was first published in Poland, Vladimir Putin, grandson of a cook, ordered his troops to invade Ukraine, and Europe's bloodiest conflict since World War II began. The divisions between the main characters in this book—those from Ukraine, Georgia, and Estonia, and those from Russia—became even deeper. As I have already said in the foreword, now it would be impossible for me to enter either Russia or Belarus.

But I have been traveling to war-torn Ukraine, mainly as a volunteer.

World events have raced forward since the book came out, and so have the lives of its main characters.

Following the outbreak of the war, Alexandra Igorevna Zalivskaya, the great-granddaughter of a man who cooked for the last tsar, decided that her conversation with me was a mistake. She refuses to answer my calls.

Only one of the women who survived the Great Famine is

still alive: Hanna Basaraba. But she's not living in Rostivka anymore—her children have moved her to the city.

Tamara Andreyevna, the baker from Leningrad, is also still alive. She's very upset about what's happening in Ukraine, but naturally she sees it through a Russian lens: consistent with Russian propaganda, she believes that Russia had to attack Ukraine, or otherwise it would have been attacked itself by NATO. It's impossible to explain to her that this is absurd.

Just before the attack on Ukraine, the longtime Kremlin cook Viktor Belyaev passed away. He was a wonderful interlocutor and a good man. He died of COVID in a Moscow hospital.

At the start of the war I spotted Erfan Kudusov, the Tatar, in a Reuters photograph, taking part in an anti-war protest in Kyiv. Later on he came to see me in Warsaw. He is heavily involved in humanitarian aid.

And Olga, the cook from Chernobyl, had a dream about the war on the very night it started. "When friends started calling to tell me there were bombs falling, I already knew," she told me.

I have always thought cooks see more than other people. Here we have yet more proof.

ACKNOWLEDGMENTS

My thanks for their help in writing this book and for supporting me while I was working on it are due to:

Viktor Belyaev, Marcin Biegaj, Andriy Bondar, Jadwiga Barbara Dąbrowska, Natalia Denysiuk, Anna Dziewit-Meller, Arek Jakimiuk, Roman Kabachiy, Elżbieta Kalinowska, Taciana Kalinowska, Walery Kalinowski, Vyacheslav Kebich, Piotr Kędzierski, Wiktoria Kołpak, Krzysztof Leśniewski, Anastasia Levkova, Daniel Lis, Antonia Lloyd-Jones, Izabela Meyza, Maciej Musiał, Gabriela Niedzielska, Andrew Nurnberg, Masza Pistunowa, Anna Rucińska, Taras Shumeyko, John Siciliano, Aniela Szabłowska, Marianna Szabłowska, and Ida Świerkocka.

BIBLIOGRAPHY

I. The Last Tsar's Chef

For information about the work and organization of Nicholas II's kitchens, as well as for some of the recipes for dishes served at his court, my sources were:

Ilya Lazerson, Igor Zimin, and Alexander Sokolov. *Императорская кухня. XIX—начало XX века. Повседневная жизнь Российского императорского двора* [Imperial cuisine, 19th to early 20th century: The everyday life of the Russian imperial court]. Moscow: Centerpolygraph, 2014.

I also used the following sources:

Dmitry Fakovsky. "Дневник охранника: каким человеком был Николай II" [Diary of a bodyguard: What sort of a man was Nicholas II]. GardInfo, April 2, 2020. http://guardinfo.online /2020/02/04/dnevnik-oxrannika-kakim-chelovekom-byl -nikolaj-ii.

"Как повар Николая II отдал жизнь за царя, разделив участь царской семьи" [How Nicholas II's chef gave his life for the tsar, sharing the fate of the imperial family]. Kulturologia.ru. https:// kulturologia.ru/blogs/090819/43865.

Bartłomiej Garczyk. "Życie—polityka—władza. Rytuał dnia codziennego ostatniego cara Rosji Mikołaja II w świetle jego dziennika" [Life—politics—power: The ritual of the daily life of the last tsar of Russia Nicholas II in the light of his diary]. *Kultury Wschodniosłowiańskie—Oblicza i Dialog* 7 (2017).

Lev L. Kolesnikov, Gurgen A. Pashinyan, and Sergey S. Abramov. "Anatomical Appraisal of the Skulls and Teeth Associated with the Family of Tsar Nicolay Romanov." *The Anatomical Record* 265, no. 1 (2001): pp. 15–32. (This article shows the exact locations of the remains of the imperial family and their accompanying persons.)

II. Lenin's Cook

The statements by the tour guide at Gorki Leninskiye are in fact a compilation of the accounts of three people: senior specialist Svetlana Generalova, senior specialist Tamara Shybina, and the director of the museum, Boris Vlasov.

William Pokhlebkin's text about Lenin's diet was published in the Russian weekly magazine *Ogonyok* in 1997: "Что ел Ленин" [What Lenin ate]. *Огонёк* 39 (1997).

Yevgeny Zhirnov. "Мы гоняли соловья, который не давал спать Владимиру Ильичу" [We chased away the nightingale that kept Vladimir Ilyich awake]. *Коммерсантъ Власть*, January 19, 2004.

III. The Great Famine

Anne Applebaum. *Red Famine: Stalin's War on Ukraine*. New York: Doubleday, 2017.

Wacław Radziwinowicz. "Rosja ma w genach pamięć o głodzie. Do dziś część Rosjan suszy chleb na czarną godzinę" [Russia has the memory of the famine in its genes: To this day some Russians dry bread for a rainy day]. *Gazeta Wyborcza*, March 5, 2018.

IV. A Meeting in the Mountains; and V. Beauty and Beria

I discovered the story of Alexander Egnatashvili and his wife, Liliana, in a book by Egnatashvili's stepson, Liliana's son Ivan Alikhanov: *Дней минувших анекдоты* [Anecdotes of past days]. Moscow: Agraf, 2004.

Most of the facts about Sasha's and Liliana's lives are sourced from this book. I also made use of information provided in conversations with Ivan Alikhanov's son, Sergei, who is a well-known Russian songwriter.

The stories about Stalin's life in exile were told by Nikita Khrushchev in his memoirs and reproduced in the Russian journal *Вопросы истории* [Questions of history] 1 (1992).

Other sources:

Henri Barbusse. *Stalin: A New World Seen through One Man.* Translated by Vyvyan Holland. London: Workers' Bookshop Limited, 1935.

Boris Bazhanov. *Byłem sekretarzem Stalina* [I was Stalin's secretary]. Warsaw: Niezależna Oficyna Wydawnicza, 1985. (The Polish edition of Bazhanov's memoirs.)

Roman Brackman. *The Secret File of Joseph Stalin: A Hidden Life.* London: Routledge, 2003.

Vladimir M. Loginov. *Тени Сталина. Генерал Власик и его соратники* [Stalin's shadows: General Vlasik and his associates]. Moscow: Sovremennik, 2000. (The author conducted interviews with Pavel "Pavelek" Rusishvili and also with Alexander Egnatashvili's son, Georgy Egnatashvili.)

Simon Sebag Montefiore. "Stalin, His Father and the Rabbit: The Bizarre Story of Stalin, His Possible Biological Father, His Food Taster." *The New Statesman*, September 6, 2007.

Simon Sebag Montefiore. *Stalin: The Court of the Red Tsar.* New York: Knopf, 2004.

Anatoly Ovcharov. *Душа вождя* [The leader's soul]. Self-published, Strelbytskyy Multimedia Publishing, 2019.

Joshua Rubenstein. *The Last Days of Stalin*, New Haven, CT: Yale University Press, 2016.

VI. A Baker in Besieged Leningrad

The story of the Putin family during the war and the blockade are from an account by Vladimir Putin (taking him at his word), published in a Russian newspaper: "Жизнь такая простая штука и жестокая" [Life is such a simple and cruel art]. *Русский пионер* [Russian pioneer], April 30, 2015.

The story of Kyyttinen the Finnish baker, whose first name in his own language was Taneli-Juho, was told on YouTube by Tatiana Vatanen, a Russian of Finnish origin. The title of the video is *Даниил Кютинен. Пекарь-легенда блокадного Ленинграда. ч. 1 ГОЛОД і Даниил Кютинен; Блокада Ленинграда. Судьба его семьи. Эвакуация. ч. 2* [Daniil Kyyttinen: the legendary baker of blockaded Leningrad, part 1, famine; and Daniil Kyyttinen: The Leningrad blockade, the fate of his family, part 2, evacuation]. February 16, 2021. YouTube video, 28:14. https://www.youtube.com/watch?v=jsiQWzUaYxQ.

Richard Bidlack and Nikita Lomagin. *The Leningrad Blockade, 1941–1944: A New Documentary History from the Soviet Archives.* New Haven, CT: Yale University Press, 2012.

I also interviewed Nikita Lomagin in Saint Petersburg in 2019.

VII. Exhumation

Ksenia Dementyeva. "Полевая кухня времен Великой Отечественной: как и чем питались советские солдаты" [The field kitchen during the Great Patriotic War and what Soviet soldiers ate]. *RusBase*, May 4, 2015.

Ivan Dmitrienko. "Чем кормили солдат во время войны по обе стороны фронта" [What soldiers were fed during the war on both sides of the front]. *Profil*, May 9, 2019.

Sergei Glezerov. "Кровопролитие за рубеж. Исследователь – о неизвестных фактах Нарвской битвы" [Bloodshed Abroad: Unknown Facts about the Battle of Narva]. *Sankt-Peterburgskie Vedomosti*, July 24, 2019. https://spbvedomosti.ru/news/nasledie/krovoprolitie-za-rubezh-issledovatel-o-neizvestnykh-faktakh-narvskoy-bitvy.

Olga Lipchinskaya. "Шел второй год войны. Хлеба—400 граммов, лампочки—25 ватт" [The war was in its second year: Bread—400 g, lightbulbs—25 watts]. *Komsomolskaya Pravda*, February 2, 2015.

Anna Reid. *Leningrad: Tragedy of a City under Siege, 1941–44.* London: Bloomsbury, 2011.

VIII. The Feast at Yalta

S. M. Plokhy. *Yalta: The Price of Peace*. New York: Viking, 2010.

William Pokhlebkin. *Кухня века* [Cuisine of the century]. Moscow: Polifakt, 2000.

IX. Gagarin's Cook

The only journalist to have conducted an interview with Faina Kazetskaya was the Ukrainian Volodymir Shunievich in 2002: "Ночью накануне гибели Юрий Гагарин попросил стакан своего любимого сырого молока" [The night before the death of Yuri Gagarin he asked for a glass of his favorite raw milk], *Факты*, October 24, 2002.

Kazetskaya's statements to the commission that investigated the causes of Yuri Gagarin's death remain classified.

Several weeks before she died, Maria Kritinina, who cooked at Baikonur, was interviewed by Olga Gopalo for the Russian newspaper *Komsomolskaya Pravda*. The interview was published on April 11, 2013.

I also sourced information from the following conversations and articles:

S. M. Belotserkovsky. *Гибель Гагарина: Факты и домыслы* [The death of Gagarin: Facts and suppositions]. Moscow: Mashinostroyenie, 1992.

Piers Bizony and Jamie Doran. *Starman: The Truth behind the Legend of Yuri Gagarin*. New York: Bloomsbury, 1998.

A. T. Gagarin. *Слово о сыне* [A word about my son]. Moscow: Yunatstva, 1986.

Yuri Gagarin. *Road to the Stars*. Moscow: Foreign Languages Publishing House, 1962.

Y. Golovanov. *Королёв: факты и мифы* [Korolev: Facts and myths]. Moscow: Fond sodeystviya aviatsii Russkiye vityazi, 2007.

Natalia Nekhlebova. "Вкус—космический. Чем питаются на орбите и как это готовят" [Cosmic taste: What's eaten in orbit and how it's prepared]. *Огонёк*, April 8, 2019.

Anton Pervushin. *Империя Сергея Королева* [Sergei Korolev's empire]. Moscow: T8 Russian Titles, 2020.

Anton Pervushin. "'Не могла скрыть заплаканных глаз': как Летала Терешкова, За что Королёв ругал Валентину Терешкову" ["She couldn't hide her tears": How Tereshkova flew, why Korolev scolded Valentina Tereshkova]. Gazeta.ru, June 16, 2018. https://www.gazeta.ru/science/2018/06/16_a_11803717.shtml.

Anton Pervushin. *108 минут, изменившие мир* [108 minutes that changed the world]. Moscow: Eksmo, 2011.

Lena Porotikova and Alexey Sokolov. "'Здравствуй, Рита': первая встреча Гагарина после возвращения из космоса" ["Hello Rita": Gagarin's first meeting after returning from outer space]. TASS, April 12, 2016. https://tass.ru/kosmos/3189731.

Ewelina Zambrzycka-Kościelnicka. "60 lat temu Jurij Gagarin został świętym" [60 years ago Yuri Gagarin became a saint]. *WP Magazyn*, April 9, 2021. https://magazyn.wp.pl/informacje/artykul/60-lat-temu-jurij-gagarin-zostal-swietym.

XI. The Cook from the Afghan War

Svetlana Alexievich. *Zinky Boys: Soviet Voices from the Afghanistan War*. Translated by Julia Whitby and Robin Whitby. New York: W. W. Norton, 1992.

Rodric Braithwaite. *Afgantsy: The Russians in Afghanistan 1979–89*. New York: Oxford University Press, 2011.

Wojciech Jagielski. *Modlitwa o deszcz* [Praying for rain]. Kraków: Znak, 2016.

XIII. The Fairy-Tale Forest: Cooking at Chernobyl

Kate Brown. *Manual for Survival: An Environmental History of the Chernobyl Disaster*. New York: W. W. Norton, 2020.

Igor Kostin. *Chernobyl: Confessions of a Reporter*. New York: Umbrage Editions, 2006.

Serhii Plokhy. *Chernobyl: The History of a Nuclear Catastrophe*. New York: Basic Books, 2018.

XV. Wild Boar Goulash, or the Soviet Union's Last Supper

Vyacheslav Kebich. *Искушение властью* [The seduction of power]. Minsk: Paradoks, 2008.

Olga Korelina. "'Лучше бы они охотились'. Бывшие работники 'Вискулей'—о том, как 25 лет назад не стало СССР" ["It'd be better if they'd gone hunting": Former employees of Viskuli on how 25 years ago the USSR ceased to be]. Virtualny Brest, December 8, 2016.

V. V. Semakov. *Беловежская Пуща. Век XX* [The Białowieża Forest: 20th century]. Minsk: Izdatelstvo Belarus, 2011.

Adam Wajrak and Andrzej Kłopotowski. "Puszcza Białowieska za drutem kolczastym" [The Białowieża Forest behind barbed wire]. *Gazeta Wyborcza*, April 5, 2017.

XVI. The Sanatorium Cook

Alexander Gamov. "Путин носил еду Ленину" [Putin took food to Lenin]. *Komsomolskaya Pravda*, April 22, 2019.

XVII. Crimean Tatar Cuisine

Natalia Gumenyuk. *Потерянный остров. Книга репортажей из оккупированного Крыма* [The lost island: A book of reportage from occupied Crimea]. Kyiv: Vidavnictvo Starogo Leva, 2020.

PHOTO CREDITS